I0816779

ALSO BY EUGENE ROBINSON

Disintegration
Last Dance in Havana
Coal to Cream

FREEDOM LOST, FREEDOM WON

A Personal History of America

EUGENE ROBINSON

SIMON & SCHUSTER
New York Amsterdam/Antwerp London
Toronto Sydney/Melbourne New Delhi

Simon & Schuster
1230 Avenue of the Americas
New York, NY 10020

For more than 100 years, Simon & Schuster has championed authors and the stories they create. By respecting the copyright of an author's intellectual property, you enable Simon & Schuster and the author to continue publishing exceptional books for years to come. We thank you for supporting the author's copyright by purchasing an authorized edition of this book.

No amount of this book may be reproduced or stored in any format, nor may it be uploaded to any website, database, language-learning model, or other repository, retrieval, or artificial intelligence system without express permission. All rights reserved. Inquiries may be directed to Simon & Schuster, 1230 Avenue of the Americas, New York, NY 10020 or permissions@simonandschuster.com.

Copyright © 2026 by Eugene Robinson

All rights reserved, including the right to reproduce this book or portions thereof in any form whatsoever. For information, address Simon & Schuster Subsidiary Rights Department, 1230 Avenue of the Americas, New York, NY 10020.

First Simon & Schuster hardcover edition February 2026

SIMON & SCHUSTER and colophon are registered trademarks of Simon & Schuster, LLC

Simon & Schuster strongly believes in freedom of expression and stands against censorship in all its forms. For more information, visit BooksBelong.com.

For information about special discounts for bulk purchases, please contact Simon & Schuster Special Sales at 1-866-506-1949 or business@simonandschuster.com.

The Simon & Schuster Speakers Bureau can bring authors to your live event. For more information or to book an event, contact the Simon & Schuster Speakers Bureau at 1-866-248-3049 or visit our website at www.simonspeakers.com.

Interior design by Wendy Blum

Manufactured in the United States of America

10 9 8 7 6 5 4 3 2 1

Library of Congress Control Number: 2025945406

ISBN 978-1-9821-7671-6
ISBN 978-1-9821-7679-2 (ebook)

Let's stay in touch! Scan here to get book recommendations, exclusive offers, and more delivered to your inbox.

To my sons, Aaron and Lowell,
the next generation

CONTENTS

THE ROBINSON & FORDHAM FAMILIES

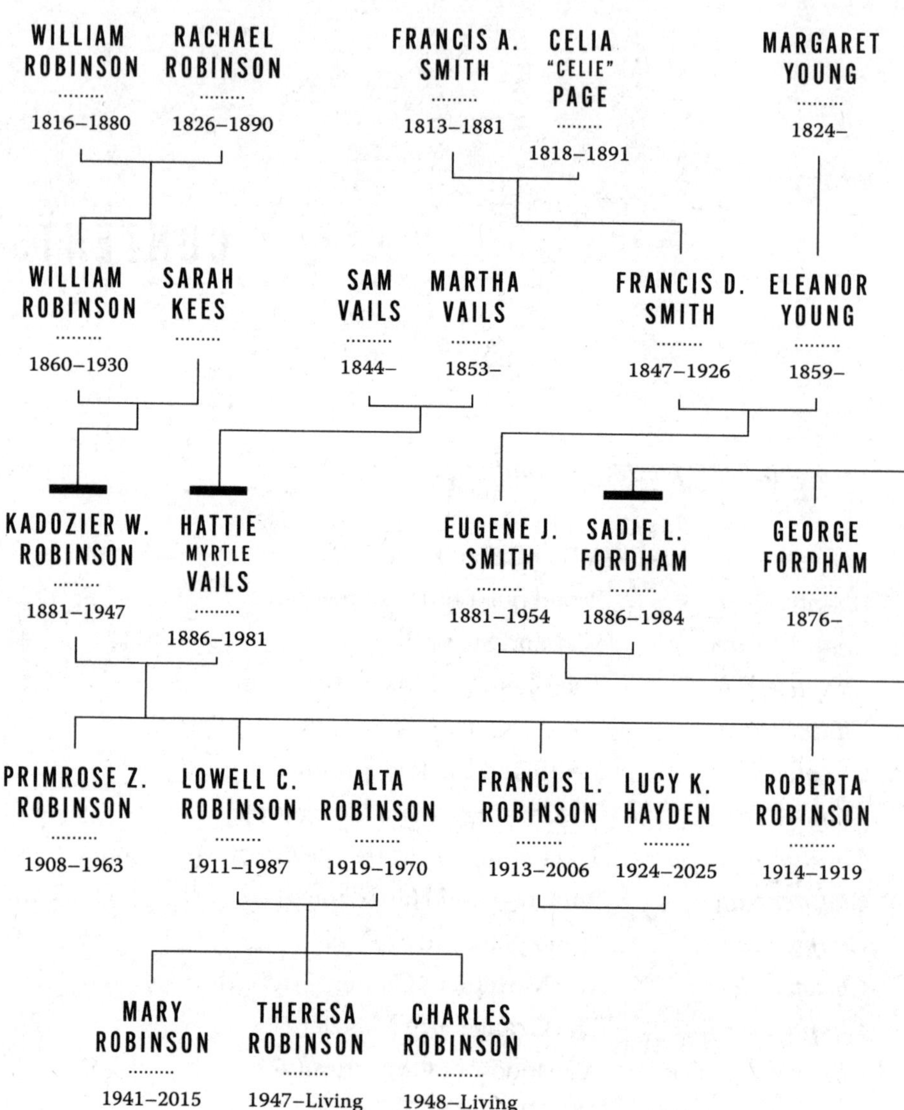

Featured prominently

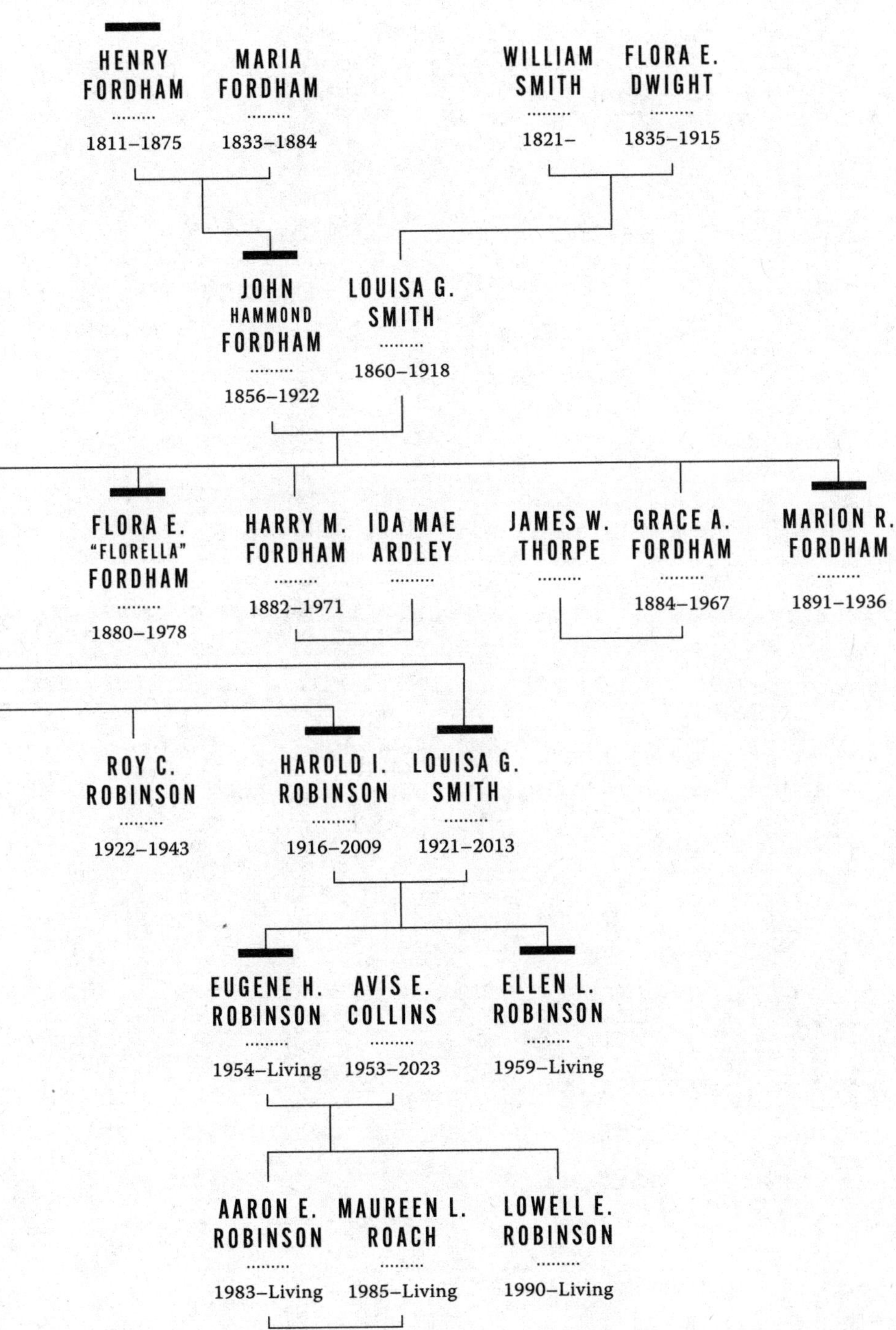

HENRY FORDHAM
1811–1875
MARIA FORDHAM
1833–1884
WILLIAM SMITH
1821–
FLORA E. DWIGHT
1835–1915
JOHN HAMMOND FORDHAM
1856–1922
LOUISA G. SMITH
1860–1918
FLORA E. "FLORELLA" FORDHAM
1880–1978
HARRY M. FORDHAM
1882–1971
IDA MAE ARDLEY
JAMES W. THORPE
GRACE A. FORDHAM
1884–1967
MARION R. FORDHAM
1891–1936
ROY C. ROBINSON
1922–1943
HAROLD I. ROBINSON
1916–2009
LOUISA G. SMITH
1921–2013
EUGENE H. ROBINSON
1954–Living
AVIS E. COLLINS
1953–2023
ELLEN L. ROBINSON
1959–Living
AARON E. ROBINSON
1983–Living
MAUREEN L. ROACH
1985–Living
LOWELL E. ROBINSON
1990–Living

Chapter One

A BOY CALLED HARRY

On March 27, 1829, a wealthy white planter and entrepreneur named Richard Fordham purchased four enslaved African Americans from a woman named Isabella Perman. One of them was my great-great-grandfather, a boy called Harry.

This transaction in human flesh, as with many thousands of other such sales over nearly two centuries, took place in Charleston, the metropolis in the Low Country of South Carolina that was the port of entry for an estimated 40 percent of all enslaved Africans brought to toil in this country. A document recording the sale was filed with the South Carolina secretary of state several days later, on April 7. It does not say where in Charleston the sale took place—on the steps of the Old Exchange and Provost Dungeon perhaps, or at the Cooper River docks, or in one of the thriving markets where people were bought and sold. The individuals bought by Fordham are listed as "a Negro boy named Harry and a Negro woman named Jenny and her two children named Hager and Margaret." For the lot, Fordham paid $1,080.

Founded in 1670 as Charles Towne by English colonists from Bermuda, Charleston occupies a narrow peninsula flanked by two navigable rivers, the Ashley and the Cooper. The rivers meet at the city's southern tip, which is protected by a wide and deep natural harbor; Charleston could not have been better situated to become a center of seafaring commerce. In 1829 it was a bustling place with a population of nearly thirty thousand, the most important Atlantic port in the South and the sixth-largest city in the nation, behind only New York, Baltimore, Philadelphia, Boston, and New Orleans.

Richard Fordham was the owner of Moonham Plantation and Shipyard, a large landholding on flat and fertile Daniel Island, just across the Cooper River from the city. Excavations there have found remnants of a pre-colonial Native American settlement believed to have been occupied by a clan called the Ittiwan; they were gone well before Fordham arrived, having been displaced by European settlers and unpaid Black workers. At his plantation, Fordham used enslaved African Americans to grow two of South Carolina's most lucrative cash crops, indigo and Sea Island cotton. An ambitious and busy man, Fordham also used the people he held in bondage to build watercraft (small cargo vessels that he sold for use in the maze of shallow Low Country waterways) and to work at the blacksmith's forge he and a partner owned in the heart of the city, on Chalmers Street, near the end of the peninsula.

Not far from the forge, on that same street, a man named Thomas Ryan and a major slave trader named Ziba B. Oakes operated a huge establishment, Ryan's Mart, where Black human beings were bought and sold. The business was colloquially known as "Ryan's nigger-jail." Buyers entered through a wide stone archway into premises that stretched the full width of a city block. Across an expansive yard stood a four-story dormitory-style prison, or barracoon, where African Americans were warehoused pending their sale; the cells were outfitted with shackles to prevent escape. To the right was a low building that housed a busy kitchen; the enslaved were fed relatively well in the days before their sale, so they would look as strong and healthy as possible. To the left was a small morgue—as with any trade in livestock, a certain percentage of inventory loss was factored in as an inevitable cost of doing business. And at the front of the yard, near the entrance, was the part of Ryan's Mart that customers were meant to see: the auction gallery, where men, women, and children were presented for purchase. That was the showroom where husbands and wives were separated, where sons and daughters were taken from their mothers, and where fathers were led away in chains to a future of servitude, abuse, and punishment—a life they could realistically expect to escape only through death.

Harry, whose proper name was Henry, spent nineteen years as Richard Fordham's chattel. The young man proved to be quick of mind and good with his hands: He mastered the art of blacksmithing. At the Chalmers Street forge, his skills eventually made him Fordham's de facto right-hand man. He had a talent for making unyielding iron bend to his will.

On July 10, 1848, Fordham sold "a Negro man named Henry" to Otis Mills and Co., a grain wholesaling business with multiple warehouses near the Cooper River docks. The sale was recorded with the secretary of state seven days later. The Mills company's eponymous founder, one of Charleston's richest men, went on to build the city's grandest and most luxurious hotel, the Mills House. The price Mills paid for my great-great-grandfather was $2,000, which was a lot of money for a single Black man. Henry was now Henry Fordham—he had taken Richard's surname as his own—and he clearly had attributes that made him worth nearly three times the going local price of $725 for a field hand. It was the kind of money that a wealthy Charleston tycoon would pay for an experienced and gifted blacksmith in his prime. According to family lore, Henry had somehow circumvented the state's strict law against educating the enslaved and become literate. And he had become deeply religious. He had not only learned to read the Gospel of Jesus Christ but also heard the call to preach it.

This extraordinary Henry Fordham is *my* Henry Fordham, my direct ancestor on my mother's side. Three years after being acquired by

Otis Mills, he was purchased one final time—by himself: Sometime in 1851, he bought his own freedom.

I've always known through my family's rich oral history that my great-great-grandfather obtained his liberty at some point before the Civil War. For a long time, however, attempts to find out exactly when and how he cast off his chains ran into dead ends. In Charleston, there was no systematic collection of manumission records, legal documents marking an enslaved person's freedom, and by 1841, the state of South Carolina had passed laws that effectively made manumission illegal. That did not entirely end the practice, but it did mean there would be no official document recording the moment of Henry Fordham's freedom in the archives of the secretary of state.

I knew about his 1848 sale to Otis Mills from research that my "Aunt" Grace—actually one of my mother's many first cousins—painstakingly conducted years ago, though she never laid eyes on the actual document. And I knew that Henry indeed was free before the Civil War and Emancipation, because I found his name in the 1861 Charleston city census, appended with the notation "f.p.c."—"free person of color." By then, I reasoned, he must have been a free man for some time, because the census showed that he already owned two wood-frame houses in the city, one on Desportes Court and the other on Washington Street; it must have taken him at least a few years to accumulate such assets, starting from zero. But exactly when, in that thirteen-year gap between his final sale and his first appearance in the census, had he become free? I pored through real estate records, scoured the family Bible, searched archives in reading rooms and digital databases online, looked everywhere I could think of—and didn't find a hint, much less a clue.

The South Carolina Historical Society, a private institution founded in 1855, has long been the biggest and richest repository of historical documents in the state. It is the mandatory first stop for researchers seeking information about the antebellum period. I visited the society's grand neoclassical headquarters on Charleston's main thoroughfare, Meeting Street, several times over the years to look for traces of Henry

Fordham's manumission, or for records pertaining to Otis Mills or his company, or anything about my great-great-grandfather that might pin down even the year of his freedom. No luck.

In 2014, the society's collection was moved across town to the College of Charleston so that the archive's original home, a landmark 1822 structure known as the Fireproof Building, could be turned into a museum. Slowly but surely, more records were digitized or at least preserved on microfilm. In February 2023, I visited the collection at its present location, a hushed sanctum on the second floor of the college's Addlestone Library, in the hope that more of the hit-or-miss manumission records from Henry Fordham's time might have been found, catalogued, and made accessible. I was overjoyed when the helpful librarians at the desk found that the stacks held a folder labeled with Henry Fordham's name—but then immediately deflated when they brought it out, because I saw that it contained only a long, speculative, and largely inaccurate account of Henry's life compiled by a distant relative whom I'd never met. I was already familiar with that document, and I knew it said nothing about when he had liberated himself.

Finally, one of the librarians at the historical society suggested I look through editions of Charleston's "Free Negro Book." I had no idea such a thing existed: a yearly list of free African Americans residing in the city who had paid a required poll tax. It was an exercise in data collection born of paranoia. The fact that Blacks outnumbered whites in South Carolina during the decades before the Civil War meant that white officials lived in constant fear of a Haiti-style Black uprising, which they assumed would be led by free African Americans. The free were a tiny minority—roughly 95 percent of Black people in the state were enslaved—but it seemed to make sense that any rebellion would be led by conspirators with independent resources and the liberty of unsupervised movement. Whites took great pains to keep track of men and women like Henry Fordham.

The helpful librarian sat me in front of a microfilm reader and brought out roll after roll of film. I sat there for hours, squinting to decipher the records' graceful archaic handwriting. It was actually called the "Free Negro Book." The names in each year's edition were alphabetized, but only roughly, by first letter—all the surnames starting with *A* came before all the surnames starting with *B*, but the name Agee might come before the name Anderson or it might come after. I began with the edition from 1848, the year of my great-great-grandfather's sale to Otis Mills, but there was no listing for a Henry Fordham. The same was true of the book for 1849. Same for 1850. But as I slowly made my way through the *F* section of the 1851 edition, I let out a shout that shattered the library's decorous hush: "Yesssss!" Then quickly, to the startled patrons and librarians: "I'm so sorry, excuse me, I'm so sorry." And then, more softly, "Yes."

I had found him.

Henry Fordham was recorded as a free Black man for the first time in 1851. I doubt I will ever be able to pin down the month and the day, but finally I knew the year. I can be quite sure my great-great-grandfather was still enslaved when free African Americans were counted in 1850—and that he had become a free man, a proud free Black man, by the time the Free Negro Book was compiled in 1851.

WHEN I WAS GROWING up, it never occurred to me to go looking for my family's history. It was already right there, all around me. My younger sister, Ellen, and I were surrounded by the material objects of our heritage and immersed in family lore. Our history was beneath our feet and above our heads; it crammed every cabinet, rested on every surface, and hung from every wall. We were raised in a world of legacy.

I was born and raised in the town of Orangeburg, seventy-five miles northwest of Charleston, in the house that Henry Fordham's son, a formidable man named Major John Hammond Fordham, built for his family in 1903. There were six of us in the household. Our grandmother Sadie Fordham Smith and our great-aunt Florella Fordham were two of Major Fordham's daughters; they had lived in the house since it was brand-new, when Sadie was seventeen and Florella was twenty-three. Our mother, Louisa Smith Robinson, had been born in the house and lived there her entire long life, except for two years when she was away studying for master's degrees and one year when she was a newlywed. Our father, Harold Irwin Robinson, had moved into the house after marrying Louisa in 1952 and trying briefly, and unsuccessfully, to convince her to settle in the Detroit area where he'd grown up. I came along in 1954, Ellen in 1959, and today the Fordham home, with all its history and all its ghosts, belongs to the two of us.

Anchoring the corner of Boulevard and Oak Streets, the house is a characteristically southern structure—one and a half stories, with white wooden siding, two graceful bay windows, four dormers poking through the roof, and a wide, curving wraparound front porch that serves as an auxiliary living room during the hot months. I marvel at the integrity and durability of the building materials they used back then. After my father died and my mother had no one living in the house with her, I decided to install some motion-sensor lights for added security. What I thought would be maybe a two-hour job took all day, and not just because of my lack of aptitude as a handyman. I had to make a couple of trips to the hardware store to find a power drill with sufficient torque and a sharp-enough bit to make more than a dent in the wood siding, which is only slightly more yielding than granite.

When I was young, the porch was always furnished with rocking chairs, a wooden swing big enough for two people, and a piece of furniture that still remains. We called it a "glider"—a wide metal seat, painted white, that gently swayed back and forth in a floor-mounted frame instead of being suspended from the ceiling. While Ellen and I spent long summer nights in the swing, straining to touch the ceiling with our toes, the adults sat in the rockers and the glider moving softly to the quiet rhythms of conversation.

Above the glider is a narrow little window too high to look through without straining on tiptoes. Inside, on the other side of that wall, Major Fordham installed a massive black upright piano, which was still there when I was young, after half a century. The window was designed into the house, my grandmother once told me, because of the belief at the time that pianos needed to "breathe" fresh air. The piano had a textured, ebonized finish that was fashionable around the turn of the twentieth century, and I recall its being slightly out of tune. My grandmother once had been such a talented pianist that she taught music and played at church on Sundays, and my mother also knew how to play. Neither of them sat down at the black piano often, though. For me, it was an object of fascination. I liked to open the front panel and explore how the mechanism worked—the keys activating the felt-tipped hammers that struck the metal strings to make all the different notes. When I was in my teens, my family bought a new, much smaller spinet piano, mostly for Ellen to learn on, and they put it in a different room. They donated the old piano to Trinity Methodist Church, our family's church, three blocks away down Boulevard Street. The instrument sat there for years, breathless, in the basement activity room.

On our family room wall, near the old piano's window, there is a large photographic portrait of Louisa Fordham, my great-grandmother, Major Fordham's beloved wife. Surrounded by an oval frame of polished wood, it shows her wearing a high-collared blouse and the kind of searching, romantic look associated with Victorian heroines. Her eyes gaze into the room with emotion and what looks like a touch of sadness.

On another wall in the same room—the first wall you see when you enter the house—is a similarly formal, slightly larger portrait of Major Fordham. It is an artifact that defines the house, at least for me, and in many ways our family. The frame ringing his image is circular and also of polished wood. Welcoming visitors to his domain, or perhaps judging them, Major Fordham projects no romance. His eyes are as dark as pieces of coal, his skin just a shade lighter. He looks self-possessed, confident, proud, uncompromising. He was all those things, and this powerful image of him is as much an integral, structural element of our family home as any brick or timber.

When Ellen and I were growing up, those portraits always seemed to be taking our measure. Their gaze was unrelenting and scrutinizing—his, impatient and stern; hers, more generous but still formidable. The images constantly reminded us that the Fordhams' hard work and remarkable achievements were never to be forgotten, never to be dishonored.

We knew that important family talismans lay in a big black safe that Major Fordham kept in the main bedroom. It looks like a cartoon safe, the kind the Road Runner used to drop on Wile E. Coyote's head; and it is incredibly heavy, which is probably why it still sits today where the Major left it. When he died in 1922, he took the combination to his grave in Orangeburg Cemetery. A locksmith had to be called.

When I was growing up, the safe was always closed but never locked. That bedroom was my grandmother's; and because the safe had belonged to her father, I had the sense that it now belonged to her. The contents, therefore, seemed private. At the same time, though, I was curious about everything, and so, sometimes, while my grandmother was busy in the kitchen, I would peek inside. The old, yellowed papers I found didn't mean anything special to me; there were papers and photographs stashed away everywhere throughout the house—boxed under beds, loose in desk and dresser drawers, long forgotten in the attics or in the backyard shed. The safe was just one of many places where my mother or grandmother would search for a document, picture, or keepsake when she wanted to tell us something about the family.

I knew that my mother's side of the family was from Charleston. I knew that Major Fordham was the patriarch who had built our house. I knew that he had been a Reconstruction-era success story, that he had been a prominent man, that he had been a loving but demanding father to his six children. I knew he had been a character. I knew, vaguely, that *his* father, Henry Fordham, had been a free man before the Civil War. I knew myriad discrete facts about our family, I thought I had grasped the broad outlines of our history, and I had met more Fordham relatives than I could count. But I had no sense of how it all fit together, no sense of what it all meant.

That was the state of my knowledge for a long time—through high school, college at the University of Michigan, and my first journalism job, at the *San Francisco Chronicle*. In 1980, I was hired by *The Washington Post* and moved back east—with my Baltimore-born wife, Avis Collins Robinson, whom I'd met at a coffee shop near Golden Gate Park.

Being so much closer meant that I saw my family more often. Avis and I had been married for a couple of years, and my mother kept asking when we'd start presenting her with grandkids; my grandmother Sadie was ninety-four, and her health was finally beginning to fail. On one of our frequent trips to Orangeburg, I finally took another look at the papers in Major Fordham's safe and found some items that intrigued me: the construction contract for the house, a letter to Major Fordham from Theodore Roosevelt, the Major's handwritten draft of a powerful speech he gave in 1908. These facts and papers and pictures and stories began to coalesce into a narrative, and that narrative wanted to be written down.

The *Post* had a Sunday section called Outlook, and as a break from ponderous arguments about public policy and foreign affairs written by éminences grises, the section's editors welcomed extended essays by staff members that observed the world through a wider lens. In 1981, I wrote a long Outlook piece in which our house in Orangeburg was the main character. I traced the outlines of Major John Hammond Fordham's life, related some of the stories Sadie had told about her illustrious father, recounted what I knew of our family's history, and ended with a tragic episode from the civil rights struggle, the Orangeburg Massacre, which happened a few hundred yards from our house when I was a sophomore in high school. The focus, the "so what" of the piece, was the house itself—its longevity, its profound connection with my family, its lessons in the value of permanence.

The essay was well received, both by my *Post* colleagues and, to my surprise, by readers who wrote to offer their reflections. In those days, of course, reacting to something one read in the newspaper involved more than scrolling down to the comments section and batting out a few quick sentences; it required taking out a sheet of paper, typing one's thoughts or writing them out in longhand, folding the paper neatly and putting it into an envelope, addressing the envelope, affixing a postage stamp, and dropping the letter into a mailbox. None of that felt as onerous in 1981 as it sounds today; still, it took time and effort—and letters about my house and its history continued to arrive for weeks.

Within the family, meanwhile, the piece entered the annals of family lore. It was sent out by the *Post*'s syndicate, the Washington Post Writers Group, and far-flung family members sent me copies of the article as it had appeared in newspapers across the country. When I reread the piece now, I wince at the details I got wrong. But I take pride in the fact that those mistakes are few. It was the first time anyone had tried to assemble and organize the fragments of our family's story, and I got the big things right.

For me, that essay had two big, lasting impacts. First, it inspired my mother's first cousin Grace Manggrum, who lived in Cincinnati, to embark on a decade-long quest to unearth and chronicle everything she possibly could find about our genealogy. At a time when most of her research had to be done through correspondence with librarians and heritage buffs, Aunt Grace did extraordinary work that holds up as remarkably accurate. For years, she wrote back and forth with my mother, cross-checking her own findings against whatever my mother knew, suspected, or might once have heard. In 1990, Aunt Grace assembled all her discoveries into a seventy-page report. She made copies, put them neatly into binders, and sent one to every household in the family.

The other impact of the Outlook piece was that seeing the way it resonated for others made me realize that my family's house, documents, photographs, and oral history constituted an extremely rare and precious gift and also imposed a responsibility. All that material told a bigger and more important story. I didn't know what that larger story was, but I had the sense that I was destined to find it and share it. I remember that feeling because it was so odd. I was a journalist; I dealt in facts, events, accidents, misdeeds, consequences. I knew how a random encounter or a missed connection could change a life, and I didn't believe in destiny. Yet there was a disconnect between what I believed and what I felt.

In any event, I didn't return to the subject for nearly forty years. Life and career have a way of intervening: Avis and I had a son. I became an editor at the *Post.* We spent a year at Harvard, where Avis earned a master's degree and I was a Nieman Fellow. We spent four years in Buenos Aires, where I was the *Post*'s South America correspondent, and two years in London, where I was the *Post*'s bureau chief. We had another son. We came home, and I spent five years as the number two editor on the foreign desk and six years running the Style section. I started writing a column, won a Pulitzer Prize, became a talking head. I wrote two books plus a third, *Disintegration*, in 2010.

I did want to return to the family story in earnest, but there was always something that took priority—the insatiable maw of my *Washington Post* column, a new election cycle to write about, a second job as a television commentator, another new election cycle, nine years of enormously gratifying but time-devouring service as a member of the Pulitzer Prize Board. I simply didn't have the bandwidth for anything else. It was never the right time to take a deep, immersive dive into my history—until, finally, that moment came.

The first push toward family and the past was the Covid-19 pandemic. In March 2020, when workplaces suddenly shut down and we all got sent home, I was like a lot of people: I went inside and stayed there for months, both physically and psychologically. Isolation bred reflection, and I found myself thinking more about heritage and history. Over the years, I had taken a few items from Major Fordham's safe, brought them to my house, and tucked them away in a cabinet in my study. One day, I pulled them out for the first time in years—an old Orangeburg city directory, with the Major and his adult children listed; a powerful and heartbreaking speech the Major gave in 1908; a little leather-bound notebook in which he kept his accounts. I came across a faded copy of the Outlook section with my essay about the house on the front page, and I pulled that out, too. At the time, I didn't quite know why, but I needed to think about our past.

Then came the second big shove: the murder of George Floyd. The excruciating, infuriating cell phone video of a white police officer kneeling on the neck of an unarmed Black man for nine and a half endless minutes, slowly choking the life out of him, set off massive protests across the nation. Huge multiracial crowds marched in every major city; Senator Mitt Romney of Utah, of all people—a conservative Republican and a lifelong member of the Mormon Church—joined demonstrators as they marched in Washington, D.C. On Sixteenth Street, visible from the White House just across Lafayette Square, D.C. mayor Muriel Bowser blocked off traffic and had city workers paint "BLACK LIVES MATTER" in fifty-foot letters on the pavement. The country's political, cultural, and intellectual leaders—with the glaring exception of President Donald Trump—all spoke of the need for a national reckoning on the issue of racial justice.

I allowed myself to hope that we would finally have that reckoning. But a voice in the back of my head kept saying, "We've been here before. We've been here before. We've been here before . . ." Just twelve years earlier, in 2008, I had been so hopeful when Barack Obama became the first Black man to be elected president of the United States. I'd never dreamed I would live to see that milestone; I'd never dreamed such a thing was even possible. But then, almost immediately, I witnessed the white backlash—the rise of the Tea Party, the implacable opposition to Obama's agenda, and finally the election of Trump. I didn't know how to interpret all this except as a reaction to the great leap forward of Obama's presidency—a revanchist taking back. I saw how this pattern had repeated itself over the centuries: African Americans would make a major advance, would begin to be seen as full American citizens—but then, in short order, that full citizenship would be revoked.

And I realized that what I knew of my family's history—the little I knew, compared with what I know now—traced this recurring cycle of hard-won progress and forced retreat. I was beginning to see the outlines of a much larger narrative, a quintessentially American history that I seemed destined to tell, given the wealth of documentation my family had kept for more than two centuries. I saw how doggedly my ancestors, like other African Americans, had clung to American ideals—and how hopefully they had pursued the American dream. It felt as if I had been given both a privilege and a responsibility. I had the outlines of a story that I wanted to tell and that I felt I had an obligation to tell.

I NEVER STOPPED WONDERING about my deeper history—before the time of Major Fordham, before the time of his father, Henry. I wondered about my first African ancestor to set shackled foot on this continent. He or she had a name. He or she came from *somewhere*—not "Africa" in general but a specific place, a community that was situated in its own particular landscape, strung alongside a river or hugging a coastline or nestled amid dry interior hills. He or she had a mother, a father, grandparents, siblings, cousins, friends. He or she had a clan, a language, a culture, a faith. All this history had been obliterated by one act of violent separation followed by many acts of deliberate erasure, and it is forever gone.

That missing part of my heritage—that missing part of *me*—had not been lost. It had not somehow been mislaid like a set of housekeys or absentmindedly left in an Uber like a cell phone. It had not been accidentally wiped when someone clicked Delete instead of Save. There had been nothing at all inadvertent about its disappearance. It had been stolen.

Enslavers in the English colonies of the New World went to great lengths to sever any ties their captives had with the past and with one another. They wanted us to be empty vessels they could label with new names and fill with new words, new deities, new Commandments, new rituals, and a new, false, diminished sense of our worth and our place in the world. From the white captors' point of view, this was done not so much out of contempt or animus as out of necessity. Their fortunes and their lives depended on being able to control large numbers of able-bodied Black men, women, boys, and girls who locally outnumbered them—twenty, forty, sixty Black bodies crammed into drafty, leaky slave shacks versus maybe a dozen white family members in the big house, aided and abetted by a few white overseers. Firearms gave whites some protection, but they were no guarantee that a plantation owner wouldn't be awakened in the middle of the night by the point of a sharp knife against his throat. Our captors could not allow us to feel confident in the strength of our numbers. They wanted us to feel small, weak, powerless, overwhelmed, ungrounded, disconnected, and thus easier to control.

I feel the absence of my deep, pre-American history. I feel it the way an amputee suffers phantom pain in a missing limb. I keep looking for what was stolen from me. And occasionally, I glimpse what might be fragments of it.

Family legend says that Henry Fordham's lineage may have arrived in Charleston from Barbados, one of the British islands in the Caribbean where some Africans were "seasoned" (conditioned to the lash) in the sugarcane fields. When Avis and I went on vacation to Barbados in 1996, I decided to look for traces of my family in the Barbados National Archives. We drove around for quite a while (on the wrong side of the road) until we found the place, which I remember as a graceful old building filled with natural light. In a big reading room, we sat at a long table while helpful staff members, accustomed to visits from Americans seeking their roots, brought out materials they thought might help us with the search. A day of poring through records, however, gave up nothing more than hints and shadows.

Discouraged, we went back to our hotel, and I called Aunt Grace, who by then was firmly established as the family's chief genealogist. I had been looking for records of slave owners named Fordham. But on that phone call, she made me understand for the first time that the Fordham name hadn't attached itself to our family until after Henry's 1829 sale to Richard Fordham. Instead, she said, I should look for a Black woman named Jenny, the "Negro woman" who was sold at the same time as Henry. Jenny had been owned by Isabella Perman, whose maiden name had been Isabella Fell. So, I should look for a woman named Jenny who had some connection with those two surnames.

We returned to the archives, and a senior researcher named Shirley "Archer" Griffith helped us renew the quest, bringing out reels of microfilm and precious old ledger books recording births, baptisms, and deaths. We finally did find a family named Fell who lived in Barbados around the right time, in Saint Philip Parish. We also found a family in the same parish named Perreman—pretty close to Perman. And we found that on November 27, 1793, an enslaved adult named Kitty Fell was baptized at Saint Philip's Church; she would have been the right age, I thought, to be Jenny's mother. We could find no definitive records linking Kitty Fell to the Fell family, although it was no great stretch to infer some connection. We also found no record of Kitty having a daughter, and no record of Kitty being sold away to Charleston. We had bits and pieces that might fit together, but we couldn't figure out how.

The English kept meticulous records of the sires and dams of the Thoroughbred horses they bred and raced, but they couldn't be bothered to keep even rudimentary family histories of the human beings they claimed to own. Yet it's not as if they were admitting that they were ashamed of slavery; they knew in their hearts that it was wrong, but they rationalized it to themselves by claiming it was somehow divinely ordained, or at least divinely permitted, and thus was no sin that had to be hidden. Perhaps they just saw the enslaved as more interchangeable, and infinitely more disposable, than their prized stallions and mares. Or maybe they thought that if they kept no records, future generations would have the option of pretending the centuries-long holocaust had never happened.

My family's story, like any epic narrative, had to start at the beginning. And I had no idea when that beginning was.

Not specifically, I mean. I am a descendant of enslaved African Americans, so, obviously my deepest roots lie in Africa. But saying that is almost as vague and unsatisfying as saying that my ancestors lived on planet Earth. Africa is the world's second-biggest continent, home to fifty-four sovereign nation-states, hundreds of ethnicities and languages, and a vast, kaleidoscopic array of diverse cultures. It is safe to narrow the range of possibilities to West Africa because that is where the transatlantic slave trade primarily operated, but this is roughly like saying one's ancestors came from "Europe" or "Latin America." Somewhere on that continent, there is a city, town, or village where Henry Fordham's progenitors lived and died for hundreds or thousands of years, where they were grounded and rooted, where distant relatives walk the streets today. That place exists, and I know I will never find it. I might be able to get closer than was possible even a few years ago, though, because today there are powerful research tools that no one could have dreamed of when I wrote that Outlook piece in 1981.

The most revolutionary new resource is DNA testing. I mailed away my saliva sample and waited, impatiently, with no real expectation of an aha moment. When the results came back, they offered no surprises, but they did confirm my general assumptions. According to the lab I used—and I know that results can vary—34 percent of my DNA comes from what is now Nigeria, 20 percent comes from what is now Mali, and another 26 percent comes from other places up and down the west coast of Africa. That doesn't depart from what I'd have predicted, and it doesn't narrow things down meaningfully.

The remaining 20 percent of my DNA comes mostly from Germany, with a small contribution from the British Isles—again, no surprise: I knew I had white ancestors as well as Black. Someday, perhaps, the collective human genome will be sufficiently catalogued to trace my DNA to some specific Nigerian village or English hamlet. Until then, science tells me what I always knew: I am an amalgam of the enslaved and the enslaver. I am an African American.

So, I had confirmed—as I had suspected—that modern science could tell me next to nothing definitive about my deepest history. Genetics could pin down no specifics about the lives my West African ancestors led before being kidnapped, chained, and brought to the New World. All I had were possibilities and probabilities based on the places in West

Africa my genes came from. But that was better than nothing. Over the years, I had come across what I imagined were hints of my possible past—when I was a child in Orangeburg, when I was a foreign correspondent in Latin America. The DNA test couldn't rule in any of these histories, but it made clear that I should not rule them out.

One example: When I was little, among the out-of-town visitors who would occasionally drop by to visit my grandmother and great-aunt were two women from Charleston. These ladies were friends of my grandmother's relatives, I think, or maybe there was some Methodist Church connection. I don't remember their names. What got my attention was that when they spoke to each other, they fell into an incomprehensible, rapid-fire patois. It definitely wasn't English. As far as I was concerned, they might as well have been speaking ancient Greek.

They had been speaking Gullah (also called Geechee), a creole language based on English but laden with a hodgepodge of West African vocabulary, grammar, and syntax. "Gullah" is possibly a corruption of "Angola," a region and culture from which many Africans were seized; or it might refer to the Gola people, an ethnic group living on land that is now in Liberia and Sierra Leone. If you have ever referred to peanuts as "goobers," you are using a Gullah word that comes from the Kongo term for peanut, *nguba*. On the islands around Charleston—including Daniel Island, where Richard Fordham had his plantation and where my great-great-grandfather grew into manhood—something of Africa survived three long centuries after the first Africans worked those abundant fields.

Gullah evolved as a lingua franca that allowed enslaved Africans from different cultures and language groups to communicate with one another. Linguists have been able to make definitive linkages between Gullah and African languages such as Ewe, Efik, Gā, Twi, and Yoruba. Henry Fordham almost surely would have understood every word those women who visited from Charleston were saying. So would have other ancestors whose names I do not know: At least two other branches of my family tree on my mother's side and one on my father's side lead back to the Charleston area.

Researching the Gullah linguistic survival, I learned that a pioneering African American scholar named Lorenzo Dow Turner, working in the 1930s, concluded that a traditional Gullah religious dance called the "ring shout"—in which worshipers form a ring and circle counterclockwise while singing and clapping—was brought to the islands by enslaved Muslims. Turner wrote that the dance mimics the way pilgrims on the hajj circumambulate the sacred Kaaba in the Grand Mosque of Mecca.

As many as one-third of the Africans brought here in chains were taken from lands that were predominately Muslim. Both my mother and my father gave me genes from Mali, according to the DNA test I took, and Islam arrived in Mali in the ninth century, long before the transatlantic slave trade began. So, one or more of my distant ancestors could have been Muslim.

Or not. It was, as I said, a glimpse. Of a possibility.

I had more hints during the years I spent working as *The Washington Post*'s correspondent in South America, from 1988 to 1992, and later researching the book I wrote about Cuba. What I saw then was the vibrancy of syncretic religions that melded the traditional beliefs of enslaved Yoruba men and women, kidnapped from what is now Nigeria, with the Roman Catholicism imposed by their captors. In Brazil, the faith is known as Candomblé or macumba; in Cuba, as Regla de Ocha or Lucumí; in Haiti, as vodou. The American lexicon reduces the last religion to two terms I never once heard from the lips of actual practitioners, "Santería" and "voodoo."

I spent a good deal of time and effort (and a decent amount of the *Post*'s money) trying to understand as much as I could about this worldview, and I knew at the time that I was doing so mostly for personal reasons. I wasn't really looking for news stories; I was looking for heritage and connection. The idea of a fully elaborated African theology having endured and prospered despite centuries of slavery and oppression seemed to me nothing short of a miracle. Spending time with a holy man or woman versed in the Yoruba faith never made me believe. But it always made me *feel*.

I thought back to these experiences decades later, when I got those DNA results and saw that one-third of my DNA came from Nigeria, where the Yoruba deities would have been present and active in most people's lives. I knew that this might be as close as I would ever get to the very beginning of my African American history. I looked up at a small figurine from Cuba that I keep in my study, a stylized representation of one of the orishas, or demigods—Eleguá, the gatekeeper who opens the doors to the spirit world. And I *felt* again.

THE FACT THAT 20 percent of my genetic inheritance comes from Europe makes me like most Black Americans: According to the National Human Genome Research Institute at the National Institutes of Health, "an African American individual in the United States has, on average, about 75–80 percent West African ancestry and about 20–25 percent European ancestry." I am right at the midpoint of the bell curve. Toward the extremes, I know Black Americans who have been told by DNA testing that they have few European genes, if any; and I also know African Americans who have been surprised to learn that they are well under 50 percent African.

I am also like most African Americans in that it is difficult to trace my white ancestry. A couple of distinctive names that came down through oral history on my mother's side—DesVerney, Vanderhorst, Chisolm—have been impossible to pin down, and I have had to conclude that they are dead ends. My mother's maternal grandmother and paternal grandfather were so light-skinned that they obviously had recent European ancestry, but they both happened to have been born with the all-too-common surname of Smith. Efforts to trace them back, and to tease out connections with white slave-owning families that can only be imputed, get lost in a vast sea of Smiths. On my father's side of the family, I have met relatives who could pass for white at a Klan rally; again, though, I run into brick walls when I try to identify white forebears.

The DNA test did find that I have a handful of distant white relatives, fourth to sixth cousins with whom I share less than 1 percent of my genetic inheritance, just enough to establish the relationship. But we have been unable to identify any common ancestors—or, for that matter, common geography that would put our progenitors in the same place at the same time. These links do exist, as DNA does not lie, but they are lost—at least for now: As more people decide to get tested and make their results open to possible matches, I may someday find a white lineage I can trace.

The most important thing that DNA reveals is that all of us, all living humans, are related. We all descend from a small group of common ancestors, no matter how much melanin we have in our skin or how tightly curled our hair might be. Aside from infinitesimal blips in the genome, like the sickle cell trait or susceptibility to skin cancer, we are all the same. Race has never been a biological fact of any import. It has always been a social construct, a relatively recent invention that allowed the powerful to justify exploitation of the powerless.

In 1776, Thomas Jefferson, famously an enslaver of human beings, wrote that "all men are created equal." Just a few years later, in *Notes on the State of Virginia*, Jefferson invented a pseudoscientific justification for his hypocrisy:

> I advance it therefore as a suspicion only, that the blacks, whether originally a distinct race, or made distinct by time and circumstances, are inferior to the whites in the endowments both of body and mind. It is not against experience to suppose, that different species of the same genus, or varieties of the same species, may possess different qualifications. Will not a lover of natural history then, one who views the gradations in all the races of animals with the eye of philosophy, excuse an effort to keep those in the department of man as distinct as nature has formed them? This unfortunate difference of color, and perhaps of faculty, is a powerful obstacle to the emancipation of these people.

If he was being honest, Jefferson would have admitted that a far greater obstacle to emancipation was that the unpaid labor of African Americans—and the license to summon at least one of them, Sally Hemings, to his bedchamber—made his life more prosperous, comfortable, and enjoyable than it otherwise would have been.

It was race as a social construct, an elaborate fiction, that gave Richard Fordham the "right" to purchase my great-great-grandfather in 1829. It was race, a manufactured distinction, that required Henry Fordham to purchase his own freedom in 1851. And it is race, a weaponized fairy tale, that so far has kept me from knowing with any certainty even the names, let alone the hopes and dreams, of Henry's predecessors in my American history.

So, I begin with him. Henry's self-liberation staked a claim on the rights and freedoms that Jefferson—and most white Americans—wanted to deny him. The partial citizenship he was able to seize allowed him to build a good life for himself and his family. But over the next decade, as the city and the nation spiraled toward war, America steadily and remorselessly took that freedom back.

Chapter Two

PROUD BUT TENUOUS FREEDOM

In the fraught decade before the Civil War, my great-great-grandfather owned a tidy wooden house at 12 Washington Street, near the Cooper River docks, where he lived with his wife, Maria, and his young son, John. Barely a block away was Gadsden's Wharf, the notorious pier where at least one hundred thousand enslaved Africans were brought ashore during the peak years of the slave trade—more than at any other landing in North America. Men, women, boys, and girls in shackles would have passed within yards of Henry Fordham's front door as they were led in chained coffles, disoriented and terrified, from the hellish ships to the crowded holding pens where they would be groomed for the auction block.

Henry's busy city was a place of contradictions. There was the quotidian horror of commerce in human beings at infernal marketplaces all around town, including on the steps of the grand old colonial-era Exchange, downtown on East Bay Street. Most of the people bought there were destined for shortened, brutish lives, spending their days in sunbaked fields and their nights in squalid slave quarters, sequestered from the world beyond the fences of the plantations where they toiled.

In dense and cramped Charleston, however, even grand mansions lacked enough space to shelter all the household's enslaved workers. Many of the enslaved lived off-site, in run-down and spartan boardinghouses, which meant they had to walk to and from the residences, shops, and warehouses where they worked. Others, especially those with specialized skills, were often rented out by their owners to other white employers; these enslaved men and women were required by law to wear little copper badges announcing the kind of work they were permitted to do—"Porter" or "Servant" or "Mechanic." It was normal to see enslaved African Americans in the streets, unsupervised but hardly free, commuting to their workplaces or running their assigned errands. Their prison was the entire city, the entire state, the entire South.

The 1861 Charleston city census reported that there were 409 individuals living on Washington Street, which ran less than a quarter mile from Laurens Street at the southern end to Chapel Street at the northern. One hundred ninety of those residents were classified as "White Persons," 174 were listed as "Slaves," and 45, including Henry and his family, were "Free Colored." Those numbers approximated the demographics of the city as a whole: Within Charleston's city limits, which had recently been expanded to include the upper section of the peninsula known as the Neck, the census counted 26,969 white people and 21,400 Black people. Of the African Americans residing in the city, according to the census, 17,655 were enslaved and 3,785, or roughly 20 percent, were free.

It is likely that the enslaved were undercounted. They were anonymous, as far as the official enumerators were concerned, and the fact that so many lived apart from the Charlestonians who owned them or belonged to planters whose rural households were not included in the city census meant that many Black people would have been missed. The tally of "Free Colored" was probably quite accurate, though, and the presence of so many Black men, women, and children who were not enslaved made Charleston a striking anomaly in the antebellum South.

According to the 1860 U.S. census, in the fifteen slaveholding states there lived 4,201,000 African Americans, of whom 3,950,000, or 94 percent, were enslaved—and just 251,000, or 6 percent, were not. In other words, the free Black population in the South amounted to little more than a rounding error. Nineteen out of every 20 African Americans living in states where slavery was still legal were classified as property, not citizens, and were forced to endure involuntary confinement, forced labor, corporal punishment, physical and psychological torture, and vile sexual abuse.

The few free African Americans in the South were concentrated in the cities, especially the cosmopolitan ports such as Savannah, Mobile, New Orleans, and Charleston. In this aspect, too, Henry's city was full of contradictions.

There were basically two ways for African Americans to become free. The less common was the way my great-great-grandfather did it: Skilled enslaved artisans, such as blacksmiths, were sometimes jobbed out by their owners and allowed to keep a small fraction of the money paid for their labor. Henry would have taken on as many outside jobs as he could, sustained the focus and discipline to hoard his earnings as savings, and eventually amassed enough money to effectively buy himself from his owner. My assumption is that Otis Mills, a very successful businessman, probably drove a hard bargain.

The other route to freedom was via the wills and testaments of deceased owners, a gesture most commonly performed for children born of the rape of Black women by the white men who held them as property. Sex between enslaver and enslaved is rape by definition, as there can never be consent without the possibility of its withholding.

Another of my great-great-grandfathers, also on my mother's side, was a tailor named Francis A. Smith. He also lived in Charleston, and he shows up in editions of the Free Negro Book more than a decade before Henry liberated himself. My family has a photograph of his son, also named Francis, who was so light-skinned, with such "good" wavy hair, that it is no stretch to assume the elder Francis's emancipation resulted from partial white parentage. One branch of the Smith family tree—not the one that leads through my maternal grandfather to me—was even able, and inclined, to successfully "pass" for white; we have a photograph of them, too.

By contrast, a Freedman's Bank document I found lists Henry's complexion as "Black." We have no photograph of him, but his son had cocoa-dark skin, coarse hair, and African features. Henry could not have been any plantation owner's bastard son.

The divergent paths to antebellum freedom taken by my ancestors Fordham and Smith trace two long, unbroken strands of African American history. One is the story of hard work, perseverance, creativity, skill, struggle, and victory against impossible odds—the reality, as I was taught growing up, that to rise half as high as a white man in this country, a Black man must be twice as good. The other is the story of the truly unspeakable crimes committed against Black people on these shores, beginning in 1619, when the first captive Africans were bartered to Virginia colonists in exchange for provisions—and also the occasional willingness of white enslavers to assuage their consciences with individual kindnesses, though not with anything that might aspire to comprehensive justice.

Henry Fordham was free, as of 1851, but what kind of free man was he? That is not a rhetorical question, because some free persons of color in Charleston had a sense of themselves as special and superior, occupying a privileged intermediate racial stratum between white and Black.

Only a very few had any significant wealth. The College of Charleston scholar Bernard Powers, in his book *Black Charlestonians: A Social History, 1822–1885*, highlights a free Black man named Jehu Jones Sr. who owned a hotel on posh Broad Street. Jones had purchased his freedom from his owner, a tailor, and built his assets by buying and selling real estate before seeing that there was greater profit to be made as an innkeeper. According to the *South Carolina Encyclopedia*, "Jones and his wife Abigail turned 33 Broad Street into a popular hotel, catering to travelers on extended visits, such as the portrait artist Samuel F. B.

Morse [better remembered as one of the inventors of the telegraph]. Elite white society patronized the establishment and praised it highly for its comfort and fine food."

Jones's story shows what free Black Charlestonians could do when given the opportunity—but also how very tenuous the condition of being simultaneously "free" and "Black" inevitably was in a society based on racial hierarchy and subjugation. In 1822, at the peak of Jones's career, one of the pivotal events in South Carolina history derailed his life.

This turning point was the discovery, at the last minute, of a plan for a massive uprising of the enslaved. Led by a free Black man named Denmark Vesey, the revolt was meant to be more than just an escape to liberty. Vesey wanted to ignite an Armageddon that would reduce prideful Charleston to a smoking ruin. His plot was for a mutiny by thousands of enslaved African Americans, in both the city proper and the surrounding countryside, especially the fertile Sea Islands, where enslavers like Richard Fordham had their plantations. White slave owners were to be slain without quarter. The fields and the streets were to be soaked with the blood of tyrants, made to run free by weapons that Vesey intended to pillage from the city's well-stocked Meeting Street Arsenal. As their final act, the rebels planned to seize ships at the wharf and sail away to freedom in Haiti, the revolutionary Black republic whose very existence whites in the South saw as a mortal threat. Vesey originally scheduled the uprising for July 14, Bastille Day, in honor of the French Revolution. Concerned about the potential for betrayal, he moved the date back to June 16.

Vesey's worries were justified. In May, two enslaved men who knew about the plan—and doubted its wisdom—had begun meeting with local authorities and keeping them informed as the conspiracy ripened. Before Vesey could make his move, he and thirty-four of his fellow conspirators were arrested, tried, and hanged. As if that were not enough of a warning to anyone thinking about rebellion, an African Methodist Episcopal church that Vesey had used as a headquarters for his secret meetings was burned to the ground.

It is hard to overstate how deeply traumatic the discovery of the Vesey plot was for whites in Charleston. At the time, they were outnumbered by African Americans across the Low Country. The ultimate nightmare of a mass revolt, the "servile insurrection" that whites constantly feared, had narrowly been averted.

And this was not the first time: The city's historical memory was still haunted by a previous near miss.

In 1739, Charleston witnessed the Stono Rebellion, the biggest and bloodiest enslaved uprising in the Deep South during the colonial period. On September 9 of that year, just south of the city, a group of about twenty Black men gathered near the Stono River, determined to escape their bondage. They went to Hutcheson's country store, took guns and ammunition, and killed the two shopkeepers. Heading south toward Spanish Florida—where freedom was being promised to escapees from slavery in the British colonies—they collected more recruits as they walked, until they numbered nearly one hundred. The rebels killed more than twenty white people who tried to get in their way, sparing one innkeeper who "was kind to his slaves," according to one historian, Peter H. Wood. A militia of white planters caught up to the insurrectionists at the Edisto River and defeated them after a running battle. Up to fifty of the Black insurgents were killed in the fight or later executed, and some others were sold away to planters in the West Indies. At least a few are believed to have disappeared into the wilds. I like to imagine that they made it all the way to Florida and that their descendants live among us today.

South Carolina's panicked colonial authorities enacted a harsh "slave code" that other colonies used as a model. The legislation codified the inferior status of the enslaved, making clear they had no rights or standing under English common law. Murder of an enslaved African American by a white person was reduced to a misdemeanor, punishable by a fine; murder of whites by Blacks was to be punished, unsurprisingly, by death. Rebellion also was officially made a capital offense for the enslaved, along with arson and giving instruction in the use of poisonous plants. And for whites, teaching an enslaved African American to read and write was made punishable by a hundred-dollar fine and six months in prison. Many years later, after the Revolutionary War, which was fought under the banner that "all men are created equal," the nascent South Carolina state legislature upheld the colonial slave code and made it "perpetual."

Over time, many of the code's toughest strictures proved impractical, inconvenient, or simply unenforceable. Whites in Charleston gradually let down their guard. But now came the terrifying Vesey plot, incubated in the heart of the city, planned not just as a mass escape but as an act of brutal vengeance. Even with Vesey and his fellow rebels now dead, how was anyone to be sure there were not others out there secretly planning an uprising and a bloodbath? And wouldn't the leaders of any new conspiracy likely be free Black men, like Vesey, who had money of their own and could move around the city and the countryside as they pleased? Vesey, after all, had been a respected carpenter who ran his own business and was trusted to work in white people's homes. How many other free African Americans might be walking Charleston's streets by day and scheming for revolution by night?

The state legislature quickly passed a law putting new strictures on free persons of color—among them the requirement that every free African American man over age fifteen have a white "guardian," who had to appear at the local courthouse and attest to the Black man's character. Another new law prohibited free African Americans who left the state from ever returning. My great-great-grandfather was unaffected; in 1822, he was still a young boy called Harry enslaved by the Perman family. But high-profile free Black men, including the hotelier Jehu Jones Sr., were squarely in the crosshairs.

Jones's wife, Abigail, his three sons, and his stepdaughter, Ann, were visiting relatives in New York when the new laws were passed, and as a result, they were barred from coming home to Charleston. Given his wealth and prominence, Jones was able to find a powerful "guardian"—South Carolina's incumbent governor, John Lyde Wilson. With Wilson's help, Jones successfully petitioned the legislature for permission to visit his family in their New York exile and return to Charleston; there is no record, however, of his ever having risked the journey. One of his sons did come home, in 1832—and was promptly thrown in jail for violating the no-return law. Jehu Jones Sr. died in 1833, and the governor allowed family members to come back to Charleston and take over management of the Jones Hotel.

There were a few other free African Americans who achieved similar status in antebellum Charleston—Eliza Lee, for example, who had such talent as a chef and such a head for business that at one point she was managing four restaurants, including the dining room at the Jones Hotel, and catering the annual banquet of the whites-only South Carolina Jockey Club. But these were rare exceptions, the unicorns and black swans of their time.

The majority of free African Americans in Charleston made their living with their hands. They were artisans and shopkeepers—blacksmiths like Henry Fordham, tailors like Francis A. Smith. Most had only rudimentary education. Only a few, including Jones and Lee, were themselves unabashed slave owners in the full sense of the word—they bought fellow dark-skinned human beings and exploited their uncompensated labor. Some other free Black men and women purchased and "owned" relatives as a way of securing their de facto freedom. For most free Black Charlestonians, however, it was all they could do to make a living for themselves, keep a roof over their heads, and walk the narrow, obstacle-strewn path their status permitted them to walk, the societal isthmus between bondage and citizenship.

It is hard to get as full a sense of the texture of Henry's life as I would like. He was forty years old when he wed his wife, Maria, who was thirty-seven—an unusually late marriage for both. It may have been his second marriage. He may have waited to marry Maria until he had secured his and her freedom. No photograph of him has survived, so I have to extrapolate my mental image of him from passed-down descriptions and from images of his son, my great-grandfather. While I know the addresses of the houses where he lived and the other properties he owned at various times, those structures are long gone. His old neighborhoods have been through multiple transformations.

I do know that his was a prayerful household. In addition to being a blacksmith and an entrepreneur, Henry was also a lay preacher; he was addressed as "Rev. Fordham," and for years he funded and operated a small storefront church. I know that he was literate, and I know that Maria was not; I managed to find her will, and she signed it with an *X*. I know that there must have been bookshelves in the house, because he valued education; he made sure that his only son was prepared for the best schooling available. I know that Henry doted on young John but did not coddle him, insisting that he hew to a strict moral code. And given the life Henry lived, given what he had endured and what he achieved, I know that at his center there must have been a core as hard as diamond.

As far as I can tell, Henry was not among the free African Americans in Charleston who validated their status and position by belonging to an exclusive "Brown" social club. Whether or not he wanted to join one of these cliques, I suspect his dark skin would have made him ineligible.

Colorism was a strong and pernicious prejudice in the Black community—one that whites encouraged as a way of keeping African Americans less unified and, thus, less of a threat. Light-skinned free African Americans were allowed to imagine that they were neither truly Black nor white, defining themselves with the colorist term "Brown" to signify their elevation. This fantasy was encouraged and validated by a wave of free mulatto émigrés from Haiti, who had been deprived by Toussaint L'Ouverture's revolution of the status and privileges they had enjoyed in a French colonial society with three sharply delineated racial castes—whites on top, mixed-race elites in the middle, and the Black masses on the bottom. French surnames are overrepresented in the membership lists of Charleston's Brown social clubs.

Jehu Jones Sr. belonged to the most elevated of these groups, the Brown Fellowship Society. Founded in 1790 by five mulatto members of St. Philip's Episcopal Church, the society performed only one practical service: It purchased and maintained a suitable burial ground for its members, who because of their race were ineligible for interment in the white cemeteries. The society's less tangible but more important function was to confirm its members' status in the uppermost tier of the free Brown elite. The membership was kept artificially small, and dues kept artificially high, to maintain the Brown Fellowship Society's aura of exclusivity.

My only other free great-great-grandfather whom I know of, Francis A. Smith, did belong to a Brown social club, albeit one that was less exalted: the Friendly Moralist Society. Unlike Henry Fordham, Francis was light-skinned enough to pass the "paper bag test"—no darker than that. In a city where whites and non-whites alike were acutely conscious of pedigree and social position, the Friendly Moralists occupied a middle tier. And like those both higher and lower in the Brown pecking order, they took themselves far too seriously. Along with the idea of occupying a middle racial stratum between Black and white came something of a persecution complex, a feeling of being loathed from above and below.

A vice president of the Friendly Moralists lamented, in an 1848 speech, that he and his fellow members were caught between "the prejudice of the white man" and "the deepest hate of our more sable brethren." If that was how the free Brown elite regarded the dark-skinned, to say nothing of the enslaved, then they were probably right that a certain antipathy was mutual. Nonetheless, demand for membership in the Friendly Moralists was always high—and despite that "sable brethren" speech, not all members agreed that light skin should be an absolute prerequisite for membership. That same year, a dark-skinned man named Edward Logan Jr. applied to join. He was of controversial hue but impeccable character, and a two-thirds majority of members—including Francis A. Smith—voted to admit him. An adamant minority objected strenuously, almost desperately, insisting that all who belonged to the society must visibly be of both white and Black heritage.

The "paper bag test" absolutists refused to accept their loss, and they found a technicality they could exploit: An examination of the books showed that one of the members who had voted to admit Logan was delinquent in his dues—as it happened, the laggard was my ancestor Francis Smith—and this meant that the vote had been conducted in contravention of the bylaws, making it null and void. Logan was out. The traditionalists' triumph was short-lived, however; Smith paid his back dues, the Friendly Moralists held another vote, and Logan was again invited to become a member. The losers were so upset, and so insistent on color as a proxy for status, that they broke away to form their own new social club, one that would uphold what they saw as the hallowed pure-Brown standards. The remaining Friendly Moralists continued their association with a new, more inclusive ethos.

None of this concerned Henry Fordham—it happened the year he was purchased by Otis Mills—but the various Brown societies were still going strong in 1851, when Henry finally became free. Over the next few years, he became a successful tradesman and property owner, achievements that fit the profile of a society member. Yet there is no evidence in the Fordham papers, in writings about the Brown societies, or in our family's oral history that he ever sought to join the Friendly Moralists, the Brown Fellowship, the Humane Brotherhood, or any of the other clubs. Maybe he assumed his skin color ruled him out. Maybe he was taking a principled stand against pretentiousness and colorism. Or maybe he had just decided that the social clubs' admission fees and membership dues were a waste of good money.

THE SENSE OF SECURITY, well-being, and unlimited prospects that Henry finally achieved when he bought his freedom was short-lived. As the tumultuous 1850s marched grimly toward apocalypse, the nation was fulfilling its manifest destiny through westward expansion—and tearing itself apart over the original sin of slavery. Free African Americans in Charleston would suffer collateral damage.

Congress had passed the Fugitive Slave Act in 1850, legally compelling free states to deny refuge to African Americans who fled from bondage—effectively making slavery once more a national institution, as it had been at the time of the Revolution, and not just a regional one. This law was a mandatory, nonnegotiable measure from the point of view of the southern states, and it was completely unacceptable to many in the North. Then, in 1854, Congress passed the Kansas-Nebraska Act, which revoked the 1820 Missouri Compromise prohibiting slavery in the vast lands of the Louisiana Purchase north of latitude 36°30'. The law allowed residents of the newly delineated Kansas and Nebraska territories, and others who would inevitably follow, to decide for themselves whether to permit slavery. This sparked a shocking wave of political violence in what the *New-York Tribune* dubbed "Bleeding Kansas."

Three years later, in 1857, the Supreme Court's decision in *Dred Scott v. Sandford* legally consigned all African Americans to inferior status, everywhere denying them the rights and protections enjoyed by white citizens. Chief Justice Roger Taney could not have been clearer, writing that Black people in the United States had "no rights which the white man was bound to respect."

Abraham Lincoln, a rising star in the new Republican Party, vividly laid out the stakes in an 1858 speech at the Illinois State Capitol that quickly became famous: "A house divided against itself cannot stand. I believe this government cannot endure, permanently half slave and half free. I do not expect the Union to be dissolved—I do not expect the house to fall—but I do expect it will cease to be divided. It will become all one thing, or all the other."

In state capitals across the South, elected officials understood Lincoln's words as calls for abolition. In South Carolina, with its Black majority, legislators thunderously proposed the unthinkable: secession from the Union. And in Charleston, with its chilling memories of the Stono Rebellion and the Vesey plot, city officials went beyond words to action. Still obsessed with the danger of free African Americans as potential leaders of a new revolt, authorities began arresting free Black men and women who failed to pay the annual capitation tax of $2.75 per individual. Henry Fordham continued to be listed in the annual Free Negro Book, meaning he must have paid the tax as required.

In October 1859 came the coup de grace: white abolitionist John Brown's bloody raid at Harpers Ferry. That attempt to spark a general uprising of the enslaved sent South Carolina's political and economic power structure into full-fledged, hair-on-fire panic.

White leaders in Charleston formed a Committee of Safety, a corps of vigilantes, and gave it the power to arrest anyone, white or Black, who displayed abolitionist sympathies. Whites who ran or in any way supported schools for Black children were especially targeted, along with households that received anti-slavery newspapers. The state legislature even debated radical proposals to seize all free African Americans and force them into slavery—including those, like Henry's son, John, who had been born free. And in August 1860, with the most pivotal presidential election in U.S. history approaching, the city of Charleston sent marshals door-to-door to canvass the homes of free Black people and demand that individuals produce proof of their freedom. Those who lacked the right papers were to be taken into custody and sold into slavery.

Free African Americans in Charleston, once so sure of their footing, suddenly found themselves navigating quicksand. Many who lacked the proper papers went out and bought slave tags, hoping the copper badges—identifying the wearer as enslaved and stating his or her trade—would at least protect them from cursory inspection while they were in the streets. Some who had limited means and options went so far as to sell themselves to local white owners, seeing that as a far better fate than being "sold down the river" to harsh plantation slavery in Alabama, Mississippi, Louisiana, or Texas. With local owners, they would at least be near family and friends; and the work, however arduous and demeaning, would be less punishing than the hell of the cotton fields.

Hundreds of free African Americans, some with all their documents in order, decided the prudent course of action was flight—to the free northern states, to Canada, to Haiti. They packed what they could and set off, by rail or by ship. This was a drastic move, however, because according to South Carolina law, there was no coming back for free persons of color. Everything they had built in Charleston, everything they had achieved, everything they had acquired, would be surrendered. And forever lost.

Henry Fordham stayed put. Surely, he would have prayed over that decision, but he also would have weighed the earthly pros and cons. I can only imagine the calculations he had to make. The document certifying his manumission, his passage from slavery to freedom, must have been unimpeachable. But it would have been difficult to have confidence that a piece of paper alone would guarantee protection, especially given that his freedom had been attained at a time when there were laws on the books intended to forbid manumission. What he had done—freeing himself and remaining in Charleston—was not supposed to be possible. Given the success of his business, he had relationships with wealthy and powerful white men—probably including his former owners, Richard Fordham and the tycoon Otis Mills. Perhaps Henry thought his influential connections were enough to make him and his family safe.

Or maybe the answer is simpler: Charleston was all that he had and all that he knew.

He wasn't a privileged mulatto of Haitian descent who could decide to take his chances in his family's homeland. He wasn't some plantation owner's mixed-race son or grandson, with family who had already moved away to New York or Philadelphia and who could help him get a fresh start up north. He had been born enslaved. He had lived in the Low Country at least since he was a young teenager, probably since his birth. Charleston and its environs constituted his known world. It was where he had made his life, won his freedom, and built his success. He had assets—two houses, a stake in a blacksmith's forge, valuable tools and equipment. He had a wife and son who would have to be uprooted if he decided to leave. He was still close to the two girls, Hagar and Margaret—now women—with whom he had been sold, all those years ago, to Richard Fordham; there are records that suggest he may have eventually "purchased" the women to set them free, that he may have given them lodgings in his house on Desportes Court, and that he felt close enough to them that he would have been reluctant to leave them behind. Perhaps most important, he had bet on himself all his life—had bet on his resourcefulness, his determination, his luck—and that wager had paid off. Henry may have been confident enough in his own abilities to double down.

In any event, the man must have had nerves of steel as he stayed in Charleston and watched the nation tear itself apart. War was coming. There would be blood.

ON DECEMBER 20, 1860, a convention of delegates from across the state of South Carolina, meeting in a grand auditorium in Charleston, approved a brief and legalistic ordinance to "dissolve the Union between the State of South Carolina and other States united with her under the compact entitled The Constitution of the United States of America." The ordinance formally repealed the state's 1788 ratification of the Constitution and its subsequent ratification of all amendments, including the Bill of Rights. *The Charleston Mercury* rushed out an "extra" that proclaimed, "THE UNION IS DISSOLVED!"

Four days later, on Christmas Eve, the convention issued a longer and more florid document that it called a "Declaration of the Immediate Causes Which Induce and Justify the Secession of South Carolina from the Federal Union." Those "immediate causes" involved one nonnegotiable issue: slavery. The declaration noted that a section of the Fourth Amendment to the U.S. Constitution mandated that "No person held to service or labor in one State, under the laws thereof, escaping into another, shall, in consequence of any law or regulation therein, be discharged from such service or labor, but shall be delivered up, on claim of the party to whom such service or labor may be due." Federal laws had been enacted to enforce this provision, including the Fugitive Slave Act.

> For many years these laws were executed. But an increasing hostility on the part of the non-slaveholding States to the institution of slavery, has led to a disregard of their obligations, and the laws of the General Government have ceased to effect the objects of the Constitution. The States of Maine, New Hampshire, Vermont, Massachusetts, Connecticut, Rhode Island, New York, Pennsylvania, Illinois, Indiana, Michigan, Wisconsin and Iowa, have enacted laws which either nullify the Acts of Congress or render useless any attempt to execute them. In many of these States the fugitive is discharged from service or labor claimed, and in none of them has the State Government complied with the stipulation made in the Constitution.

And now, the declaration said, came the despised president-elect Lincoln, who was not mentioned by name:

> A geographical line has been drawn across the Union, and all the States north of that line have united in the election of a man to the high office of President of the United States, whose opinions and purposes are hostile to slavery. He is to be entrusted with the administration of the common Government, because he has declared that that 'Government cannot endure permanently half slave, half free,' and that the public mind must rest in the belief that slavery is in the course of ultimate extinction. . . . The guaranties of the Constitution will then no longer exist; the equal rights of the States will be lost. The slaveholding States will no longer have the power of self-government, or self-protection, and the Federal Government will have become their enemy.

It is my habit to quote from the South Carolina declaration whenever someone tries to argue that the Civil War was about "states' rights" or impingements on sovereignty or some implicit constitutional right for states to secede. It was about those things only insofar as they bore on the ability of white people in the South to continue to own Black people as their property and compel their unpaid labor. That unholy privilege was under dire and intolerable threat.

The grand Italianate building on Meeting Street where the convention met was officially called South Carolina Institute Hall. After December 1860, though, everyone knew it by another name: Secession Hall. South Carolina had become the first state to officially leave the Union.

The other states of the Deep South quickly followed, and as the Confederacy came together, it became obvious that Charleston would be one of the proto-nation's most vital ports. Also obvious was the fact that the entrances to Charleston Harbor could be controlled from Fort Sumter, the island citadel just offshore; and that Fort Sumter was presently occupied by federal forces, which would soon be under the command of the hated Abraham Lincoln. The Confederacy had little chance of winning international recognition as an independent country if it could not claim dominion over its own most strategic assets. Something had to give.

Chapter Three

WAR AND SURVIVAL

At four thirty in the morning on April 12, 1861, Henry Fordham; his wife, Maria; and their son, John, would have been sound asleep in their home on Washington Street when gunners on James Island fired a single shell that exploded above Fort Sumter. That blast was a cue for Confederate batteries around the harbor to begin hurling a deafening, nonstop barrage of cannon fire at the tiny, Union-held island stronghold. The whole city was awakened by the terrible explosions. People threw on their clothes and ran down to the battery at the tip of the peninsula to watch the fireworks. Suddenly, violently, the world had changed.

The opening shots of the Civil War were shocking, but at that point they were anything but a surprise. The hated Lincoln had been inaugurated and installed in the White House, and while he spoke of unity and compromise, his Republican Party was implacable in its loathing of slavery. Now rebel Charlestonians were committing the first armed act of aggression in the deadliest conflict in the nation's history—a war that would become, ultimately, a second American Revolution and a second founding of the republic.

Supplies and matériel that Lincoln had dispatched to replenish Fort Sumter were tantalizingly close. The ships' masts could be seen on the horizon, but their skippers dared not approach within range of the rebel artillery flanking the harbor. For all its sound and fury, the Confederate bombardment didn't kill a single Union soldier at Fort Sumter. But the outgunned and outnumbered Union commander, Major Robert Anderson, knew it was just a matter of time before he began taking heavy casualties and running out of food and ammunition. He saw no choice but to surrender the last major coastal redoubt in the South still under Washington's control. Anderson and his men agreed to depart, but only after firing a thunderous, defiant hundred-gun salute to the American flag.

Half of Charleston—the white half—erupted in celebration. Boaters sailed and rowed out to watch the Stars and Stripes replaced by the new Confederate flag, the Stars and Bars. For weeks, hostesses threw lavish dinners and gala parties for the rebels who had taken Fort Sumter; singled out for special celebration and praise was the popular local regiment known as the Palmetto Guard. In truth, the Confederates had not done any real fighting—they had just fired cannonballs in the general direction of the island—but no matter. It was a victory, and the infant Confederacy needed heroes to celebrate. Food and libations for these gay affairs were prepared and served, of course, by the Black women and men whose bodies were the war's prize and plunder; *they* surely had a very different reaction to the outbreak of hostilities. Soon, some of those same enslaved workers who shucked bushels of oysters and cooked heaping platters of meat and fish for the secession festivities would have been among the legions of African Americans forcibly pressed into service building new fortifications around the city's perimeter—an attempt to guard against the ever-present threat of a Union invasion.

In any event, the euphoria among the white people of Charleston dissipated as the realities of war set in. That summer and fall, some of the young men who had looked so handsome and gallant as they marched north to the war's first major battles came home grievously wounded; some did not come home at all. And on November 7, residents heard faint but ominous cannon fire from a distance: Union forces were besieging and capturing Port Royal, an important harbor less than fifty miles down the coast, near Beaufort. For the rest of the war, with the enemy now so close, the people of Charleston lived in constant fear that Yankee marauders could storm into the city at any moment.

Then, a month later, the specter of looming apocalypse became all too real: On the night of December 11, 1861, Charleston went up in flames.

What became known as the Great Charleston Fire started near the docks. Although many whites wanted to blame phantom "Black saboteurs," in fact the blaze was accidental. Fanned by unusually brisk winds, the fire grew quickly into a conflagration that burned a wide diagonal swath across the peninsula, all the way from the Cooper River on the east to the Ashley River on the west. In the path of total destruction lay some of the most valuable real estate in the city, and there was little that firefighters could do but watch their beloved Charleston burn. Destroyed were elegant mansions, historic churches, and much of the central business district. One building in the path of the fire, but somehow spared by the capricious flames, was Mills House—the grand hotel built by Otis Mills, Henry's onetime owner—where Confederate general Robert E. Lee happened to be staying during a visit to inspect coastal defenses. Lee and his staff watched nervously from a balcony as the flames approached. Worried locals, protective of the man they were counting on to keep the Union hordes at bay, rushed to hustle their Great White Hope away to safety.

Reduced to charred rubble, though, was Secession Hall, the grand auditorium where defenders of slavery had made official the state's decision to leave the Union. Most of the damage from the Great Fire was not repaired until years later, following the South's defeat—meaning that when the war ended in 1865, Secession Hall still lay in ruins, much like the idea for which it was named.

For almost the entire Civil War, then, what had been the heart of Charleston, one of the Confederacy's and the nation's most precious urban jewels, was bisected by a desolate, ugly gash left by the Great Fire. Going back and forth across this wasteland, white citizens who had been so elated by the victory at Fort Sumter shuddered as they glimpsed a vision of the South's inevitable doom.

South Carolina was, arguably, the state with more to lose than any other. It was the most African state in the nation: At the beginning of the Civil War, 57 percent of the state's population was Black and enslaved, while another 1.4 percent was Black and free—which meant that only four out of ten South Carolinians were white. This minority knew that its wealth and privilege, and even its very survival, hinged on keeping the Black majority subservient and compliant. Whites kept for themselves all political, police, and military power, of course, and during the war, they exercised that power as ruthlessly as ever. But now, instead of just worrying about the potential threat that free Black people posed from within, they also had to worry about the threat from Lincoln and his generals, who could embolden African Americans—considered lawfully acquired property, duly assessed as to their monetary value, for tax purposes—to rise up against their white "owners." The whole point of the Confederacy, after all, was to continue the patent fiction that slavery was anything but obviously, brutally, tragically, inarguably wrong—the fiction that slavery was anything but one of history's most monstrous crimes. To "prove" the lie, it was necessary to show that the enslaved had accepted their lot.

African Americans in Charleston, enslaved and free alike, were therefore required to demonstrate or feign loyalty to the secessionist cause. There was a lot of feigning.

"Not by one word or look can we detect any change in the demeanor of these negro servants," a Charleston socialite named Mary Boykin Chesnut wrote, on one of the nights when Fort Sumter was under siege, in a diary that was published after the war. "Lawrence sits at our door sleepy and respectful and profoundly indifferent. So are they all, but they carry it too far. You could not tell that they even heard the awful roar going on in the bay, though it has been dinning in their ears night and day. People talk before them as if they were chairs and tables. They make no sign. Are they stolidly stupid? or wiser than we are; silent and strong, biding their time?"

For Henry and his family, the Civil War was a time of privation. Everything was in short supply, and established business relationships were disrupted by the demands of the secessionist armed forces. Records show that he did at least one blacksmithing job for the Confederate Army, which would have been mandatory. Before the war, he had functioned successfully within a system that was vile and repugnant, a system that deserved to be eradicated yet had stubbornly managed to continue, a system that gave him no leeway or margin for error. Rather than pick up stakes and move the family north, he had stayed put—and now that hostilities had begun, he was stuck. His future would depend on how the war ended. And secretly, working underground with other African Americans, he would do what he could to ensure a Union victory.

The South's strategy did not require winning. Only the most deluded Confederates believed that the North, with its huge advantage in manpower and industrial capacity, could be defeated. The goal was merely surviving, holding on, drawing out the conflict, and draining the Union of blood and treasure. The bet was that eventually Lincoln would weary of the fight, be pressured into relenting, or get kicked out of office. The rebels knew there were plenty of constituencies in the North that wanted to see the war end with some kind of exhausted understanding that brought the country back together or let the Confederacy go in peace, either way allowing slavery to continue. Wall Street, for example, had come to depend on massive profits from financing the enterprise of southern plantation agriculture—so much money that the powerful mayor of New York, Fernando Wood, pushed vainly for the city to declare itself independent from the state government in Albany and announce a policy of neutrality between North and South. The Confederacy counted on the ministrations of such allies, along with the casualties Lee and his generals were inflicting, to weaken the Union's resolve. Lee's early battlefield successes only reinforced the view that eventually the South would be able to get back to the unhindered practice of industrial-scale chattel slavery, the cruel and profitable "way of life" that Confederate blowhards waxed on about so insufferably.

Black Charlestonians had a cold-eyed view of the South's prospects. But they were equally realistic about the fact that many whites saw free Blacks, with their liberty of movement, as potential spies and fifth columnists who could stealthily attack the Confederacy from within. Some members of the state legislature were arguing once again that all free African Americans should be summarily clapped into bondage. Speaking out publicly against secession or, horror of horrors, slavery itself was not an option for Henry and other free Black men and women. The muzzles came off only when they spoke among themselves, where white people could not hear.

Except in the most private of spaces, Henry was required to display unqualified support of the Confederacy and all that it stood for. He had to show respect for the Confederate flag, with its three broad red-white-red horizontal stripes and its circle of white stars on a field of blue. He was not forced to make any public statement in support of the Confederate cause—no such statement that I can find, at least. But some free African Americans did make such declarations. One group of free Black men in Charleston—men who considered themselves mulatto, or Brown, and intrinsically superior to those with darker skin—went so far as to make a grandiose pledge of loyalty to the white secessionists who had gone to war to keep Black people in chains: "In our veins flows the blood of the white race, in some half, in others much more than half white blood. . . . Our attachments are with you, our hopes and safety and protection from you. . . . Our allegiance is due to South Carolina and in her defense, we will offer up our lives, and all that is dear to us."

One of the best reports I've found about the real views of many Black people in the Low Country of South Carolina who outwardly supported the Confederacy comes from a December 23, 1861, article by a *New York Times* correspondent who visited Port Royal, near the island now known as Hilton Head, while embedded with the Union forces that had seized the harbor:

> I have seen negroes who reported themselves as just escaped from their masters, who came breathless to our forces, and said they dared not go back, for their masters would kill them; who told that their masters were at that moment armed and threatening to shoot any slave that did not fly with them; who declared they had tricked their owners and came away in boats that they were bidden to take back to the whites. I have talked with drivers and field-hands, with house maids and coachmen and body-servants, who were apparently as eager to escape as any. I have heard the blacks point out how their masters might be caught, where they were hidden, what were their forces. I have seen them used as guides and pilots. I have been along while they pointed out in what houses stores of arms and ammunition were kept, and where bodies of troops were stationed. In a few hours I have known this information verified. I have asked them about the sentiment of the slave population, and been invariably answered that everywhere it is the same. . . . The absurd attempts of Southern papers to pretend that the blacks are still loyal, can only excite a compassionate smile. The poor wretches cling to this hope, the absence of which would present to them so appalling a future. The slaves not yet escaped, of course, pretend to be faithful, but some have told me how they said to their masters and mistresses on the day of the fight, "The Yankees will be whipped, Massa and Missus," but all the while they prayed and believed otherwise.

The fact that Union forces occupied Port Royal and a long stretch of the Sea Islands south of Charleston so early in the war made the enslaved Africans living there among the first Black people in the Deep South to be emancipated. From the white point of view, this was an especially terrifying blow.

The very existence of individuals who were both Black and free refuted the mythology of slavery as nothing more than a reflection of the natural order of things: white people as the superior race and Black people as the inferior, in need of the discipline that whips and shackles provided. It was possible to rationalize the class of free persons of color as being less than fully Black, given that so many were of mixed blood, and even to imagine that their professions of loyalty to the Southern cause were sincere. It was not possible to hold such illusions, however, about large numbers of unambiguously Black people who were enslaved one day, breaking their backs in the fields, and suddenly free the next. White Southerners trumpeted the notion that freed African Americans pined for their lost servitude and wished desperately for its return, but even those who professed that fantasy had to know, or at least fear, that it was utter nonsense. Whites had no reason to believe that liberated Black men and women, so close to Charleston and so terrifyingly far from white control, could truly be anything but enemies.

In the weeks following the Great Fire, Union troops began setting up a blockade of Charleston Harbor. They scuttled decrepit old hulks, mostly whaling ships brought down from New England, in the channels leading to the port to make those waterways impassible. Then they sent warships to interdict all vessels, including smaller boats with shallower drafts that did not need the blocked main channels. Local skippers knew hidden ways in and out of the harbor, so the blockade was never absolute. But it was effective enough to seriously unsettle a city whose livelihood and sense of self were so tied up with the sea, a city built on a peninsula that once had been called Oyster Point. And it certainly did not bode well for the weeks, months, and years to come. By 1863, Union outposts and vessels were close enough to bombard the city's southernmost sector with cannon fire, returning the favor of Fort Sumter. Most residents of what had been the grandest part of town were forced to pack up and move north of Calhoun Street, out of the gunners' range, turning what once had been a thriving business district surrounded by picture-postcard residential neighborhoods into mostly a ghost town.

Also in 1863, Union forces approaching from the territory they controlled around Port Royal launched one of the most storied battles of the war. They wanted desperately to take Charleston, but they knew that any attempt would be doomed unless they first controlled the two Confederate fortresses, out past Fort Sumter, that guarded the narrow entrance to Charleston Harbor like a pair of menacing pincers. The Confederates understood this geographical imperative, too, so they guarded the forts fiercely: If they could hold on to Fort Moultrie to the north of the harbor and Fort Wagner to the south, they could protect Fort Sumter—right in the middle of the harbor's mouth—and keep Charleston out of the hands of the Yankees.

On July 18, Union troops made an attempt to take Fort Wagner, the southern pincer. The assault failed, but the fierce clash is famous because the attacking Union forces included the highly trained soldiers of the most storied all-Black unit in the Civil War, the Fifty-Fourth Massachusetts Regiment. Acting as the point of the Union spear, the men of the Fifty-Fourth suffered devastating casualties. But they were celebrated in the Northern press as heroes for the bravery and fighting spirit they had shown, and their performance gave Lincoln the political support he needed to enlist, train, and arm more African Americans to fight for the Union cause. This was the South's worst nightmare: Black men with guns. The battle was immortalized in 1897 by Augustus Saint-Gaudens's epic *Robert Gould Shaw Memorial* relief sculpture, which stands in Boston Common (and has as its central figure the Fifty-Fourth's commanding officer, who was white); and again, much later, by the 1989 film *Glory*, which is memorable for Denzel Washington's Oscar-winning performance as a fictional Black private named Silas Trip who fights and dies at Fort Wagner.

Many of the Black soldiers who led the Fort Wagner attack were slain or executed on the battlefield. But a number of them—roughly twenty-five, according to most sources—were captured by the Confederates and taken into the city. After the war, Henry Fordham told that story, and described the part he played in it, when he gave sworn testimony in a case heard by the U.S. Southern Claims Commission.

"After the assault on Battery Wagner and a large number of wounded colored soldiers had been brought to the city of Charleston," Henry testified, "a committee of colored citizens was formed secretly, for the purpose of furnishing them with necessities and comforts; knowing Mr. Hamilton Slawson to be a Union man and sympathizing with us, I as the chairman of our committee applied to him for assistance to aid us in carrying out our purpose which he cheerfully gave, and by means of his assistance we succeeded in our purpose."

Those words did not impress the commissioners—Slawson's appeal for financial relief was denied—but they took my breath away. They reveal two things I hadn't known before: During the Civil War, there were African Americans in Charleston working underground to support Union forces and undermine the Confederate cause. And my great-great-grandfather, at least by his own account, was a leader in this Black resistance.

Finding that transcript was pure serendipity. When I began researching this American history, I signed up for Ancestry.com and all the other online genealogy sites I could find. They sent alerts when new collections of documents became accessible, and I got such a message about the proceedings of the postwar Southern Claims Commission, which decided on possible compensation for property seized from anti-Confederate, pro-Union Southerners during the conflict. I had no reason to expect to find anything about my family in that archive, but for some reason, I called it up, searched for Henry Fordham's name—and got a hit. Slawson, the man on whose behalf Henry testified, was a white shipowner with whom Henry had worked before the war. I love the irony: Before the war, a free Black man like Henry was required by law to have a white man attest to his character and loyalty. After the war, a white man like Slawson needed a Black man to support his claim of having held Unionist sympathies.

In their resistance work, Henry and his fellow African American fifth columnists would have been inspired by the example of Robert Smalls, a Black man who had pulled off one of the most audacious anti-Confederate exploits of the entire war—and who did his heroic deed right there in Charleston Harbor.

Smalls was born in 1839 in Beaufort. His mother was an enslaved woman named Lydia Polite, who worked as a servant in the house of a wealthy man named Henry McKee. It is not definitively known who Smalls's father was; some historians suspect it might have been Henry McKee's father, John McKee, and that this kinship might have explained why Lydia and her son were given better treatment and more privileges than the enslaved field hands who worked the McKee family's lands. Despite any laxity in the way she was treated, however, Lydia was determined that Robert not grow up with any illusions about the evils of slavery. She took her young son to the Beaufort jail yard to watch enslaved men being whipped for infractions such as insolence. She took him to slave auctions to watch chained Black men and women being bought and sold. She even asked that Robert be sent to work in the fields for a time, to understand what most enslaved Black people were forced to suffer.

In 1851—the year Henry Fordham bought his freedom—Henry McKee bought a plantation near Charleston and took twelve-year-old Robert Smalls there to work for him. McKee hired the boy out as a laborer for sixteen dollars a week, with Smalls allowed to keep one dollar for himself. The boy spent his teen years around the Charleston docks, working as a longshoreman and a rigger; and ultimately, he learned the duties of a helmsman, although African Americans were not supposed to perform that highly skilled role. He became an expert in navigating the ins and outs of Charleston Harbor.

When the Civil War began, Smalls, like many other enslaved men and women, was forced to work in service of the Confederate cause. By 1862, he was the leader of a crew of fellow enslaved seamen who had been compelled to serve aboard a small Confederate military transport ship operating out of Charleston, the CSS *Planter.* Smalls won the confidence of the ship's white officers and bided his time.

On the evening of May 12, the *Planter*'s three officers went ashore to spend the night amid the city's comforts, leaving just the trusted Black crew on board, which was not unusual. Smalls convinced the officers to let the Black crewmen's families pay a visit to the vessel, which was unusual but not unprecedented; the captain granted the request provided that the family members went ashore before curfew. When the officers were gone and the crew's wives and children were aboard, Smalls announced that they were about to flee to freedom.

In the middle of the night, while the city slept, Smalls put on one of the white captain's uniforms, including a straw hat similar to the one the white skipper always wore, and the *Planter* set sail. Smalls knew how to give all the proper signals as the ship passed Confederate vessels and batteries on its way out of the harbor. In the darkness, Smalls was just a familiar-looking silhouette—not the leader of a treasonous escape. By the time the rebel sentries at Fort Sumter realized what was happening, Smalls was already out of range. The last nervous moment came as the *Planter* approached the line of Union ships blockading the harbor. Smalls had ordered the crewmen to replace the ship's Confederate flag with a white bedsheet his wife had brought on board, and fortunately one of the Union lookouts spotted it before any of the blockade ships opened fire.

Smalls had done more than win freedom for himself, his crew, and their families. He had given the Union a propaganda coup that was celebrated in the Northern newspapers—a Black man had outsmarted the Confederates who thought themselves so superior. And he had delivered to the Union cause not only a rebel warship but also the cargo of heavy guns the *Planter* was carrying, as well as a mother lode of intelligence about Charleston's defenses. Smalls continued to serve his country in a Union uniform for the rest of the war. Afterward, he spent nine months learning to read and write, legally won possession of his former master's house in Beaufort, and went into politics, founding the South Carolina

Republican Party and winning a seat in the state legislature. In 1874, with Union troops still guaranteeing the rights of African Americans in the South, Smalls was elected to the U.S. House of Representatives.

Smalls's exploit electrified and cheered African Americans in Charleston—and sent Confederates into an embarrassed rage. Two of the officers who had left the *Planter* under Smalls's command were court-martialed. White Charlestonians already felt menaced, with Union ships blocking the sea-lanes and Union troops encamped in the Beaufort area just down the coast. Now they had to worry about the threat from within posed by enslaved and free Black people who had every reason to betray, and try their best to destroy, the Confederacy.

In January 1863 came the Emancipation Proclamation, which legally freed the enslaved millions throughout the Confederate states. As a practical matter, given the state of war, Lincoln's order did not liberate African Americans in the Low Country of South Carolina who were outside Union lines. In June of that year, however, Harriet Tubman did.

Already legendary for her work with the Underground Railroad, Tubman had volunteered to join the Union Army and gone to South Carolina to serve primarily as a spy. Based in the area around Beaufort that was under Union control, she became the first woman to plan and execute a U.S. military operation. On June 1, she led the Second South Carolina Volunteers, a Black regiment, on a daring gunboat raid up the Combahee River. Scouts had spread the word that the woman called Moses was coming, and when enslaved men and women heard her signal, they rushed to prearranged spots along the river to board the Union boats. Soldiers burned plantations, fields, and warehouses, and more than seven hundred African Americans were delivered from slavery to freedom.

White Charlestonians were proud that the Union never managed to mount a successful invasion of the city, either by land or by sea. They were proud that Lincoln's defiling troops did not tread their precious streets until 1865, when the war was already lost and the only real question was regarding the timing and terms of the South's capitulation. But if this was supposed to be some kind of victory, it was the hollowest and most Pyrrhic imaginable. The stately, beautiful Charleston that its white residents boasted of having defended was a burned and battered husk of what it had once been. And the economic basis of the city's prosperity—the legal right to own people, keep them in bondage, and compel them to work without compensation—was gone with the wind.

ON THE MORNING OF February 18, 1865, Charleston suffered a final insult designed to inflict maximum humiliation: Black troops from the Fifty-Fourth and Fifty-Fifth Massachusetts Regiments were among the first Union soldiers to march into town as conquerors. The city where four years of devastating warfare over slavery had begun was now being invaded, occupied, and ruled by proud Black men. Men who were indomitable. Who were victorious. Who were free.

The official record of the Fifty-Fifth's service in the war relates the scene:

> [A] few soldiers had come over from Sullivan's Island; but the Fifty-fifth was the first body of troops to enter the town after its evacuation. Words would fail to describe the scene which those who witnessed it will never forget,—the welcome given to a regiment of colored troops by their people redeemed from slavery. As shouts, prayers, and blessings resounded on every side, all felt that the hardships and dangers of the siege were fully repaid. The few white inhabitants left in the town were either alarmed or indignant, and generally remained in their houses; but the colored people turned out en masse. Assiduously had they been taught to regard the "Yanks" as their enemies; carefully had every channel of information been closed against them: but all to no purpose. "Bress de Lord," said an old, gray-haired woman, with streaming eyes, and hands clasped and raised toward heaven, "bress de Lord, I's waited

for ye, and prayed for ye, long time, and I knowed you'd come, an ye has done come at last"; and she expressed the feelings of all.

A provost-guard was detailed from the Fifty-fifth Massachusetts and One-hundred-and-forty-fourth New-York, and Major Nutt made provost-marshal. Little disorder, however, occurred. Some pigs, geese, and chickens came to untimely ends, both regularly and irregularly, as was to be expected, and some of the white inhabitants complained that the colored troops insulted them, which, when it is considered that they thought it an insult for a black man to address them without first removing his hat, was also to be expected; but no one was hurt, and no complaints brought against the men of the regiment were found to rest on any substantial basis. The troops had been besieging the place for nearly two years, knowing it as the birthplace and hot-bed of rebellion, yet no unusual effort was required to restrain them.

Camping grounds were assigned to the several regiments of the command; and the Fifty-fifth took its position in a level field between the village and Sullivan's Island, where air and water were good, and there was a fine place for salt-water bathing, of which the men soon availed themselves. This rest was, however, short. On the morning of Feb. 21, orders came to draw five days' rations, and prepare to move; and, the same afternoon, the tin-clads transferred the command to Charleston, where they landed just before sunset.

Daylight was fading when the line was formed to march through the city to a camping ground on Charleston Neck. Before the march commenced, three rousing cheers were given by the men of the Fifty-fifth, and given with a will. They were then told that the only restriction placed on them in passing through the city, would be to keep in the ranks, and that they might shout and sing as they chose.

Few people were on the wharf when the troops landed, or in the street when the line was formed; but the streets, on the route through the city, were crowded with the colored population. Cheers, blessings, prayers, and songs were heard on every side. Men and women crowded to shake hands with men and officers. Many of them talked earnestly and understandingly of the past and present. The white population remained within their houses, but curiosity led even them to peep through the blinds at the "black Yankees."

On through the streets of the rebel city passed the column, on through the chief seat of that slave power, tottering to its fall. Its walls rung to the chorus of manly voices singing "John Brown," "Babylon is falling," and the "Battle-Cry of Freedom"; while, at intervals, the national airs, long unheard there, were played by the regimental band. The glory and the triumph of this hour may be imagined, but can never be described. It was one of those occasions which happen but once in a lifetime, to be lived over in memory for ever.

With little straggling, the regiment reached the position assigned to it, near the line of works built for the defence of Charleston Neck, and went into bivouac for the night.

I can't imagine how any African American within ten miles of Charleston could have resisted being part of such a scene. Henry and Maria Fordham and their son, John, would have watched in awe as the Black soldiers of the Massachusetts Fifty-Fifth strode arrogantly into the city like Roman conquerors. I can only picture what Henry's reaction must have been.

I can be more certain, however, of what his son was thinking. My great-grandfather was just turning nine. Everything I know about him, and I know quite a lot, tells me that he watched those Black victors march into town and saw a bright and limitless future.

That same day, at the city's Northeastern Railroad Depot, some African American boys were playing a game with a big pile of gunpowder they had stumbled across. They grabbed handfuls to throw into a cotton fire they had set some distance away, making the blaze spark and crackle. Unfortunately, as they went back and forth between the pile and the fire, the gunpowder they spilled formed a trail, which became a fuse, which set off a huge explosion. Those killed and injured numbered in the hundreds, in what may have been the single deadliest incident in Charleston during the entire war.

ON MARCH 27, IN that year of liberation, the people of Charleston held a grand parade and celebration. The correspondent from the *New-York Daily Tribune* gave an eyewitness account:

> There was the greatest procession of loyalists in Charleston last Tuesday that the city has witnessed for many a long year. The present generation has never seen its like. . . . It was a procession of colored men, women and children, a celebration of their deliverance from bondage and ostracism; a jubilee of freedom, a hosannah to their deliverers. . . .
>
> First came the marshals and their aid[e]s, followed by a band of music; then the 21st Regiment in full form; then the clergymen of the different churches, carrying open Bibles; then an open car, drawn by four white horses, and tastefully adorned with National flags. In this car there were 15 colored ladies dressed in white, to represent the 15 recent Slave States. Each of them had a beautiful bouquet to present to Gen. Saxton after the speech which he was expected to deliver. A long procession of women followed the car. Then followed the children of the Public Schools, or part of them; and there were 1,800 in line, at least. They sang during the entire length of the march:
>
> *John Brown's body lies a moulding in the grave,*
> *John Brown's body lies a moulding in the grave,*
> *John Brown's body lies a moulding in the grave,*
> *His soul is marching on!*
> *Glory! Glory! Glory! Hallelujah!*
> *Glory! Glory! Glory! Hallelujah!*
> *We go marching on!*

This verse, however, was not nearly so popular as one which it was intended should be omitted, but rapidly supplanted all the others, until at last all along the mile or more of children, marching two abreast, no other sound could be heard than

We'll hang Jeff. Davis on a sour apple tree!
We'll hang Jeff. Davis on a sour apple tree!
We'll hang Jeff. Davis on a sour apple tree!
As we go marching on! . . .

The most original feature of the procession was a large cart, drawn by two dilapidated horses with the worst harness that could be got to hold out, which followed the trades. On this cart there was an auctioneer's block, and a black man, with a bell, represented a negro trader, a red flag waving over his head; recalling the days so near and yet so far off, when human beings were made merchandise of in South Carolina. This man had himself been bought and sold several times and two women and a child who sat on the block had also been knocked down at public auction in Charleston. As the cart moved along, the mock-auctioneer rang his bell and cried out: "How much am I offered for this good cook?" "She is an 'xlent cook, ge'men." "She can make four kinds of mock-turtle soup, from beef, fish or fowls." "200's bid." "Two hundred?" "200's bid." "250," "300," "350," "400," "450," "Who bids? who bids? 500." And so he went on imitating in sport the infernal traffic of which many of the spectators had been the living victims. Old women burst into tears as they saw this tableau, and forgetting that it was a mimic scene, shouted wildly, Give me back my children! Give me back my children! . . .

Behind the auction-car 60 men marched, tied to a rope, in imitation of the gangs who used often to be led through these streets on their way from Virginia to the sugar-fields of Louisiana. All of these men had been sold in the old times.

Then came the hearse, a comic [feature] which attracted great attention, and was received with shouts of laughter. There was written on it with chalk.

"Slavery is Dead."

"Who Owns Him?"

"No One."

"Sumter Dug His Grave on the 13th of April, 1861."

Slavery was indeed dead, its fate written four years earlier by those first shots at Fort Sumter, right there in Charleston Harbor.

The *Tribune*'s correspondent was particularly impressed by the demeanor of the many Black children in the teeming crowd: "Very few of these children had ever been at school before; not one of them had ever walked in a public procession; they had had only one hour's drill on their playground; and yet they kept in line, closed up, and were under perfect control and orderly up to the last." Among those children being complimented on their correct demeanor would have been young John Hammond Fordham, who went on to have an epic and quintessentially American life.

He was born on March 9, 1856, ninety-eight years and three days before my own birth. After the Civil War, when African Americans no longer had a knee on their collective neck, they launched themselves and they soared—until the knee was brutally reapplied. They had won their freedom and were using it to build a prosperous future. But instead of being lauded for their enterprise and accomplishment, they were despised for having the temerity to succeed.

And in due course—as had happened with my first unknown ancestor's African freedom, and as had happened with Henry Fordham's dearly purchased American freedom in the run-up to the war—my great-grandfather's freedom to fulfill his potential, made possible by the limited breathing space briefly offered by Reconstruction, was taken away.

Chapter Four

THE MAKING OF MAJOR FORDHAM

On tree-lined Bull Street in historic Charleston, amid the graceful white houses with wood siding and Greek Revival columns and side-door entrances and wide verandas, there stands an anomaly: a massive, stately, three-story redbrick building with an expansive front lawn and a whimsical cupola. A herringbone brick walkway and a wide stone staircase lead up to the second-floor entrance of this imposing structure, which houses the College of Charleston's Avery Research Center for African American History and Culture. It is the very building where, three years after the end of the Civil War, my great-grandfather went to school.

The Bull Street schoolhouse was erected in 1868 as a permanent home for the Avery Normal Institute, which was Charleston's first fully accredited secondary school for Black children. Henry Fordham's twelve-year-old son, John, was one of Avery's ambitious and determined pupils.

Representatives of the American Missionary Association, based in New York, had arrived in Charleston to establish a school for the children of freedmen in 1865, almost immediately after the city's liberation. At first, classes were taught in temporary quarters that had to be moved frequently—largely because the idea of educating the sons and daughters of freedmen was fought bitterly, and with some success, by whites determined to re-create something very like the old order. The school would set up in some house or storefront, only to be evicted when the building's white owners returned from wherever they had waited out the war's chaotic final days to reclaim their property. Unbelievably—given who had won the war and who had lost—they were allowed to take it back. The South was already launched on a new campaign to win the peace. The Civil War had given Black people in the South freedom and opportunity, and now whites in the defeated Confederacy began trying to take them away.

The slain Lincoln's successor as president, Tennessee-born Andrew Johnson, was a Democrat who sympathized with his fellow white southerners and whose idea of Reconstruction was less the creation of a new South than the restoration of the old. In the months after Lincoln's assassination, Johnson gave the defeated Confederates substantial control of their local affairs, even under Union occupation. Southern state legislatures, which of course were white-controlled—the issue of African American suffrage hadn't yet been resolved—seized the opening that Johnson gave them. Reprieved from the reckoning they should have been required to face, they quickly passed "Black Codes" designed to impose a new system of racial hierarchy and privilege that would replicate the old system of slavery as closely as possible.

South Carolina's Black Code, approved in December 1865, was used by other states as a model. It would require "persons of color" to sign contracts binding them to work as "servants" for white "masters"—those were the terms of address that had to be used, by law. Former slaves who refused to sign on as "servants" would risk being arrested as vagrants and could be jailed or forced to work. Black artisans, like blacksmith Henry Fordham, would not be allowed to practice their trades unless they paid the hefty sum of one hundred dollars for a license. Interracial marriage was, of course, strictly outlawed. Any citizen could arrest a Black person for violating the code, and special courts would be set up to establish guilt and mete out punishment.

As it happened, my great-great-grandfather was not forced to endure this system of statutory white supremacy. The Union military commander of the Department of South Carolina, General Daniel Sickles, was so outraged by the legislature's new Black Code that he struck it down a month after it was passed. Sickles had given far too much to the Union cause to see it so callously betrayed: He'd lost a leg at Gettysburg, leading his troops into the teeth of the Confederate attack on Cemetery Ridge, for which he would tardily be awarded the Congressional Medal of Honor in 1897. Having jettisoned the oppressive Black Code, he issued a new set of orders decreeing that all laws in the state must henceforth be applied equally without regard to race.

The spirit and intent behind the Black Codes never went away, though. The spirit and intent remain.

The Civil War had been fought over slavery, the North had prevailed at unthinkable cost, and Lincoln's allies in Washington were determined not to let the South behave as if none of that had happened, not to let the losers carry on as if the recent unpleasantness had meant nothing at all. The Republicans who controlled Congress refused to seat the Democrats elected in whites-only voting in the former Confederate states, an action the former rebels decried as the "end of democracy" but had no power to reverse. With veto-proof majorities on Capitol Hill, Republicans seized control of Reconstruction. Congress passed new laws that tightened military rule over the South, established the Freedmen's Bureau to aid the formerly enslaved, and guaranteed African Americans the right to vote. For the first time in U.S. history, Black people had a measure of political power and were being protected, not oppressed, by the overwhelming might of the state. Even in Charleston.

The man leading the American Missionary Association's educational efforts in the city was Francis Cardozo, a Black man who had been born free in Charleston—the son of a free Black woman and a

Jewish immigrant from Portugal—and educated in Edinburgh and London. Cardozo was determined to build a permanent home for the new school for African Americans. The missionaries managed to obtain a ten-thousand-dollar bequest from the estate of a Pittsburgh clergyman named Charles Avery—hence the school's name—and were given additional construction funds by the Freedmen's Bureau. Cardozo oversaw construction of the Avery Institute's fine building on Bull Street and became the school's principal. Young John Fordham and his classmates were able to learn their reading, writing, and arithmetic in an edifice fittingly grand for its noble and revolutionary purpose.

"School to Bull Street" is what he gave as his occupation in 1868, when he registered as a depositor at the U.S. Freedman's Bank. "John Fordham" is how he signed his name. His father is listed in the ledger as "Henry Fordham." His complexion is described as "Black." His address is given as "7 Duncan Street"—then a modest wooden house, today a pocket-size park next to a small modern office building. Each morning, John left his home and took a seven-block walk—west on Duncan, south on Pitt, west on Bull toward the Ashley River—to the education that would make possible a future his parents could scarcely have imagined.

The Avery building on Bull Street has gone through many changes over the century and a half since the school opened its doors. It was operated as a private institution until the county made it a Blacks-only public school in 1947—only to close it down in 1954, following the *Brown v. Board of Education* decision outlawing school segregation. Inevitably, the building then fell into disrepair. It might have been torn down had not a group led by alumni formed a nonprofit to save it. At one point during Charleston's recent gentrification, there were even proposals to turn the Avery into luxury condos. Finally, the College of Charleston stepped up to perform a full restoration and make the grand old building into a research archive, museum, and event space. One of the classrooms is furnished and arranged exactly as it would have been in 1868, when my great-grandfather went there.

I visited the Avery Institute in 2023 and spent time in that classroom. The students had sat three and four abreast at eleven wooden pew–like desks with writing surfaces that featured inkwells. In the front of the room, on a raised platform, the teacher would have presided in front of a wide blackboard. In the back of the room stands a potbelly stove, which would have struggled to heat the cavernous space, with its high ceilings. Tall windows flooded the room with natural light.

Being there was a moving experience for me, and I stayed as long as my tour guides would let me. I was able to sit where my great-grandfather had once sat and imagine what those days must have been like for him, just three years after the end of the Civil War. He and his classmates were pioneers, venturing without maps or guideposts into an uncharted new world.

John was a bright and diligent pupil, the perfect clay for Avery's educators to mold, and it was an exciting time for him. One thing I wonder about, though, is how he was regarded by his fellow students at the school on Bull Street. Like many of his classmates, he was from a family who had been free before the war. Unlike most of them, he had very dark skin. He sat at his desk surrounded by light-skinned teenagers who had been raised to think of themselves as Brown rather than Black, who had been taught all their lives that their beige, tan, and caramel skin tones and their pliant "good" hair made them special and superior. Would they have included a kinky-haired Black boy in their busy social lives? When the Brown elite was once again able to celebrate itself as before the war, to have its dances and balls and soirees and cotillions, would John have been invited?

There were between three hundred and four hundred students at Avery when my great-grandfather was there, and colorism was a fact of life, often seen as a rough proxy for one's prewar status. According to the book *Charleston's Avery Center*, an exhaustive history of the school, Principal Cardozo described his student body as half "free-born" and half "pure African." Some of the teachers were local; others had come down from the North, full of missionary zeal and eager to dispel the notion, pushed by bitter whites, that African Americans who were visibly mixed-race were more intelligent than those who were not. One teacher from Connecticut, a man named Mortimer Warren, boasted of the pupils he taught mathematics: "Some of them are very black, and some very white, but the blacks are the smarter." John Fordham, of course, didn't conform to anybody's neat categories—having been free before the war, but being "pure African" in appearance—and that is why I wonder just how he fit in.

The fact that John's father, Henry, had been free before Emancipation gave him status; the antebellum free, in general, had a head start over the enslaved. John's dark skin, for some, stole a measure of that status away. But as far as I can tell, color never seemed to bother my great-grandfather in the least. Nothing about how others might see him as an individual seemed to concern him—as opposed to how others might see and treat African Americans as a race, which was his obsession and his mission. He cared very much that white Americans be made to appreciate that Black Americans were in every measure their equal, that all we lacked was opportunity, not ability. But he knew, and expected others to recognize, that as an individual he was quite obviously any man's match. In all the papers he left behind, all the speeches and letters and financial records, the one thing I cannot find is a trace of self-doubt—about his color, his worth, his dignity, his intelligence, his right to be wherever he happened to be at any given moment. He knew exactly who he was.

In those papers, I do find joy and sadness, triumph and failure, confidence and worry. I find uncompromising rigor and charming tenderness. I find constant ambition, occasional modesty, and considerable wisdom. I find grave concern, at various times, about the status, progress, and persecution of African Americans. But I have never found insecurity or lack of faith in himself. Today might be a setback, a detour, even a disaster, but tomorrow would be better. And he would do everything in his power to make it so.

WHEN HE FINISHED HIS studies at the Avery Institute, John Fordham was a young man on the make. He was tall, dark, and handsome. He was smart as a whip. And he was coming of age in the 1870s, a unique moment in American history. Those were the all-too-brief years of "Radical" Reconstruction, an interlude when Black men and women in the former Confederacy were allowed and even encouraged to fulfill their potential. John was a young man at the foot of his mountain, with what looked like unlimited possibilities. Like any determined up-and-comer, though, he needed a mentor. And he was lucky: An unlikely mentor found *him*.

The Reverend Joseph Baynard Seabrook, born in 1809, was the scion of a wealthy Low Country plantation family who owned enslaved Black workers. He graduated from Princeton—which many southerners found more congenial to their views about race and slavery than the other elite northern schools—and became a lawyer. Poor health dissuaded him from pursuing a career as a practicing attorney, though, so he returned to the family estates intending to spend the rest of his life as a planter. But that plan, too, had to be changed: In 1848, the same year Henry Fordham was sold to Otis Mills, Seabrook heard the call to become an ordained minister in the Episcopal Church. To his family's dismay, he felt an obligation to serve not the wealthy whites of his own social class but the Black children of the Low Country, free and enslaved. At his own expense, he founded two churches near Beaufort to minister to his flock. And when he wasn't preaching, he was teaching Black boys and girls how to read and write.

Remarkably for a white man who had so richly benefited from the system of plantation slavery, Seabrook was a staunch and vocal opponent of South Carolina's secession from the Union. "He invariably prophesied failure, therefore was looked upon coldly by his more hot-headed relatives and friends," his widow wrote in a letter after his death. When the state decided to go to war anyway, he did what he thought was his duty, sending his sons to fight in the rebellion that he knew would lead to the South's, and his family's, utter destruction. After the war ended, he became rector of St. Mark's Episcopal Church, a congregation newly established in Charleston to serve Black Episcopalians.

Seabrook was determined to play a part in the effort to provide quality education to emancipated African Americans, eventually serving as Charleston's superintendent of schools. He took an interest in the Avery Institute, especially its brightest pupils, and among those who caught his eye was my great-grandfather. Seabrook agreed to tutor him in the law.

In our house, in the bedroom that once had been my great-grandfather's, I found one of the law books Seabrook had him study. Published in Charleston in 1843, it is a dense tome on English legal procedure, and its title is almost as long as a foreword: *An Historical Treatise of A Suit in Equity: In Which Is Attempted A Scientific Deduction of the Proceedings used on the Equity sides of the Courts of Chancery and Exchequer, from the Commencement of the Suit to the Decree and Appeal. With Occasional Remarks on Their Import and Efficacy.* The author was "Charles Barton, of the Inner Temple, Barrister at Law." The book is tattered, its pages age-spotted and water-stained from some ancient mishap, but it survives. My great-grandfather saved it among his records and belongings.

After reading law under Seabrook, John was admitted to the state bar in 1874. He was not the first Black attorney certified by the state supreme court to practice law in South Carolina—Jonathan Jasper Wright, William James Whipper, and Robert Brown Elliott had gained that distinction in 1868—but he was one of just a handful. And he was officially on his way.

The road to advancement ran through the Republican Party during the Radical Reconstruction years, and John became an active member. Government was being reorganized at every level, under the supervision of federal officials, and it was an era when jobs and promotions were doled out through a system of political patronage. For a young, hungry, able, and loyal Black Republican, opportunities were all around. It was just a matter of deciding which to pursue, and John's choice was "all of the above."

My great-grandfather established a home and base of operation seventy-five miles inland from Charleston, in Orangeburg, a crossroads town where, in 1869, Methodist missionaries had founded the first institution of higher learning in South Carolina for African Americans, Claflin College. For much of the rest of his life, John would split his time between the two cities, raising his family in Orangeburg but keeping a law office—and for decades, a federal government job—in Charleston. My grandmother told me that when she was young, he would choose one of his children each summer to accompany him on an extended sojourn by the sea while he tended to business in his hometown.

In 1874, the same year he was admitted to the bar, John was elected coroner of Orangeburg County. He ran as a Republican and was unopposed, receiving 5,640 votes, more than any other candidate for county office in that election. Meanwhile, he continued expanding his web of activities and connections in Charleston, joining several of the Black fraternal organizations that men used to establish lifelong friendships and connections; I've come across records of his membership in the Prince Hall Masons, the Knights of Pythias, and the Odd Fellows, and language in his will suggests there were even more of these "secret" societies whose meetings and ceremonies he somehow found time to attend. He also helped organize and lead fire brigades in both cities—vital civic work at a time when a single spark could lead to widespread devastation, as he had seen in Charleston before the war.

Most important, at least for the telling of his story, he was one of the founders of a Charleston-based Black militia called the Carolina Light Infantry, serving that corps for years as a judge advocate—a lawyer, essentially—with the rank of major. There are two reasons that this paramilitary service matters. First, it was an act of defiance against the whites who wanted to reclaim the power of physical intimidation they had lost after their defeat in the war. African Americans formed these militias as a way of announcing that they would defend their freedom with arms, if need be. Second, the Carolina Light Infantry gave my great-grandfather the title by which he would be most commonly known in newspaper clippings, certificates of commendation, political campaigns, and other formal contexts: Major Fordham.

That was the name by which my family spoke of him when I was growing up. That was what my mother called him when she gestured to the formal portrait staring down from the wall in the sitting room, or when my grandmother mentioned the safe in her bedroom down the hall, or when my father and I went looking for something in the dark and dusty attics and my flashlight beam fell on the disassembled parts of a bed that was as old as the house itself. Major Fordham is what they all called him. And Major Fordham is what I will call him in the pages that follow.

Amid his many and varied pursuits, the Major also found time to fall in love. In Charleston, on August 5, 1875, he married the woman who would bear him nine children, six of whom survived to adulthood, and who would be his partner and closest friend for the rest of their lives. He and Louisa Gertrude Smith (no relation to Francis and the other Smiths in my family tree) were joined in wedlock by a white minister, the Reverend William Black Yates, a Presbyterian pastor who was best known locally for the spiritual and educational uplift he offered to young, often illiterate mariners at his church near the docks. The groom was nineteen. He was robbing the cradle: His bride, a lissome beauty, was just sixteen.

A copy of the couple's marriage certificate has survived. The document is done in a nautical motif, typical for a wedding conducted by the Reverend Yates. There is a drawing of a dockside scene, over which stretches a banner: "Sailor, there's hope for thee." A flag on one of the vessels in the drawing offers wise counsel to newlyweds: "Don't give up the ship." A dozen witnesses to the ceremony are listed, most of them members of the bride's family.

It was a bittersweet moment: Less than a month earlier, on July 14, Major Fordham's beloved father, Henry, had dined on a supper of greens and buttermilk at his home on Desportes Court, suddenly fallen ill, and promptly died. Major Fordham recorded his passing in our family Bible, along with a brief eulogy:

A faithful worker in the cause of Christ.
A kind father, a loving husband.
A friend to the needy and distressed.

J.H.F.

In his massively eventful years on this earth, Henry Fordham had made the journey from slavery to freedom through sheer drive and determination. He had become literate, learned to shape hot iron into objects of utility and beauty, run a successful business, and managed a modest portfolio of real estate. He had suffered under the harsh strictures of the months immediately before the Civil War, when his freedom was effectively nullified. He had survived the nation's bloodiest conflict in the city where the conflagration began. He had persevered until Union soldiers marched into Charleston, proud Black soldiers, and gave him his freedom back with interest. He had sustained a long and happy marriage to the wife who survived him, Maria Fordham. He had sired and raised a son. He had provided for his family. The epitaph in our Bible refers to him as "Rev. Harry Fordham" because he had also presided over his small church in Stoll's Alley, working faithfully "in the cause of Christ."

THE YOUNG AND AMBITIOUS couple, Major Fordham and his bride, Louisa, wasted no time in acquiring the assets necessary for any up-and-coming gentleman and lady of their time: property and children.

They bought sizable parcels of land in Orangeburg. Much of it was registered in Louisa's name, which was not an uncommon practice in South Carolina. Major Fordham saved some of their property tax receipts: On December 31, 1879, Louisa paid to the Orangeburg County treasurer $6.56 for the annual levy on one of the several lots they owned. The receipt notes that there was a building on the lot; that would have been the "old" house, the one they lived in for a quarter century before building the larger, more up-to-date house at the corner of Boulevard and Oak Streets. The "new" house—the residence, built in 1903, where my sister and I grew up—is now listed in the National Register of Historic Places, in honor of Major Fordham's career.

Two sets of brick steps lead from walkways up to the front porch, one facing Boulevard Street, the other curved toward Oak. The east-facing front door is on the Boulevard side, framed by a surround of handmade colored glass rectangles and squares that glow in the morning light in bright reds, blues, and yellows—glass that has survived, miraculously, for more than a century. The first floor comprises the sitting room with the portraits, the larger formal living room, the dining room, the principal bedroom, a smaller bedroom, a bathroom with an ancient cast-iron enameled bathtub on claw-foot legs, a long hallway, and the kitchen and pantry. At the ends of the front porch are Dutch doors, one set leading into the living room and the other into the dining room, making it possible, at least theoretically, to open the house up wide for entertaining or just to air the place out. I don't remember those doors ever being opened, but perhaps they were in earlier times. Upstairs, there were originally two more bedrooms and two attic spaces; my father had workmen carve an additional bedroom out of the dormer above the dining room and somehow conjure another bathroom above the hallway. There is no basement; the water table in Orangeburg is far too high. In fact, the whole house sits about three feet aboveground, on a foundation of thick brick pillars, leaving an enclosed crawl space beneath the floor.

The roof is crowned with two tall brick chimneys that once served fireplaces in the living room, the principal bedroom, the sitting room, and the dining room. At some point before my time, three of the hearths were bricked in and replaced with gas heaters—all except the one in the living room, where our family burned not wood but coal. Every few weeks during the winter, a supplier would bring a load of coal and shovel it into a pile in the crawl space beneath the kitchen. One of my chores as a kid was to use an ancient metal pail called a scuttle to fetch loads of coal on cold days and nights when we wanted to warm the living room, which in those days had no other source of heat. Another of my father's eventual updates was to give the house central heating, which works well, and air-conditioning, which does not.

Major Fordham kept a copy of the construction contract for the house. The builder was named W. Wilson Cooke, and the quoted price was $1,326.54. The Major agreed to pay $400 when the foundation had been laid and the framing work completed; another $400 when the house was "raised and closed in," presumably meaning when the walls, roof, siding, windows, and doors were in place; $350 more when "floors, ceilings, piazzas and plastering" were completed; and the balance, $176.54, when all interior and exterior work save painting and plumbing was done. The contract was executed on June 18, 1903; the last payment was made on September 26. For the record, there are no piazzas.

THE PROPERTY THAT THE late Henry Fordham owned in Charleston had to be dealt with. He had died without a will, and there was a dispute between his son and his wife over the disposition of the estate. Major Fordham wanted to sell the house on Desportes Court, which had belonged to his father since before the Civil War. Maria refused to sell it. Eventually, in 1881, the Major went so far as to sue his mother to force the sale. She filed a response, and the Court of Common Pleas ruled in her favor, deciding the house was hers to do with as she pleased. Years later, when Maria died, she did leave a will—signed with an *X* in front of witnesses. In it, she honored what she said had been Henry Fordham's wishes: A lifetime earlier, in 1829, young Henry had been sold to Richard Fordham along with a woman named "Jenny" and her daughters "Hager and Margaret." It was to "Hager," whose name was actually Hagar, that Maria left the Desportes Court property.

In 1876, the Major and Louisa welcomed the birth of their first son, George Henry; the boy was born in Orangeburg, as were all but one of the Fordham children. Siblings came in rapid succession: Walter Hammond, born in 1877; Flora Ella, called "Florella," in 1880; William in 1881; Harry Mattison (the one born in Charleston) in 1882; Grace Annett Legare in 1884; my grandmother Sadie Louise in 1886; and the boy-and-girl twins, Marion and Marie Gertrude, in 1891. As was all too common at a time before vaccinations and antibiotics, three of the Fordham children died before their second birthdays. The family Bible records that Walter lived for one year, six months, and eight days; William "departed this life" exactly six months after his birth; and Marie, the twin, the youngest girl, and the apple of her mother's eye, died at the age of one year, three months, and three days.

Little Marie's death is the central event in one of the stories of her childhood that my grandmother Sadie Fordham Smith—our "Gomma," as Ellen and I called her—used to tell. I had overheard my mother casually saying to one of her friends, "You know, Mama never wears green." I thought that was odd, so I asked Sadie why.

Her father was a very important man in the Republican Party, she said proudly, so her parents traveled often for political gatherings and events. For one of these trips—my grandmother thought it was a presidential inauguration or a national Republican convention—Louisa Fordham had packed a stunning green taffeta dress to wear to the gala social events they would be expected to attend. There was a baby in the house at the time, a sickly infant whom Louisa was reluctant to leave behind. But duty and position called, so off she and her husband went. While they were gone, the baby died. When they got the news in a telegram, they were filled not just with anguish and grief but with guilt over not having been there for little Marie's final agony. The trip back to Orangeburg was endless, the sadness unimaginable. When they got home, Louisa took the unworn green dress into the backyard and burned it to ashes. She resolved never to wear green again, and so did her three surviving daughters.

As with everything I relate in this American history, I combed through records and documents to try to pin this story down. Comparing the dates of the three Fordham infants' deaths with the dates of inaugurations, conventions, and other political events the Fordhams traveled to attend, I found that my grandmother's recollection was slightly off. The gathering in question must have been the 1892 South Carolina state Republican Party convention, held in Columbia in April of that year—during the week Marie died. At that meeting, Major Fordham was chosen as a delegate to the National Republican Convention to be held a few months later. Sadie was five and a half at the time, just old enough to remember her baby sister's death and her mother's bitter grief. Just old enough to be imprecise on the details but to have an indelible memory of her mother's anguish.

Sadie may have misremembered that trip, but Major Fordham did indeed travel far and wide to Republican National Conventions as an official delegate or alternate from South Carolina. He went to Minneapolis in 1892, where President Benjamin Harrison was nominated to run for a second term; Harrison lost to his predecessor, Grover Cleveland. He went to St. Louis in 1896, where William McKinley was nominated for his victorious presidential run. He went to Philadelphia in 1900, where President McKinley was nominated for reelection, winning but tragically serving only until his assassination in 1901. And he went to Chicago in 1916, where Charles Evans Hughes was nominated to run; Hughes would lose against Woodrow Wilson. The Major may well have gone to other GOP conventions, not in an official capacity but as one of the many party activists who always descend on the host city, with or without a status that admits them to the convention floor. And for more than three decades, whenever a Republican president was inaugurated in Washington, Major Fordham was there amid the crowd.

I think a lot about that itinerary. A Black man in America, born before the Civil War, was able to journey back and forth across this vast nation with his wife—to the Twin Cities astride the Upper Mississippi; to the growing metropolis downriver that served as the gateway to the West; to the historic city where the nation itself was born; to the great hub of industry and transportation on the western shore of Lake Michigan; to the capital of the Union that Lincoln preserved and cleansed of the abomination of slavery. I think about how the Major was not a fugitive fleeing the South via the Underground Railroad, but rather a dignitary, a man in full, arriving in style by way of the most comfortable and luxurious mode of travel of the day—spending his nights in Pullman sleeping cars and taking his meals on fine china and crisp white tablecloths. I think of the couple's suitcases and trunks packed with fashionable clothes, the documents and correspondence the Major would have read and pondered en route, the mountains and rivers and prairies they passed on the long stretches between stops. I think about the fact that Major Fordham made these trips not for pleasure but to select the Republican Party's candidate for president or to witness the sacred democratic ritual of an inauguration. I think about what the GOP stood for in those days, how it fought—although with waning zeal and success—to keep alive the fading promise of Emancipation and the great leap forward of Reconstruction, the dream of an America where men and women with brown skin and coarse hair, men and women like Major Fordham himself, were universally allowed to soar as high and as far as their talent, ambition, and drive could take them.

IN 1893, THE YEAR after Major Fordham returned from his first Republican Convention as a delegate, an imposing monument was erected in Orangeburg's central square, less than a mile from his home. It was intended to mock and threaten all that African Americans had achieved.

At the initiative and expense of the Orangeburg Confederate Monument Association, a group of notable white citizens, workers installed a bronze-and-stone memorial to the Civil War dead—the Confederate dead, exclusively, who came from the Orangeburg region. The monument immediately became the most prominent landmark in town, the unmissable focal point, right in front of the imposing Orangeburg County Courthouse with its tall white columns.

On a square, tiered base stands a pedestal upon which rests a single thick column supporting a statue of a uniformed Confederate soldier. The Smithsonian American Art Museum's authoritative Inventory of

American Sculpture gives a terse description: "The figure faces southwest and leans on his rifle with both hands. A canteen and haversack hang from his proper left shoulder and a knife is at his proper left side. He carries a bedroll and a kepi rests on his head. The model for the sculpture was a Confederate soldier named John S. Palmer." The statue was created by a Prussian-born Georgia sculptor named Theodore Markwalter and cast at a foundry in Massachusetts. Chiseled into the south and west faces of the pedestal is an inscription: "A grateful tribute to the brave defenders of our rights, our honor and our homes. Let posterity emulate their virtues and treasure the memory of their valor and patriotism."

Nearly three decades had passed since the end of the Civil War, and memorials like the one in Orangeburg were suddenly being built in hundreds of cities and towns throughout the former Confederacy. Why at that particular moment? Because though the South may have lost in 1865, now the old Confederacy was winning. The monuments were boasts of victory, not lamentations of defeat.

Reconstruction, that blink-of-an-eye interlude, was already history—sweet history for Major Fordham, bitter for the white citizens of Orangeburg. It had effectively ended in 1877 with the compromise that resolved the close, contentious, and bitterly disputed presidential election of the previous November between Republican Rutherford B. Hayes and Democrat Samuel Tilden. The circumstances sound eerily familiar: There were charges of election fraud, widespread complaints of voter suppression targeting African Americans, competing slates of electors claiming legitimacy. With the trauma of the Civil War still fresh, there were even fears that the Union might fracture again. Under the agreement between party leaders that allowed the country to move forward, Democrats gave the Republican, Hayes, just enough electoral votes to defeat Tilden by the slimmest possible margin, 185–184. The GOP would retain the White House, which had been occupied for the past eight years by Ulysses S. Grant, the conqueror of the South, who as president had pressed the Reconstruction agenda, defended African Americans' hard-won rights, and ruthlessly suppressed the nascent white terrorist militia known as the Ku Klux Klan.

In return for the certification of Hayes as president, Republicans yielded to the Democrats' most persistent demand: The last of the federal troops and U.S. Justice Department prosecutors who had guaranteed the new rights of Black people across the South would be withdrawn. Hayes made that devil's bargain, and in office he kept his word.

That was how the worst election crisis in U.S. history was resolved—worse even than George W. Bush's controversial victory over Al Gore in 2000 or Donald Trump's loss to Joe Biden in 2020. There is a quote usually attributed to Mark Twain (though I can find no proof he actually said it) that keeps coming to mind when I think about how a cynical betrayal of African Americans ended the Hayes-Tilden dispute: "History doesn't repeat itself, but it often rhymes." I can't help but fear that now is rhyming with then.

In 1877, the nation faced extreme polarization. There was a seemingly unbridgeable divide between large segments of the population who had divergent and irreconcilable worldviews. In the months after the Hayes-Tilden election, there was bitter disagreement about which candidate should legitimately be sworn in on Inauguration Day. There was no sacking of the Capitol, as would take place on January 6, 2021, but there were plenty of plots and machinations, including slates of fake electors. There was no Fox News or MSNBC, of course, no Facebook or Infowars. But the newspapers of the day took sides with every bit as much vitriolic, unbridled passion as the media of today. One side, the Republicans, had extended the rights guaranteed by the Constitution to more and more Americans; the other side, the Democrats, wanted to snatch back those rights. Reverse the names of the two parties, update the disinformation technology, and you could be doomscrolling the latest news on the platform now called X.

All this is eerily, urgently familiar. We should worry, at least to some extent, that our current deep divisions might actually tear the country apart. But perhaps we should worry more that the fissures that separate us now will be bridged by another 1877-style compromise, another pact with the forces of repression, another acquiescence in the theft of expanded freedoms—including the right to vote. My great-grandfather still managed to do well for himself, at least for a time, but his children's and grandchildren's full potential had been effectively sold down the river. History not only informs but also instructs. Knowing and understanding the history of Major Fordham's time obliges me to do everything in my power to ensure that my descendants' freedoms and prospects do not suffer the same fate.

When the armed federal military presence was withdrawn in 1877, political power in South Carolina consequently, and consequentially, shifted from the Republicans to the Democrats. The outcome of the previous year's election for governor had been disputed, just like the Hayes-Tilden presidential race—only, worse. Incumbent governor Daniel Henry Chamberlain, a Republican, and challenger Wade Hampton III, a Democrat, each claimed to be the rightful winner and presumed to take office. For four long months there were two separate state governments, each passing laws and collecting taxes, each insisting on its legitimacy, and neither willing to cede an inch. Hampton had local white support and an impeccable South Carolina pedigree; Chamberlain had the inertia of incumbency. Each had his supporters in Washington, and Congress did nothing to help resolve the dispute. When the federal troops left, however, Chamberlain's position became untenable. He stepped down, lamenting the likely fate of African Americans in the state with words that soon proved prescient: "If a majority of people in a State are unable by physical force to maintain their rights, they must be left to political servitude."

Major Fordham was a prominent Black citizen and a dyed-in-the-wool Republican, which meant that in local politics, he was suddenly very much out of fashion. He lost his job as coroner and never held elective office again. The Major still had connections in the federal government, though, and managed to get a job in 1879 as a clerk in the U.S. Railway Mail Service. That gave him a steady income, and his family a stable foundation, for the next decade. Still ambitious, he became ever more active in Republican Party politics, both out of conviction and to advance himself. And he and Louisa continued buying land and subdividing it into lots, speculating that Orangeburg would still have a bright future. Nothing could ever quite snuff out his faith in the American dream.

By the 1890s, when the Confederate monument was erected on Russell Street, southern states were systematically reimposing the racist "way of life" they had fought the Civil War to defend: Whites were meant to rule, Blacks were meant to serve. New race laws were being passed. The Ku Klux Klan, previously suppressed by federal authorities with the hammer of Union soldiers, was emerging from the shadows. The "Lost Cause" mythology, the fiction that the South had done nothing but try "with valor and patriotism" to defend its rights and its honor, was being elaborated and embellished—carved in stone, cast in bronze, and placed where no one could possibly avoid it. It was being taught to white children as an inspirational fairy tale and to Black children as a warning.

The lie that the statue in the middle of my hometown told, and still tells, was not born of nostalgia. It was not born of grief for the seditionists, who by then had been moldering in their graves for many years. It was coldly calculated propaganda designed to reinforce the Big Lie about the Civil War, the lie that neglected any mention of slavery, that was being used to return African Americans to their former status. It worked.

And it endured. When I was in high school in the late 1960s—I went to the recently and grudgingly integrated Orangeburg High School, which had been the city's white public high school—there were teachers who would not say the words "Civil War." Instead, they taught lessons about "the War Between the States." They taught that the war had been fought over an abstract concept of federalism, not the concrete reality of human bondage. Many if not most of my white classmates believed this fiction. Confederate generals were remembered not for their disloyalty to the nation they had sworn an oath to serve but for their tactical skill, their leadership qualities, or their vaunted "valor"—in fighting for the right to keep African Americans in chains.

Major Fordham was in his prime in 1893, but the statue was a dire omen. He had to watch as treason and slavery were put on a pedestal in the middle of town. The opportunity he had made for himself, the freedom he had enjoyed for most of his life, the ambitious dreams he had for his children—all that was under threat.

THE MAJOR WAS, BY all accounts, a talented and accomplished attorney. A faded newspaper clipping I found in his safe—date and source unfortunately not noted—says of him, "His success in that profession has been a marked one. Owing to his intimate knowledge of law, keen, searching interrogatory, he has made criminal law a specialty and at the same time a decided success."

My grandmother, who had a way with words, described what he was like on a typical day when he was working out of his office near our house. He was by nature "too slow and lazy and aristocratic to say good morning too loud," Sadie said, so he would stroll the few blocks home at a regal pace for dinner, the midday meal, which was on the table every day at two. He cut a striking figure, tall and erect. On fair days, the sunlight would glint off his mahogany skin, highlighting his sharp cheekbones. When it rained, he would approach as slowly as ever, refusing to hurry one bit. My great-grandmother Louisa would look down the street and see him coming. She always called him by his middle name: "Hammond!" she would yell; but he was oblivious. When he finally reached the house, she would tell him he had looked like a fool strolling through the rain. "Not as much of a fool as I'd look running through it," my great-grandfather would reply. Then, removing his tailored jacket, now sopping and shapeless, he would make her exasperation complete with just the right touch of gall: "And now, madame, you may lay out some fresh clothes for me."

It was a busy household, and Sadie, as the bright and sassy youngest girl, had her own special daily chore: going to the post office to fetch the family's mail. She made the round trip in style. "I was the only colored girl in town who had a horse and buggy," she told me proudly.

The Major believed in himself and his ability to provide for his family, however difficult the circumstances. And he believed, above all, in democracy. Every year, religiously, he went to the city clerk's office and registered to vote. Louisa, like all American women, was of course ineligible, even though she was, on paper, the Fordham with the biggest stake in the outcome of elections—most of the property, after all, was technically hers. But the Major's vote spoke for the family, and he appeared in person every summer to inscribe his name on the voter rolls for the September local election. He kept the receipts, lest there be any doubt about his rights.

"This is to certify, That J.H. Fordham is a Qualified Elector of the City of Orangeburg, resides on R.R. Ave Street, is 43 years of age, and is entitled to vote in the Municipal Election on the 14th day of September 1897. Registered on the 13th day of July 1897," says one of the registration slips he left behind in his safe. (In truth, he was actually forty-one years old at the time.) The Major not only registered and voted but also encouraged other Black men in Orangeburg to do so. To vote for Republicans, of course. To vote for possibility.

The historical imagination, shaped by the limited way this country's story has traditionally been told, associates can-do American optimism with whiteness. The faces and stories that automatically come to mind are of white pioneers, entrepreneurs, dreamers, and tycoons. But that is not even half the story. African Americans whose ancestors were enslaved and legally condemned to centuries of forced labor, Native Americans whose ancestors survived genocide and the theft of a continent, Mexican Americans whose ancestors were treated like the dirt from which they coaxed agricultural bounty, Chinese Americans whose ancestors were imported to do the dangerous work of building railways through impassable mountains because their lives were considered worthless, Japanese Americans who were forced from their homes and herded into internment camps—we, the unloved and erased, are the *true* American optimists. Just to make it through the day and face another tomorrow, we have always had to be the most radical and resilient optimists on earth.

Chapter Five

"GIVE US A FAIR CHANCE IN LIFE'S BATTLE"

When he was in Charleston, Major Fordham worked at the Custom House, a majestic neoclassical pile on East Bay Street overlooking the Cooper River and the wharves. When I was little, my grandmother pointed it out whenever we went to Charleston. It was an important building, and it always demonstrated to Sadie that her father had been an important man.

Before the Civil War, the U.S. Customs Service office responsible for one of the nation's busiest ports had operated out of cramped rooms in the colonial-era Exchange building, built in 1771, on whose front steps enslaved Black people were regularly auctioned off. As the nation grew, so did the need for a new federal headquarters. Land for that purpose was acquired in 1849, and construction began four years later, but the project was abruptly halted in 1859 when Congress balked over spiraling costs. That is where things stood two years later, when the first shots were fired at Fort Sumter. The new Custom House, roughly half built, was left unfinished throughout the war. Locals could dream that someday, when the structure was finally completed, the Confederate flag would wave from its heights. But of course they were disappointed. Work did not resume until 1870—shelling by Union forces had done considerable damage during the war—and Charleston's imposing temple to the gods of commerce and taxation, and to the Union's triumphant power, was finally opened in 1879.

The Custom House is cros shaped and massive, occupying an entire long rectangular city block—imagine a cathedral with a long nave bisected by a shorter transept. There were some significant changes to the original design; a proposed dome was scrapped in favor of skylights, and the planned porticoes at the ends of the short north and south wings were enclosed to provide more office space. The longer east and west wings were built as the architects intended, each with a portico enclosed by six soaring Corinthian columns and crowned with an entablature, an architrave, and a massive pediment that would have impressed the ancient Greeks. The main-floor entrance, facing East Bay Street, is reached by climbing a monumental staircase that leads up from a formal plaza. Inside, where nave and transept meet, is an atrium paved with checkerboard black-and-white tiles and open to the skylights far above. In its grandeur—beneath the American flag—the Custom House stands as an intimidating symbol of federal victory. To this day, it reminds Charlestonians of who won the war and who lost.

In 1889, Major Fordham left his job as a postal clerk to take a more important U.S. government post as deputy collector of internal revenue, with responsibility for a sector encompassing sixteen South Carolina counties. There was at least one newsworthy thing he did as the tax man: A year after starting the job, he seized from a Charleston merchant a cargo of 106,900 cigars that had been shipped from Lancaster, Pennsylvania, without the proper duties having been paid.

Even as the white-supremacist Democrats who increasingly controlled state governments in the South went about repealing the rights and opportunities that Reconstruction had given African Americans, the ambition and energy of men like Major Fordham were still welcome in the Republican Party. Within the GOP, the Major continued to rise.

There was no Hatch Act in those days restricting partisan political activity by federal employees. Still, in his zeal, Major Fordham somehow tested the boundaries of the permissible—pushing so hard that at one point he was punished with a fifteen-day suspension "for being perniciously active in politics." A brief story in Orangeburg's local newspaper, the *Times and Democrat*, reported that disciplinary action on the day Major Fordham resumed his duties.

In his safe, the Major left behind a letter he had received in 1903 from President Theodore Roosevelt—a brief note, typed on White House stationery and signed by the president, thanking my great-grandfather for *his* correspondence of a few days earlier. I've never been able to find Major Fordham's letter that began the exchange, but the mere fact that it was offered and acknowledged gives a sense of the extent to which he had become a political insider.

Major Fordham was required to go to Charleston from time to time, but Orangeburg was where he intended to build a future for himself and his family. And one thing the growing town lacked was a proper cemetery for African Americans. In 1886, a spacious, well-landscaped, serene resting place called Sunnyside Cemetery had been inaugurated—but it was reserved for whites only. So, three years later, the Major and a group of like-minded Black citizens—the Reverend E. C. Brown, the Reverend A. G. Townsend, Abram Middleton, B. J. Lloyd, W. L. Buckley, and R. W. Jewell—formed the Orangeburg Cemetery Association, with the Major as vice president, and purchased a five-acre rectangle of land on the west side of town, not far from the Edisto River. There they laid out their graveyard, Orangeburg Cemetery. In the northeast corner, a large square plot was reserved for the Fordham family's eternal rest. Since the Jim Crow local government had no interest in tending Black graves, for more than a century the cemetery was operated and maintained privately by African American volunteers. Only in 1994 did City Hall agree to take it over as a municipal asset. My sister, Ellen, served for a time on the advisory committee that oversaw upkeep and improvements. Four generations of our family, so far, are buried there.

The arc of Major Fordham's prosperity can be traced by the financial documents he and his wife, Louisa, left behind. On January 8, 1896, they received full title to the property at the corner of Boulevard and Oak where they had established the Fordham family's homeplace. That document, which I found in the safe, certifies that they achieved this milestone by paying the sum of twelve hundred dollars to the Orangeburg Investment Company, which had held the mortgage. The property was recorded in Louisa Fordham's name, and it included not just the large lot on which the Fordham family lived but also three smaller adjacent lots stretching north along Boulevard Street, then called Railroad Avenue. In time, those lots would be parceled out to the Fordham children as they reached maturity.

In those early days, before the "new house"—the one I grew up in—was built in 1903, the family lived in what my grandmother called "the first house." There is no surviving photograph showing what that structure looked like, and the only descriptive fact I recall her mentioning is that the kitchen was in a separate building out back.

That detail came up in the context of one of Sadie's stories. She was reminiscing about the men she called "tramps" who used to ride the freight trains that would stop on the tracks across the street, where railroad workers shuffled cars for their branching onward journeys. If the tramps ventured farther into town, they could be arrested for vagrancy and held overnight. Orangeburg's jail had been built in 1860, torched by General William Tecumseh Sherman in 1865, and restored right after the war; it stood unchanged in my day. Everyone called it the Pink Palace because it looked like a miniature crenellated castle, painted a soft pastel, with turrets at the corners and thick iron bars across narrow windows. The palace's inhospitality was notorious, and nobody wanted to spend the night there.

Sadie said that the hobos were safe, though, as long as they remained on the railroad's wide right-of-way. Her mother, Louisa, kept her distance from those men and warned her daughters to do the same. One day, though, Louisa was approached by a polite and respectable tramp who asked for food, saying he hadn't eaten for days. The tramp explained that his last stop had been some other town, and the people there were so disagreeable, he didn't *want* their food. Out of compassion or amusement, my great-grandmother took him to the kitchen and gave him a good meal.

I can see from the records that the family was doing well in the decade before the turn of the century, because Major Fordham and his wife had enough disposable cash to serve as lenders to friends and neighbors. Yellowed documents detail some of the loans he made and the collateral the borrowers pledged as security. On one particularly active day, the Fordhams made four such loans:

Twenty-five dollars to L. W. Brown, secured by "one two[-]horse wagon and pair harness." Nineteen dollars to Henry Zimmermann, secured by "one milch cow, 4 hogs, one single wagon." Twenty-five dollars to J. R. Rembert, secured by "one cow and calf—one gray mule." And $12.50 to Peter Jarvis, who signed the paperwork with an *X* and secured the loan with "one sorrel mule (mare)." I don't know anything more about the debtors, including whether they repaid their loans with currency or with cows, hogs, wagons, and a mule. All of which, of course, would have been useful assets on the Fordham spread; the Major was a landowner at a time and in a place where that meant keeping livestock.

Searching through the archives of the Orangeburg *Times and Democrat*, I learned that he apparently also had some kind of machinery on the property. A brief notice reported, "The petition of J. H. Fordham and wife for permit to install a steam engine in the City limits on their premises near Oak street, was read and referred under the provisions of section 108 of the Revised Ordinances to the Committee on fire department." I can't visualize Major Fordham, in his fine clothes, actually operating a steam engine. My guess is that he would have hired someone who knew how to make the thing work.

THE FORDHAM FAMILY WAS still managing to prosper—for the time—but the racial situation in Orangeburg, throughout South Carolina, and across the whole of the former Confederacy was getting worse. Systematically and brutally, Black people were being effectively re-enslaved.

The 1896 *Plessy v. Ferguson* decision by the Supreme Court had given whites—by then once more in charge of southern state legislatures—legal permission to continue and expand a project that was already well under way: establishment of a "separate but equal" society in a way that was comprehensively designed to foreclose equality. The issue involved in the landmark case was small and local: A mixed-race man named Homer Plessy had boarded a whites-only streetcar in New Orleans, violating a recent state law that segregated public transportation by race. The High Court was asked to rule on the statute's constitutionality, and it upheld the Louisiana law. By doing so, the justices invited lawmakers across the former Confederacy to mandate segregation in other spheres of activity as well.

At the same time, courts were looking kindly upon new laws imposing poll taxes and other restrictions on voting rights, tailored to keep African Americans from exercising the franchise theoretically guaranteed them by the post–Civil War amendments to the Constitution. It was not possible to explicitly ban Black men from voting, so white legislators crafted statutes that they knew would have an adverse impact on African Americans. Most Black men were just scraping by, so they were more likely to have difficulty paying a poll tax. Black men were less likely to own a homestead, which made them more transient, which meant many of them could be excluded by arbitrary length-of-residency requirements for voting. Black men were less likely to have been able to go to school, which made them more vulnerable to literacy tests—which whites could be deemed to have passed, regardless of their ability to read and write. Black men had virtually no chance of meeting "grandfather clause" voting tests that restricted suffrage to those whose grandfathers had been able to vote. And if all else failed, Black men could easily be arrested and convicted on arbitrary charges of "vagrancy" or "disturbing the peace" and excluded from voting on that basis.

John B. Knox, a lawyer who chaired the convention to write a new

Alabama state constitution, was proud of measures like these: "If we would have white supremacy," he said, "we must establish it by law—not by force or fraud." However, the "not by force" part was a lie. Everyone could see that Jim Crow white supremacy was being imposed by a combination of legislation, brute force, and terror. In many communities, whites had no compunction about physically barring African Americans from registering to vote or casting ballots. And for those brave enough to insist on their rights, the ultimate tool of terror was lynching.

The United States had no monument remotely commensurate with the enormity of American lynching until 2018, when the National Memorial for Peace and Justice was dedicated in Montgomery, Alabama. It is a stark and striking place. Eight hundred rectangular slabs of steel hang in rows from the ceiling of a pavilion, each monolith representing a county in the South where lynchings took place. It is impossible not to see the steel slabs as representations of hanging victims themselves, impossible not to feel a sense of menace and oppression. Not since the Vietnam Veterans Memorial in Washington had there been created an American historical monument whose abstract design was so powerful and so chillingly true.

One of the slabs is inscribed "Orangeburg County." The creators of the memorial have documented eleven lynchings in the county where Major Fordham was trying to provide for his family and chase his American dream. An inscription at the entrance reads: "For the hanged and beaten. For the shot, drowned, and burned. For the tortured, tormented, and terrorized. For those abandoned by the rule of law. We will remember."

We will never know precisely how many African Americans have been lynched at the hands of white mobs. I say "have been" rather than "were," in the absence of evidence that the practice has definitively ended. For a recent example, consider the 2020 killing of Ahmaud Arbery, a young Black man, in Brunswick, Georgia; three white men saw him jogging through a white neighborhood, decided he must be guilty of something, chased and cornered him with their pickup trucks, and shot him dead. The aftermath was different from what it would have been a century earlier—the killers were arrested, tried, and convicted of murder—but the killing itself was horribly familiar.

Based on various efforts by the Tuskegee Institute, the Equal Justice Institute (which built the Montgomery memorial), and other groups to count documented cases of lynching, and taking into account how those numbers grow each year as additional decades-old incidents come to light, five thousand victims would seem to be a minimum estimate. The true number could be much higher. Lynchings took place across the South, in every state of the former Confederacy, and there were scores of lynchings in the North as well. Many of these murders were hangings, but Black lynching victims were also shot in cold blood, weighed down with rocks and thrown into rivers or lakes to drown, even burned alive—slowly, to inflict maximum pain.

For white participants and witnesses, lynchings could be festive affairs. Crowds would gather to watch, especially when a hanging was taking place. An enterprising photographer might document the occasion and make the image into postcards. These souvenir photos turn up regularly in attics, antique stores, and archives, and they all look pretty much the same: smiling white men standing around a tree from which dangles one or more battered, lifeless, often naked and mutilated Black bodies—the "Strange Fruit" that Billie Holliday sang about so powerfully years later, a fruit "for the crows to pluck . . . the sun to rot . . . the tree to drop."

How did ordinary, churchgoing, Jesus-praising white citizens justify, or at least rationalize, such inhumanity? Most Black victims of lynching were men, though hundreds of women are known to have been lynched as well. Some male victims were accused, often falsely or unreliably, of serious crimes such as murder, robbery, or rape—but not tried in a court of law, much less convicted beyond a reasonable doubt. Some were lynched for supposed impertinence or lewdness toward white women, which might have involved nothing more than a glance that lasted a second too long. Many victims, perhaps even the majority, were simply guilty of being in the wrong place at the wrong time.

One example that Major Fordham would have known about in detail: On August 16, 1899, in Greenville, South Carolina, upstate from Orangeburg, an elderly man named Tom Keith had too much to drink and passed out in a bedroom of the main house of the farm where he worked. It happened to be a room where two white children were sleeping. The white man who owned the farm awakened Keith by striking him in the head with a gun, ordered him to leave, and told him never to return. There was no evidence, or even suspicion, that Keith had harmed the children in any way, just that he had slept in the same room with them. When the news spread through the community, a white mob tracked the old man down, tied him to a tree, shot him to death, then weighed his corpse down with stones and threw it into the Saluda River. No one was ever held accountable in any way for Keith's murder. A historical marker telling the story of this atrocity was erected in 2021.

Why did white mobs think they could get away with committing murder in broad daylight? They didn't *think* there would be impunity; they *knew* it. They had the acquiescence, and often the active support, of local sheriffs and police chiefs. This was, after all, a project the entire white community participated in, at least to some extent; the intimidation and subjugation of African Americans were necessary preconditions for the establishment and maintenance of white supremacy. It wasn't required that squeamish whites participate in lynchings, witness them, applaud them, or even publicly approve of them. All that was needed was that white people do nothing to impede the vigilantes or hold them to account. Whites understood that they were immune to such rough justice as long as they stayed on the right side—the white side—of the law. If they were accused of crimes, they could be confident of being tried by a jury of their peers under the presumption of innocence. Their skin protected them and gave them constitutional rights. Dark skin left African Americans stripped of those rights and naked before mob violence. White supremacy was the goal, and white people could not be overly squeamish about what means were used toward that end. They had to be deaf and blind to the terror, and they had to be remarkably incurious. They couldn't stop to wonder why Black people would step into a muddy street so that a white man could pass on the sidewalk, or why grown Black men would so meekly accept being addressed as "Boy," or why African Americans—except a few, like Homer Plessy—would automatically shuffle quietly to the rear of the streetcar. They could imagine that these were willing signs of submission rather than humiliating acts of self-abasement performed on pain of grievous injury or horrible death.

Barnwell County, which touches Orangeburg County on the west, was the site of one of the worst mass lynchings in American history. In 1889, eight Black men were accused on scant evidence of killing a white merchant, and a white mob broke them out of jail, tied them all to trees, and shot them dead.

The eleven African Americans lynched in Orangeburg County itself included a woman whose death was reported by the *Times and Democrat* on July 14, 1914:

Lynching Caused By Brutal Murder—12 Year Old Girl Slain At Elloree—Mob Immediately Shot Negro Woman

One of the most revolting crimes in the history of Orangeburg County became known early Sunday morning when a group of searchers found the mutilated body of little Essie Bell, the twelve-year old daughter of Mr. And Mrs. Daniel Bell, a farmer near Elloree after a search which had lasted throughout the night. Saturday afternoon the little girl disappeared and her father becoming alarmed spread the news. Foul play was suspected.

Rosa Richardson, a Negress, was suspicioned and locked up. About seven o'clock Sunday morning the body was found hidden underneath some brush in a recess of the woods and horribly beaten and crushed. . . .

Suspicion pointed to the Richardson woman as knowing her whereabouts, though she and her sister denied any knowledge of the little child. They were brought to Elloree and locked up for safe keeping, however, while the hunt progressed. . . . The body of the victim was found near a large oak, and was covered with bark, grass, leaves and brush. Her head was beat in a pulp, and beside the body was the lightwood knots presumably used as the instrument of infliction. . . .

After the sadness, a cry for revenge rang from the large gathering of citizens, who had almost fastened the guilt upon the Negress brute. They came towards Elloree with determined vengeance for the woman. Policeman Ballard and the magistrate attempted to take charge of the prisoner and preventing [*sic*] lynching, but were overpowered by superior force. The keys of the guard house were not surrendered by the officers, but the locks were broken by the mob and the prisoner placed in a waiting automobile, which sped back to the place where the murder had been committed. . . .

She and Mrs. Bell had had some words a few days before over the payment of some rent, and the little girl was the victim of the woman's malice against the mother. . . . The body of little Miss Essie Bell, with her head beaten into a pulp by a lightwood knot, lies prepared for burial in the quiet home of Daniel Bell, while two hundred yards away near the scene of the crime, swinging to [*sic*] a tree is the body of her alleged assassin, Rosa Richardson, riddled with bullets. . . .

This is the first lynching that has ever occurred in this section and one of the most nauseating and brutal crimes that ever happened in the community. The people are energetic, slow-going and Christian, not given over to such brutal and rash acts.

Note that the focus of the article's sympathy and outrage is the alleged killing of the white girl, not the extrajudicial murder of the "negress brute" who was "suspicioned," apparently based solely on a dispute she had with the victim's mother. Note also that there is no evident attempt to publicly identify, let alone hold accountable, the members of the "large gathering of citizens" who abducted Rosa Richardson, hanged her, and used her corpse for target practice.

The heinously brutal lynching of a Black postmaster and his young child in Lake City, South Carolina, led African American leaders to meet in 1898 in Rochester, New York, and found the first nationwide civil rights organization in U.S. history, the National Afro-American Council. The council existed for nearly a decade, eventually involving virtually all the Black luminaries of the age: activists W. E. B. Du Bois and Mary Church Terrell, journalists Ida B. Wells and William Monroe Trotter, and educator Booker T. Washington. It dissolved in 1907, unable to reconcile differences over strategy and tactics—essentially, the fundamental struggle between the ideas of Washington, who wanted to prioritize slow and steady economic process over political rights, and those of Du Bois, who believed Black Americans should demand, not request, the full equality the Constitution theoretically guaranteed. Members of the faction that agreed with Du Bois later joined with him in 1909 to form the National Association for the Advancement of Colored People.

In November 1898, just months after the founding of the Afro-American Council, the group's raison d'être was illustrated in the most horrifying way. North Carolina's largest city at the time was Wilmington, located on the coast near the mouth of the Cape Fear River. Black residents outnumbered whites, and there was a thriving African American business community that included shops, restaurants, seafood wholesalers, and one of the only Black daily newspapers in the country, *The Daily Record*. While the architects of Jim Crow had succeeded in reestablishing white supremacy in the western part of the state, the coastal region had resisted; African Americans even held elective office in Wilmington, as part of a coalition of Republicans and Populists. To the state's most powerful white leaders, and to the dominant Democratic Party, this was unacceptable.

On November 10, a white mob burst into the offices of *The Daily Record* and burned the place to the ground. The rioters went on to destroy Black businesses and then rampage through Black neighborhoods, killing men, women, and children indiscriminately. In what amounted to a localized coup d'état, the biracial local government was intimidated into resigning and was replaced by the segregationists who led the putsch. The white press in Wilmington and Raleigh, which had shamelessly whipped up anti-Black sentiment, tried to portray the violence as a riot by African Americans. Black people always knew that was a lie, but it was nearly a century before the full extent of the racist carnage was acknowledged: Between sixty and three hundred African Americans were murdered in cold blood.

In 1903, Major Fordham joined prominent African Americans in South Carolina in forming a Negro Council, which tried to use its members' fast-waning power and influence to stop the wave of lynchings and anti-Black violence. The topic for the Negro Council's meeting in Columbia was "Is lynching ever justifiable or does it lessen the crime for which it is done?" Major Fordham delivered a speech titled "Is the charge the Negroes refuse to assist in apprehending criminals of their race true? If so, why?"

Today, that sounds hopelessly mild and defensive—having to take seriously, and earnestly refute, the notion espoused by many whites of Black people somehow being responsible for their own lynchings and of white mobs somehow being justified in taking the law into their own hands. But at the time in South Carolina, it was brave and provocative to speak up on the subject at all, even if doing so required debating the undebatable. The Negro Council delegates all knew the truth, even if they could not risk saying it plainly: No, lynching was not in any sense justifiable. No, it was not true that Black people protected criminals. But yes, African Americans might do their damnedest to hide and protect an innocent man from a murderous white mob. And they did so at the peril of their own lives.

WHITE-SUPREMACIST TERROR AGAINST AFRICAN Americans was not limited to the steady drumbeat of isolated lynchings. Frequently it erupted into an orgy of killing, a deadly "race riot." That phrase, in those days, was understood to mean the spasms of white-on-Black violence that took place in cities across the country. An even better term, in many cases, would have been "massacre."

Perhaps the worst such horror of the early years of the century happened in 1906 in Atlanta, the burgeoning metropolis of the South, where Major Fordham had friends and connections—and where African Americans were amassing numbers, confidence, and a growing share of economic power. For some white citizens of Atlanta, that would never do.

Rebuilt after being razed by Sherman on his scorched-earth march through the South, Atlanta had established itself as a major rail hub and was growing rapidly. Workers who came from around the country seeking opportunity had piled into the city faster than infrastructure to accommodate them could be built, so Atlanta was a crowded place. Whites were determined that African Americans remain on "their" side of town—and they especially wanted Black-owned stores and shops out of the central business district, where they were taking trade away from white establishments.

In the summer of 1906, the issue of race was very much in the air. The governor's mansion would be up for grabs in November, and a heated campaign was under way for the Democratic nomination—which would be tantamount to election—between two of Atlanta's biggest power brokers. Clark Howell, the editor of *The Atlanta Constitution*, was running against M. Hoke Smith, the onetime publisher of *The Atlanta Journal*. Their respective newspapers amplified their campaign messages, which were variations on a theme of white fear and anger. They warned that nearly a third of the city's voting-age population was African American, which meant that Black people potentially could have real political power—and thus, according to both candidates, somehow had to be kept from voting. Georgia had already imposed a poll tax and other Jim Crow measures to limit Black voting, but Howell and Smith were calling for some way to fully eliminate Black suffrage and be done with it. The newspapers sought moral justification by portraying Black neighborhoods and places of business as unholy dens of vice and iniquity—places where there was gambling and drinking and illicit sex.

On Saturday, September 22, Atlanta papers reported four alleged assaults against white women by Black men. Not one was ever substantiated, and all may have been wholly fabricated. But the lurid, sensationalized stories had a dramatic effect: Thousands of white men and boys gathered downtown, ready to exact the white man's vengeance. The Associated Press reported what happened next: "The mob began its work early in the evening, pulling negroes from street cars and beating them with clubs, bricks and stones. . . . Negroes were beaten, cut and stamped upon in an unreasoning, mad frenzy. If a negro ventured resistance or remonstrated, it meant practically sure death."

The white mob smashed Black-owned businesses left and right, deliberately taking aim at one in particular. The Crystal Palace was the most opulent barbershop in the city, located on Peachtree Street, in the heart of downtown. It was patronized by the white elite yet owned by a Black man, an entrepreneur named Alonzo Herndon. The establishment was closed, and Herndon had already gone home for the day, so the rioters trashed the place and then moved on to another Black-owned barbershop, across the street, where they wrecked everything—and killed the unfortunate Black barbers who were trapped inside. The mob chased at least one group of fleeing African Americans onto a bridge and over the railing, sending victims plunging to the railroad tracks far below.

Rioters stacked Black bodies near the statue of Henry W. Grady on Marietta Street. Grady was an Atlanta newspaperman and civic leader who had played a big role in the city's rebirth after the Civil War and had helped establish the city's guiding philosophy and ethos: economic growth and white supremacy. The statue still stands today, and most Atlantans barely bother to notice it.

The rampage of killing and destruction continued late into the night, quelled only by a heavy rain that began falling at two in the morning. By noon, the state militia had been deployed to restore order and was mostly successful, though isolated groups of white vigilantes continued to raid Black neighborhoods, destroy businesses, and kill anyone who stood in their way. The following day, amid rumors that some African Americans in the Brownsville area were stockpiling weapons for the community to use in self-defense, a white mob—now "deputized" to aid law enforcement—waded into the neighborhood, smashing windows, dragging women and children from their homes, and beating and killing those who resisted.

For many years, the official story that Atlanta's civic leaders told themselves was that perhaps twenty-five Black people were killed in the riot. Historians now believe that at least a hundred innocent Black victims, and perhaps many more, were slaughtered. Much of the hard-won economic progress African Americans had made was erased, and the city became more racially segregated—and racially unequal—than at any time since the Civil War.

The shocking Atlanta riot made headlines across the nation and the world. In France, *Le Petit Journal* ran a cover story on the massacre in its October issue, with a drawing of white thugs beating and choking African Americans above the caption "Les 'Lynchages' aux Etats-Unis." The scholar and activist Du Bois, who had been teaching at Atlanta University but was out of town at the time of the massacre, wrote a searing poem, "The Litany of Atlanta," that evoked the bloody terror that Black people in the city had just suffered: "Red was the midnight; clang, crack and cry of death and fury filled the air."

Then, as now, Atlanta wanted to present itself to the world as a relative model of racial harmony—an image that was good for business. But even city boosters who claimed to be open-minded and forward-looking found ways to justify the massacre, based on the purported "provocation" of Black-on-white sexual assaults that historians have been unable to document.

John Temple Graves, editor of *The Atlanta News*, wrote an exculpatory piece that appeared days later in *The Minneapolis Journal*: "To the tranquil reader of your paper, looking on at a great safe distance, it seems an awful outrage against civilization and no thoughtful citizen fails to deplore and condemn it. But if one of you who read had lived for one week with the dear women of your household under the shadow and terror of the crime you would have found an explanation of a lawless revolution which cannot be legally justified. . . . The race question is more threatening now than it has been in twenty years. The tension is sharper, the antagonism deeper between the races. . . . The horror of Saturday has doubtless left a blot on our civilization, but it will clear the atmosphere and keep the negro in order for five years."

In Orangeburg, the riot of white violence in Atlanta, the regional metropolis, must have felt like local news. *The Times and Democrat*, which Major Fordham read every day, took a more-in-sorrow-than-in-anger tone: "There is only one thing as appalling as these outbreaks," a front-page article read, "and that is the seeming impossibility of solving the problem involved in the presence of 10,000,000 people lately from the wilds of Africa dwelling among 10,000,000 people of another race, color and civilization." The paper lamented that "the worthless negro vagabond . . . brings upon the heads of the innocent a terrible vengeance" and declared, "The negro wild beast must be eliminated."

African Americans, in other words, were to be blamed for their own persecution and violent death at the hands of the white mob. The argument in southern newspapers for sharper, more comprehensive repression of Black people was that if such violence could be provoked in Atlanta, of all places—the city of elite Black institutions of higher learning, including Morehouse College, Spelman College, and Atlanta University; the city of thriving Black businesses and accomplished Black professionals—then the same thing, or worse, could happen anywhere.

However, the opposite was true. It was precisely *because* Atlanta had become a mecca for Black achievers that white supremacy felt threatened enough to lash out in murderous rage.

THIS WAS THE CONTEXT for a speech my great-grandfather gave at the Columbia Opera House in 1908. The Major clearly thought it was an important moment and an important message, because of all the speeches he gave over the years, this was the only one whose handwritten draft he kept in his safe. It was a touchstone, a reference point, a vision of possibility, a reckoning of what had been won since the Civil War—and what was now being stolen away.

Major Fordham was fifty-two years old. African Americans had made tremendous progress over the course of his lifetime, creating for themselves widening spheres of political, social, and economic freedom. Now that space was being compressed, being reduced. The Major knew that this was in no one's best interest. It was tragic for Black people but also counterproductive for whites. He was a classic, old-school Republican; he believed with every fiber of his being that a rising tide lifted all boats and that greater prosperity and freedom for African Americans meant greater prosperity and freedom for all Americans. He also knew that he was preaching to a white audience whose minds would be firmly closed to what he had to say. But he had achieved enough prominence to assemble and address that audience, gathered in the grandest venue in the capital. Built in 1900, the Opera House was an ornate theater inside a hulking Second Renaissance Revival building on Main Street that also housed Columbia's City Hall. It hosted shows by traveling troupes, concerts by leading musicians, and performances by Broadway stars; it was also the place where citizens came to hear lectures and debates about the issues of the day. Major Fordham was going to speak truth to power. He called the speech "Our Progress as a Race." This is what he said:

> Mr. Chairman, Ladies and Gentlemen,
>
> It gives me pleasure to be here today and to speak a word for my race, a word of encouragement, to bring you a message from which you may take heart and go on living in this unequal struggle of life, a message from which you can take courage, redouble your efforts, gird up your loins, close up your ranks and labor earnestly, faithfully and conscientiously for the betterment of our condition.
>
> Left just after the war without a hand to guide, drifting on an

unknown sea, no rudder, no compass, no captain, no beacon light of hope, ignorant and superstitious, a prey for designing men who fattened on our weakness; such were the conditions from which we came. That we have made mistakes and are now making mistakes goes without saying, but we are profiting by these mistakes to list higher and higher in the scale of Christian civilization. Like the Apostle Paul in his appeal to King Agrippa, I today appeal to our white friends of the South land and say "that I think myself happy, because I shall answer for myself this day before thee, touching all the things whereof I am accused, especially because I know you to be expert in all the customs and questions which are among us, wherefore I beseech you to hear me patiently, my manner of life from my youth you all know." What we are, you have made us, from savages. You have molded and fashioned us into men and women, you carried us to your churches and taught us the way to the cross, in your homes you taught us how to cook, wash and tidy the house. You hired men to teach us the various trades, these and other things too numerous to mention, you taught us.

How well we learned our lessons. You have but to look around you in this South land and behold the brick, iron, stone and wood structures that still remain monuments of our handicraft. I know that you have not forgotten that the mechanics, the workers in wood, iron and stone, the painters, cabinet makers, shoemakers, tailors and the dressmakers of the South were none other than your own Negro slaves.

You know us as no one else in the whole wide world. To you I appeal to give us a fair chance in life's battle, and as those of us struggle to rise, reach down a helping hand, for in rising we help you as well as ourselves. . . .

Hon. John Sharp Williams of Mississippi, minority leader in the House of Representatives is authority for this statement. He is really a representative Southern leader, who has commanded attention because of the strength of his mind and force of his reasoning. He says:

"Fully ninety per cent of the Negro race is behaving itself as well as could be expected. It is at work in the fields, on the railroads, and in the sawmills." Now add a few percent to this ninety for the Negroes engaged in teaching, preaching, other professions and business callings, and you will readily see that we are surely advancing higher and higher. We have much to be thankful for and much to learn. We must learn to separate ourselves from the wicked good for nothing criminal class, and that class of boys and girls who we are making so much sacrifice to keep in school and educate, who return home with so much impertinence and a desire to shun work, unwilling to cook a meal, help mother wash the clothes, or cut a stick of wood or hoe the garden. The sooner the preacher says dust to dust, ashes to ashes, over their worthless carcass, the better for them, the better for the race.

Somehow or other we have slowly and steadily marched forward up the difficult hill of success, and it gives me pleasure to unfurl our banner in the breeze today, on which is inscribed the following:

Forty years ago, the Negro of the South did not own a square foot of ground nor a roof to cover them. Now, on the other hand, there are 130,000 farms owned by Negroes, valued at $350,000,000; 150,000 homes outside the farm ownership, valued at $265,000,000; and personal property valued at $165,000,000; 12 Negro banks, 3 magazines, 450 newspapers, 800 physicians in practice, 300 lawyers, 30,000 school teachers, 300,000 books in the home. So starting from nothing, here is an accumulation of a billion dollars.

When the work began, not one per cent of the Negro adults of the South could read or write. Today, 50 per cent can do so, 55 per cent of the children are attending school, and with more facilities more would attend, and with longer terms the percentage would increase. It can be said to our lasting credit, that no matter what the cost, if we have to do with one meal a day and one suit a year, we are determined to educate our children.

In every community we have high-toned blue-blooded Christian white men, who believe in the Golden Rule, and who stand for law and order and justice to all. Let us get close to these men, obtain their friendship and stand with them and by them in all matters for the uplift of humanity and the betterment of conditions.

That speech summed up the man at the apex of his influence, such as it was—the peak of his power to be heard, if not heeded. Major Fordham knew that most of those white men in the South who considered themselves Christians found nothing incompatible about also considering themselves superior to African Americans and justified in returning them to "their place." He had to know that his appeal to better angels would fall mostly upon deaf ears. But he was a lawyer who believed in the power of argument. And he was a man who believed in dignity and respectability as weapons in the fight for justice.

The debate over how to combat Jim Crow repression and terror was, to Black leaders of the time, a matter of life and death. The Booker T. Washington approach, on the one hand, was to build slowly from the ground up. In his view, African Americans should concentrate on obtaining primary and secondary education, working the land, and acquiring marketable skills in the trades. He believed it was too soon, and ultimately would prove counterproductive, to make maximalist legal, political, and social demands. He did not believe integration was the ultimate goal, preferring to aim for self-sufficiency. The W. E. B. Du Bois approach, on the other hand, was to insist on what the Thirteenth, Fourteenth, and Fifteenth Amendments to the Constitution had guaranteed in black and white: equality. He believed there was no such thing as "separate but equal." He was tired of asking patiently for our rights, and he was tired of waiting until America felt like granting them. He wanted our freedom, and he wanted it now.

Major Fordham was somewhere in the middle. He saw, as Washington saw, that far too many African Americans were still in need of basic education and skills. In his speech, he made no demands except to be left alone, asking only for "a fair chance in life's battle" and perhaps an occasional "helping hand." He did not detail the nature of the unfairness that Black men, women, and children faced; everyone was painfully familiar with the specifics. At the same time, though, he was a lawyer. He knew the Constitution and the law, and he believed in their power. The fact that he had taken a highly visible role in the state's Negro Council would have marked him, to whites, as a "troublemaker"—and troublemakers, like Du Bois, were exposing themselves to risk, especially in the South, where the Ku Klux Klan was ascendant.

The Major's prominence gave him some protection, as did his position as an official of the federal government. But he was a Black man in South Carolina, born at a time when Black men were chattel. He was a Black man who had tasted real freedom during the interlude of Radical Reconstruction, who now saw that freedom being taken away, and who during the Civil War had seen firsthand, as Mao Tse-tung would later say, that "political power grows out of the barrel of a gun." He knew he had to choose his words very carefully indeed.

Chapter Six

DEATH AND THE RED SUMMER

Major Fordham rose no higher. At a time when white leaders in the former Confederacy were reestablishing the old racial hierarchy and claiming ever-greater autonomy from the federal government, there was no path to advancement for a Black man who was the U.S. deputy collector of internal revenue in South Carolina. Quite the opposite: In 1911, the Major was summarily demoted, with most of his responsibility and power taken away. The following year, he retired from federal service to the full-time practice of law and the tending of his family's properties in Orangeburg and Charleston—and also to the guidance of his children, who by then were young adults. John Hammond Fordham was fifty-five. He had come of age during a fleeting moment, right after the Civil War, when opportunity for a young Black man with ambition and drive was limited only by the size of his dreams. Now that interlude was a fading memory. His three daughters and three sons would have to negotiate a Jim Crow world. Possibility was circumscribed by a color line that had become, as before the war, an unbreachable wall.

In this new environment, the Major could still earn fees as an attorney. More profitably, he could still speculate in real estate. Orangeburg continued to grow and develop, making the acreage the Fordhams had acquired an increasingly valuable asset, one that could be leveraged to buy and sell more land or to host other enterprises. Not for the last time, property would help the family make it through lean times.

Orangeburg was an unusual place, a demographic and cultural anomaly. By the time the Major retired, the town had already cemented its two distinct, separate, and coexisting identities, which endure today. Its original raison d'être was to serve as an agricultural hub, where farmers could obtain the supplies they needed, sell their crops to brokers—cotton in its heyday, of course, but also tobacco, peanuts, soybeans, and assorted produce—and ship that bounty down the Edisto River to the Port of Charleston or load it onto railcars headed north. But after the Civil War, Orangeburg took on an added function: Claflin College, now Claflin University, was founded in 1869 as the first institution of higher education for African Americans in the state—a private school, affiliated with the Methodist Church. Then, in 1896, on land adjacent to the Claflin campus, the state legislature created the Colored Normal, Industrial, Agricultural and Mechanical College of South Carolina—now South Carolina State University—as the state's first public college for Black students. Suddenly, Orangeburg became an educational hub as well.

The very first institution of higher learning for Black students in the nation, Cheyney University, had been opened near Philadelphia back in 1837; the first established in the former Confederacy was Shaw University, founded in Raleigh, North Carolina, in 1865. Both survive to this day.

On the white side of Orangeburg, there were mostly farmers, merchants, tradesmen, and laborers, plus a few professionals like bankers and lawyers. On the Black side—where people on average were poorer, to be sure, and had been robbed of the political power they had briefly enjoyed back when Major Fordham was elected coroner—there were laborers and sharecroppers and farmers, too, but also increasing numbers of professors and administrators who came to teach and work at Claflin and South Carolina State. And soon there was a growing population of Claflin and SC State graduates, young men and women who had come from around the state to be educated and who had decided to stay in Orangeburg, many of them teaching at the colleges or at the city's Black elementary and secondary schools. As a result, Orangeburg's intellectual firepower became concentrated in the Black community—while its actual firepower, in terms of political control and the coercive might of the state, was monopolized by whites.

In this small city with a split personality, Major Fordham was determined to build an enduring legacy by using his instinct for risk and reward. All along, even while he was working his full-time government job, participating in GOP politics, serving in various leadership roles at Trinity Methodist Church, attending meetings as a Mason and an Odd Fellow, and being the head of a busy household, he had somehow found time for wheeling and dealing in search of profit.

I know this because of the paperwork the Major left behind. When I was five or six, I would sometimes sneak into my grandmother's room—which had been where her parents slept—to see if there was anything interesting in the many boxes she kept under the bed. Every time, there was the same disappointment: old papers and photographs. On other nothing-to-do days, if my parents were at work, I'd get a flashlight and head upstairs. I'd go either into my room, where I'd venture through a little hobbit-scale door and into the attic space in the gable above Sadie's room, or across the hall and through a similar door into the unfinished dormer above the dining room. I was (technically) forbidden to explore these places, and (I now see) for good reason. They were dark, the flooring was uneven, and inside were lots of things I could either have tripped over, hit my head against, cut myself with, or clumsily smashed into pieces. There was mostly old furniture and furnishings—bed frames, worn-out chairs, a disassembled table, a lamp, a couple of vases. And there were more boxes like the ones in my grandmother's room, full of old papers and photos.

When I began researching this American history, I knew I'd have to really examine these papers for the first time. Beginning with my great-grandfather's generation, my family kept everything: loan agreements, bank statements, canceled checks, tax receipts, letters, ledgers, funeral programs, brochures from tourist sites they visited on their travels. I found papers all over the house, crammed into desks and cabinets, tucked away under beds, stuffed into dresser drawers, piled on top of wardrobes. There were also hundreds of photographs, the oldest crumbling into dust; some were organized in albums, but most were loose in boxes.

The primary bedroom is where I found most of the papers from Major Fordham's era. The other first-floor bedroom, where my great-aunt Florella slept, is where documents from her and Sadie's time predominate. The pull-down desk in the living room is where my mother kept mementos of her life before she met my father, including papers she wrote in college and even a few circumspect billets-doux from would-be suitors.

The biggest trove of photographs was in boxes behind the living room sofa, beneath the bay window looking out onto Boulevard Street. And many of them were already annotated: After I got married, my mother saw that my wife, Avis, had a passionate interest in Black history and a fascination for the caches of documents and pictures stored around the house. Whenever we visited, at some point Momma would bring out a selection of old family photographs and summon Avis to sit beside her. She would explain to Avis who the people in the photos were, how they were related to us, and approximately when the picture was taken. Avis made notes on the backs of many prints. One year, when she and I drove down for a holiday visit, she even went so far as to bring a scanner. When she wasn't pampering my father by baking fresh rolls, she would be at the scanner, capturing every photograph she could find, even if she had no idea who was in it. She thought it was imperative that this history be archived in digital form, which would allow it to live forever.

Inevitably, some irreplaceable material has been lost since my childhood—including one special image that spoke volumes about the Major and his family. There used to be a large wooden storage shed in the backyard, probably at least as old as the house itself. I wasn't supposed to go in there, because some of the things inside were rusty and sharp and probably teeming with tetanus, but sometimes I disobeyed. There were miscellaneous old household items—more furniture, bedsprings, kitchen utensils that must have dated to Louisa Fordham's time. And there was a very large photographic portrait of the family: Major Fordham, Louisa, and their adolescent children posed formally as a group.

In my recollection, the picture was at least three feet wide and almost as high. Some of the Fordham children were still quite young when the picture was taken, which would date it to sometime in the 1890s. I remember that the whole family was dressed as if for an important occasion. And I remember the powerful sense of pride and ambition the Fordhams displayed. Over the years, I've longed to revisit that image because it said so much about the family and their times. I know it was still in the shed in 1970, when I left to go away to the University of Michigan. But by the time I became interested enough in our history to appreciate the picture's importance, which was at least two decades later, the sagging old shed had finally been torn down. I hold out the hope that someone, at some point, might have brought the photo inside the house and stuck it in some undiscovered cranny, but I've looked and looked and can't find it. I intend to keep searching.

The documents, on the other hand, had been easier to find but proved harder to decipher. With close reading, they, too, present a striking portrait of the family—a moving picture, an image that evolves over time.

As I put the papers into a timeline, I was eventually able to tease out a fundamental change in the nature of the many business transactions that Major Fordham and his wife, Louisa, conducted: During the 1880s and '90s, when the Major was on the rise and his law practice was busy, the Fordhams were almost always lenders and buyers. But later, as the

Jim Crow system tightened its grip, they became frequent borrowers and sellers.

The shift becomes clear shortly after the turn of the century. In 1903, Louisa Fordham—or, probably, the Major acting in her name—took out a $300 mortgage on one of the lots they owned down the street from the spanking-new house at Boulevard and Oak. The loan, from a John F. Rickenbacker, was at 8 percent interest; given the timing, I wonder if the Fordhams might have needed cash to finish the home's construction or to buy furniture. The following year, Louisa took out a $175 mortgage against the new house and its lot from a lender named L. M. Dunton. That was followed by several similar loans, some paid off very quickly, others remaining on the books for years.

In 1912, Major Fordham, in his own name, borrowed $295 from Banks and Wimberly Co., an equipment retailer in the nearby town of St. Matthews. The Major put up a long list of items as collateral: one steam grist mill, one fifteen-horsepower tubular boiler, one twelve-horsepower Liddell-Tompkins engine, one thirty-inch Straub grist mill, one bolting machine, one thirty-inch saw, one Chattanooga double wood splitter, one eight-year-old sorrel mule, and one dark-colored nine-year-old mare. The Major attested that the equipment and livestock were at the Boulevard Street property, meaning the acreage I grew up knowing as purely residential—to the extent that my grandmother referred to one of the lawns as "the croquet ground," where the family played that leisurely game—had been, at some point, more of a multiuse compound. Local farmers, after all, needed mills; local builders needed lumber. The steam engine permit the Major and Louisa had applied for years earlier had evidently been granted and put to use.

The Major was doing what he could to build wealth for his family at a time when doing so was increasingly difficult for African Americans in the South. On paper, given his skills as an attorney, he should have been the man to give legal advice to the biggest merchants and growers of Orangeburg County. He should have been the defense attorney sought out for the most high-profile cases by clients in Charleston, in

Columbia, and across the state. But of course that was unthinkable. The idea that a Black man could represent white clients, before white judges and white juries, was as ludicrous as the notion that Major Fordham could jump over the moon. To build his assets and make a legacy, he had to scramble harder and faster.

As I looked deeper into the Major's papers, I noticed some transactions that were anomalous and puzzling. On January 27, 1913, he borrowed forty-five dollars from a Mrs. Mary E. Edwards. It was a short-term loan, at 8 percent, which he agreed to pay back on March 1, five weeks later. As collateral, he pledged the same items he had used to secure the larger Banks and Wimberly loan a year earlier. I have no idea why he needed such a relatively small amount of money so urgently that he would encumber, even briefly, possessions worth much more; my assumption is that the loan may have been related to some larger and more complicated deal, probably involving land, whose outlines I cannot fully reconstruct. But the strange thing is that a series of scribbled notes on the Edwards loan document indicate that it was not fully repaid until 1920, seven years after the Major had borrowed the money.

That was unusual, because earlier documents showed that the Major had always made a point of paying creditors punctually. It was unlikely to be an oversight; nothing I had heard about him or seen in his papers suggested he was the sort of person to lose track of details. I looked through the pile for other pieces of business that had languished for months or years, and I found several—all of which were wrapped up in 1920, as if they were part of a general settling of accounts. The outcome, when all was said and done, appeared in the aggregate more negative than positive for the family's balance sheet. If you knew nothing else about the Fordham family but were able to spend a few days following the paper trail, you would conclude that something must have happened around 1918 or 1919. Things must have changed.

And they had, both in the Fordham house and across the nation. In terrible ways.

THE FIRST BLOW TO the family was Louisa Fordham's death. She passed away on April 24, 1918, at fifty-eight years of age, from what her death certificate says was chronic endocarditis—an infection, usually bacterial, of the lining of the heart. The condition is life-threatening even today, with the best modern care. Before antibiotics, it was dire.

In the final blink of a beloved eye, Major Fordham's soulmate, best friend, and partner in life was gone. As young children in Charleston, he and Louisa had witnessed the chaos and destruction, and ultimately the liberating glory, of the Civil War. On their wedding day, federal troops still occupied the South, and the couple's rights were protected by force of arms. Everything seemed possible. For more than forty years, they had cared for each other, stubbornly clinging to the dream that they could build a world of lasting freedom, justice, equality, and prosperity for their children. Even as the flame of that dream flickered and dimmed, they kept it alive.

While Major Fordham worked and politicked and strove, Louisa organized and kept the busy Fordham household. During the long stretches while he was away, in Charleston or elsewhere, she managed the family's real estate holdings and attended to civic and church duties. She watched over and cared for her mother, Flora Elizabeth Smith Dwight, having set her up in a house just down Oak Street; she buried "Grandma Dwight" in Orangeburg Cemetery, the well-tended African American resting place that Major Fordham had helped establish. She raised six children, who all turned out well. She was an expert cook and seamstress, and she played the old black piano in the sitting room quite well; she had insisted that her daughters—Florella, Grace, and Sadie—learn those skills, too. Her old foot-operated Singer treadle sewing machine is still in the house today, beneath the window in one of the first-floor bedrooms. Louisa's fin de siècle taste and refinement remain evident in a few surviving marble-topped tables and chests; her intellect is reflected in the 1909 Harvard Classics set of great books, comprising fifty-one volumes—from Plato and Homer to Tennyson and Whitman—that fill the living room shelves. She, more than the Major, made our house a home.

Major Fordham buried his wife in Orangeburg Cemetery. He and Louisa had looked forward to growing old together. Now he would go on alone.

The second calamity came the following year, and it affected not just the Fordham family but African Americans across the country: the blood-soaked "Red Summer" of 1919. By the time it ended, Major Fordham could have had no shred of doubt that his vision of an America where Black people and white people had equal rights and opportunity would be, as Langston Hughes wrote decades later, "a dream deferred." The Major was too much of an optimist to accept the notion that his American dream had been extinguished for all time. But he was too much of a realist to hope any longer that he would live to see it come true.

The Red Summer was a series of detonations of deadly violence by white mobs against African Americans in more than three dozen cities across the country. There were riots, pogroms, and massacres, beginning in the spring and continuing into the fall—a fast-spreading and all-consuming wildfire of hatred that marked a turning point in race relations in the United States.

A federal government report was compiled in September of that awful year by George Edmund Haynes, who was the first Black man to earn a PhD from Columbia University and a cofounder of the National Urban League. In 1919, Haynes was serving as director of the Division of Negro Economics at the U.S. Department of Labor. Assigned to quantify and analyze the crisis that was still unfolding, Haynes tallied thirty-eight separate anti-Black riots, in big cities and small towns alike, with different particulars but a common pathology. More violence was yet to take place in October, including the deadliest episode of all—an indiscriminate massacre in rural Arkansas. When the Red Summer finally ended, hundreds of Black men, women, and children had lost their lives. Thousands more had seen their homes and businesses destroyed. And *all* African Americans understood two things, wherever in the country they lived: First, white supremacy was here to stay, both in the South and the North. And second, African Americans, when under attack, could band together to stand their ground and fight back.

The context for the Red Summer was a confluence of events and megatrends that made the country into a tinderbox. World War I had ended in 1918, on the eleventh day of the eleventh month, and two million American soldiers were coming home from the battlefields of Europe. Some segregated Black units had gone overseas—notably one that included Major Fordham's youngest son, Marion—but most of the returning servicemen were white. And after the homeward-bound Atlantic crossing, those ex-soldiers disembarked from their crowded transport ships, freighters, and ocean liners onto the bustling docks of a radically changed nation.

The Great Migration of African Americans fleeing the South for opportunity in the North greatly accelerated during the war. By 1919, a half million Black people had already made the trek to the northern and midwestern industrial centers where factories of all types were desperate for labor during the war years. Many others were on the way, including my father's family, who were in the middle of their journey northward to Michigan. Black men were now filling the jobs those returning white soldiers had left behind and now wanted to reclaim. The fact that the Black migrants were willing to work for lower wages—they had no choice—meant that many employers were happy to keep them on.

At the same time, serving in the military during the war had left nearly four hundred thousand Black men with new skills and broadened horizons. Those Black doughboys now had a radically different sense of themselves and their place in the world. They had faced discrimination in the segregated armed forces—they were not given the chance, as a decades-later recruiting slogan put it, to "be all you can be"—but they had been soldiers and sailors all the same. They had worn the same uniforms as whites and had risen to the same ranks, as far as they were allowed. They had been awarded the same commendations and medals. In their all-Black units, they had learned military discipline and leadership skills. They had shown their bravery—to the enemy, to their fellow Americans, and to themselves. They had performed the ultimate duty of U.S. citizenship, and now they felt entitled to the fruits. They held their heads high as they walked down the street, and they looked passersby in the eye.

The ever-observant Du Bois recognized the importance of the moment and captured it in searing prose, publishing an essay titled "Returning Soldiers" in *The Crisis*, the magazine of the NAACP:

> For America and her highest ideals, we fought in far-off hope; for the dominant southern oligarchy entrenched in Washington, we fought in bitter resignation. . . . We return from the slavery of uniform which the world's madness demanded us to don to the freedom of civil garb. We stand again to look America squarely in the face and call a spade a spade. We sing: This country of ours, despite all its better souls have done and dreamed, is yet a shameful land. . . . We *return*. We return *from fighting*. We return *fighting*.

For Major Fordham, the death and destruction of the Red Summer began alarmingly close to home in his native Charleston. During the war years, the Navy Yard on the Cooper River had been greatly expanded with the addition of an adjacent Naval Training Center; thousands of sailors passed through the city on their way to and from Europe. They were an alien presence in a city that was—and, in many aspects, remains—insular and set in its ways.

According to most accounts, the 1919 Charleston race riot began on May 10 with an angry confrontation between two young white sailors from the Naval Training Center and a Black man named Isaiah Doctor. Most sources say the sailors gave Doctor some money to procure liquor for them—a year before Prohibition took effect nationwide, South Carolina was already "dry" by state law—and Doctor pocketed the cash without delivering the booze. However, a history of the riot published by the Charleston County Public Library tells a different story: Doctor had failed to humbly give way as he passed the sailors on a downtown sidewalk and, instead, had "jostled through" the "two bluejackets." The sailors yelled angrily at Doctor, he yelled back, and the ruckus drew the attention of more white sailors and more Black passersby, until it became a standoff. Doctor may have thrown a brick in the direction of the white crowd. Somebody fired a gun into the air. As night fell, a rumor quickly spread through the narrow, crowded streets that a Black man had shot and wounded white sailors.

A crowd of sailors, joined by increasing numbers of white civilians, bulled their way into a pool hall to grab cues for use as bludgeons and raided commercial shooting galleries for guns and ammunition. The swelling mob went looking for Doctor, found him, and shot him fatally. The correspondent for *The State* newspaper estimated that some two thousand white rioters, in and out of uniform, soon were marauding through Black commercial and residential neighborhoods, shouting, "Get the Negroes!" They destroyed a prominent Black-run barbershop, Fridie's Central Shaving Parlor, because they thought they had seen a Black man duck inside it. Rioters beat and robbed an African American streetcar driver and took his vehicle for a joyride. They pulled a Black passenger off another streetcar and shot him dead.

A brave Charleston civil rights activist named Septima Clark—described by the Reverend Martin Luther King Jr. as "the mother of the Movement"—was twenty-one years old at the time and witnessed the riot. "We had trolley cars then, and these sailors got on and started beating every Black they could find," she told an interviewer in 1981. "They killed one or two of them. That Sunday night, nobody could go out, you had to stay in. The Citadel Square was filled with screaming and hollering and we ran back into the house."

African Americans did not shrink from this fight. In the absence of police protection, they fiercely defended themselves and their community. Twenty years later, a Black witness named James Hollaway gave this account: "When the news went out in the Negro community what was happening, armed men came running through the streets with knives, hammers, hatchets, guns, razors, and sticks, and wholeheartedly joined the fight. On every street in that section, blood was shed. Negroes and white boys who were eager for excitement entered and fought until they were beaten and exhausted."

Black men armed themselves and patrolled their neighborhoods in cars. According to Hollaway, when one white police officer's commander asked him why he had not arrested those self-appointed Black guardians and confiscated their weapons, the officer replied, "Yes, sir, but every car I stopped was filled with either revolvers or guns—which were pointed directly at me!"

The death toll was lopsided and relatively small—at least six African Americans were killed, while no whites are known to have lost their lives. But it was the worst violence Charleston had seen since the Civil War. South Carolinians, both Black and white, were shocked and alarmed.

And the Red Summer was just beginning.

On July 3, in Bisbee, Arizona, a mining town near the Mexican border, white police officers attacked Black troops from the Tenth U.S. Cavalry—one of the two "Buffalo Soldier" units—who were there to march in an Independence Day parade; four of the Black men were shot, but none died.

On July 10–12, in Longview, Texas—where returning African American soldiers had encouraged Black farmers to demand fairer prices from white brokers—white mobs suddenly attacked Black neighborhoods, burning homes and businesses and murdering a sixty-year-old man.

On July 14, in Indianapolis, hundreds of white men and boys attacked the predominately Black neighborhood of Garfield Park. A seven-year-old Black girl was shot but survived.

Next came the first big explosion. In Washington, D.C., a Black man named Charles Ralls was arrested for allegedly assaulting a white woman. The arrest came after a string of sensationalized stories in local newspapers, including *The Washington Post*, about a purported "Negro fiend" who was supposedly at large in the nation's capital committing sex crimes. Police subsequently decided there was not enough evidence to charge Ralls with the attack, and they let him go. On Saturday, July 19, news of Ralls's release spread through the city. At a bar near the busy Navy Yard teeming with white sailors and Marines just back from the war in Europe, the mood turned sour, then violent. The crowd of servicemen, now a mob, spilled out into the street and headed a few blocks west, toward Ralls's working-class Black neighborhood, growing in numbers as they went along. A lynch party was coming to mete out justice.

After searching for a while, harassing Black people at random, they spotted Ralls, who was taking a walk with his wife. They chased the couple, but somehow Ralls and his wife escaped and made it home, barricading the doors. The mob was unsatisfied—but they were no longer unopposed: Black residents of the neighborhood converged at the scene, bearing arms to defend their homes and families from the invaders. The white rioters opened fire first. African Americans raised their pistols, rifles, and shotguns and shot back, wounding a white sailor.

That insult to white supremacy sparked a serious escalation. What started as localized white mob violence quickly spread across Washington and continued overnight into Sunday morning, with rioters storming into heavily Black residential and commercial neighborhoods, attacking people on the street or dragging them out of their cars and beating them savagely. One witness to the fury of the racist violence was the dean of students at Howard University, Carter G. Woodson, the Black scholar who went on to pioneer rigorous study of the African diaspora and who is considered "the father of African American history." He recalled watching as a Black man was seized "as one would a beef for slaughter . . . conveniently adjusted for lynching," then coldly shot dead. Police did effectively nothing to stop the rioting. Abandoned by their nominal protectors in law enforcement, whose sympathies seemed to be more with the assailants than with the assailed, Black Washingtonians armed themselves for self-defense.

On Monday, still under attack and unprotected by the authorities, African Americans made a stand at the intersection of Seventh and U Streets NW—the commercial, cultural, and intellectual heart of Black Washington, just south of the hilltop Howard campus. Black war veterans used their military knowledge to set up defensive positions, occupying the high ground by stationing snipers on the roof of the grand Howard Theatre to fire down on approaching columns of white rioters. Some of the vets took control of key intersections, while others launched offensive forays, sending carloads of armed Black men to shoot up white neighborhoods. In a very real sense, the recently ended Great War had come home.

By Tuesday, the violence had begun to peter out. President Woodrow Wilson—himself a white supremacist who had screened D. W. Griffith's epic racist film celebrating the Ku Klux Klan, *The Birth of a Nation*, at the White House—finally ordered two thousand federal troops into the streets to restore order. In the end, ten white people, including two police officers, and five African Americans had been killed. The fact that more whites died than Blacks was an anomaly in the Red Summer riots. But the fact that African Americans had fought back, with deadly arms and effective tactics, was a template for what would come.

On July 19, the same day the Washington riot started, there was a near riot in New York City. In Harlem, on 127th Street, a Black man and a white man were arguing about World War I. Things got so heated that the Black man drew a gun and began firing down the street, injuring several bystanders. By the time police arrived, hundreds of African Americans, many of them armed, were waiting in the streets and on the rooftops to defend their neighborhood.

And on July 21, with Washington still a war zone, African Americans in Norfolk, Virginia, home to the nation's biggest and most important naval base, were holding a grand celebration to welcome home returning Black sailors and soldiers. White police suddenly descended in force, supposedly to quell violence in the crowd. Once again, African Americans fought back, and clashes led to two deaths and many injuries.

Then came Chicago, which made what had gone before a mere prelude.

During the war, tens of thousands of African Americans had come to the city from the South looking for work and finding it. Their numbers grew from forty-four thousand in 1910 to more than a hundred thousand by the end of the decade. They settled mostly on the South Side, near the stockyards, meatpacking plants, steel mills, and factories that were offering jobs. The European immigrants, mostly Irish, who had gotten there first resented their growing presence, seeing the Black newcomers as invading what had been *their* territory and taking what they considered *their* paychecks. Racial tension mounted as white and Black veterans came home to the city from their wartime service equipped with military experience and bristling with the bearing of conquerors. All that was needed to ignite a conflagration was a single spark, which came on July 27.

It was the kind of sweltering day, before the advent of air-conditioning, when the heat was unbearable—amid all the asphalt and concrete, it felt like being inside a kiln—and Chicagoans of all races sought relief at the city's Lake Michigan beaches. By custom, there were separate stretches of sand for whites and Blacks. Everyone knew where the dividing line was, even if there were no "Whites Only" signs, and everyone observed it.

A seventeen-year-old Black youth named Eugene Williams and his friends were among the crowd at a South Side "Colored" beach having great fun, diving from a homemade raft and climbing back aboard and diving again. They were so wrapped up in their game that they failed to notice when the raft drifted into a whites-only sector. They realized where they were only when irate white men on the beach began pelting them with rocks. The boys scrambled back to the safety of the Black sector, but Williams didn't move fast enough, and a rock hit him in the head. He was in the water, swimming for his life, and more rocks kept coming in a sustained fusillade. Panicked, stunned, and disoriented, Williams drowned.

When police officers arrived, they refused to arrest the white man who had thrown the rock that hit Williams in the head. News of the killing spread quickly, and an angry Black crowd gathered. The clash that ensued sparked a white race riot that raged for eight long, deadly days.

White mobs marauded through Black neighborhoods; African Americans counterattacked in white districts. For more than a week, the city was lawless. Black Chicagoans believed the police were deliberately allowing white mobs to wreak havoc as a way of putting African Americans in their place. For the first four days, Mayor William Hale Thompson refused to ask the governor to send in the National Guard, even though the Guard was in position and ready to intervene. There were scores of tit-for-tat shootings, beatings, ambushes, lootings, and incidents of arson, mostly confined to the South Side. On July 31 alone, the fire department responded, or tried to respond, to thirty arson fires *before noon.* The overwhelming majority of the violence involved attacks by whites against Blacks. When the rioting finally ended, thirty-eight people had been killed—twenty-three Blacks and fifteen whites—and more than five hundred had been injured.

The Chicago riot shocked the nation. It was covered extensively not only by the big newspapers and news services but also by *The Chicago Defender,* one of the most authoritative and widely read African American newspapers in the country. The *Defender*'s reports were picked up by Black papers in cities like Pittsburgh, Baltimore, and St. Louis, which meant that Black people from coast to coast could follow the violence as it unfolded from the viewpoint of friends, relatives, and former neighbors; at that point, in Black America, everybody knew *somebody* who had moved to Chicago.

Governor Frank Lowden, a Republican, convened an interracial blue-ribbon commission to investigate the causes of the violence and propose solutions to improve race relations. It was a worthwhile exercise, but it solved nothing. The most concrete result of the 1919 riot was greater racial separation. Black neighborhoods became blacker, white neighborhoods whiter. Some African American families were so traumatized by the riots that they packed up and moved to other cities—or even back to the South. But these were drops in the bucket compared to the steady flow of African Americans from Texas, Mississippi, Louisiana, Arkansas, and Tennessee still arriving every day at Chicago's busy train stations. The newcomers were coming to an increasingly segregated and unequal city.

On July 31, there was an ugly white riot in Philadelphia that seemed minor only in the context of what was happening in Chicago. In August and September, there were white riots in smaller cities in Alabama, Arkansas, Mississippi, Texas, Georgia, Tennessee, and Louisiana.

On September 28, in Omaha—where African Americans, during the war years, had filled jobs in the stockyards that returning white veterans thought belonged to them as a birthright—a white mob demanded to be allowed to lynch a Black man, Will Brown, who had been accused of raping a white woman. The rioters, who far outnumbered and outgunned the police, set Omaha's courthouse on fire and threatened to hang the mayor. Officials pleaded and negotiated with the mob, ultimately choosing safety and survival over sworn duty: They surrendered Brown to the crowd. He was promptly murdered, his corpse strung up on a lamppost, riddled with bullets, doused in oil, and set ablaze.

And finally, on September 30 and October 1 came the worst horror of all. In Elaine, Arkansas, a small town near the Mississippi River, Black farmers and sharecroppers had joined a union that demanded fairer prices for their cotton. About a hundred of them held a meeting with union representatives at a church outside town, and they stationed armed guards around the building to protect the gathering. When two white deputies approached, shots were exchanged; one of the white men was killed and the other injured.

White local officials heard about the shooting and responded with pure terror, not just against the shooters, not just against the farmers at the meeting, but also against African Americans in general. They formed a posse to hunt down anyone who might be part of this "Negro uprising," roaming the area and murdering Black people indiscriminately. An authoritative tally was never compiled, but most historians believe at least two hundred innocent African Americans, and perhaps many more, were killed in what became known as the Elaine Massacre.

The Red Summer's bloody events were covered in all the newspapers. Major Fordham would have followed them and understood their implications. Jim Crow had already shattered African Americans' hopes and dreams in the South. Now the color line was being drawn, and enforced by violence, in cities all over the country, including those in the North that once were thought of as sanctuaries of freedom and opportunity.

To the extent that the Major once had the power to help bring about his vision of a better, fairer America, that power was waning. Now in his sixties, he had no federal position to give him authority. His Republican Party had been relegated to bystander status by the dominant Democrats across the South. The brief era of Black elected officials was over. Major Fordham had achieved much, but the times were passing him by.

In that awful year of 1919, Major Fordham took at least one extended trip. On August 22, he wrote a warm letter to his daughter Sadie from Atlantic City, where he was attending a meeting or convention of some sort, perhaps a gathering of one of his fellowship organizations. Like every visitor, he would have promenaded along the famed Boardwalk and enjoyed the hospitality of one of the city's grand hotels. I know that he spent time on the beach. He may well have taken in a baseball game, because Atlantic City was known as one of the best towns in the country to watch top-quality teams from the Negro leagues in action.

The Major opened his letter with a recitation of the high prices being charged in what was then America's premier resort destination: $0.75 for breakfast, $1.25 for dinner, $2 a night for his hotel room. The room charge was set to go even higher the following day, all the way to $3. "But I leave here tomorrow 12:15 for New Orleans," he wrote, so he would not have to pay the increase. He was heading off to another meeting, another long train ride to a city full of diversions, another responsibility in which he now sought respite and joy. It must have been a sad undertaking, this journey without Louisa, but not as sad as sitting at home without her.

The Major was nothing if not resilient—or, at least, determined to show resilience to his family. "Hope you and all at the home are well," he wrote to Sadie. "I am quite well and having the best time of my life. Was reelected leading the ticket, and am one of the leaders now." Whether he meant being a leader of Republicans, Masons, Odd Fellows, or some other group he belonged to, I do not know.

"Hope you keep well. You must take some rest from that stove these hot days. Kindest regards to all who ask of me." He listed eight individuals, apparently names Sadie would recognize, who were "all in the surf today—you meet people from everywhere."

He signed off as "Dad." Then he added a postscript naming more people from South Carolina he had run into, and in his final line, he returned to practical matters: "I hope Corbin has finished my job." For Corbin's sake, whoever he was, I hope so, too.

Chapter Seven

THE NEXT FORDHAM GENERATION

In our house I found an old Orangeburg City Directory from Major Fordham's era that opens with a boosterish preface. It claims that the town, with seven thousand residents, was first in production of cotton in the state of South Carolina and second in the United States in the number of individual farms. "Orangeburg business men are alive, wide awake, active, energetic and progressive," the directory boasts, "and the Chamber of Commerce urges business enterprises and manufacturing interests to investigate our advantages when seeking locations."

The preface also informs the reader that an asterisk is used to designate the names of "colored persons." And there, on page 130, are the Fordhams, duly asterisked: John H., listed as an attorney (the only Black lawyer in town), his daughter Florella (the only Black nurse in town), son Marion (proprietor of one of two Black pharmacies in town), and Sadie (the only Black music teacher in town).

The Major's children were taking advantage of the opportunity their demanding father had created for them. I believe that if he had been asked to diagram his hopeful vision of African American progress, the

Major would have drawn a rising line without a wobble, a line unperturbed by the end of Reconstruction or the rise of Jim Crow or any other setback. He required that his children make something of themselves, so he sent them the short distance across the railroad tracks to be educated at Claflin College. He required that they comport themselves as ladies and gentlemen, that they be both respectful and respectable, and that they be churchgoing and reverent, so he took them down the street to Trinity Methodist Church every Sunday. The Major could be stern and uncompromising, especially with his boys. With the girls, though, he could also be indulgent.

THE MAJOR'S OLDEST DAUGHTER was a star. Her given name was Flora Ella, but everyone called her Florella, personally and professionally—except for her younger sister Sadie, my grandmother, who shortened it even further, to "Frella." The two of them lived with us when my sister, Ellen, and I were growing up. More accurately, because they had lived in the house since it was built in 1903, *we* lived with *them*—and we and our parents had a different name for Florella: Aunt Doc.

She was born in 1880. For an ambitious and career-minded young Black woman in those days, in both the North and the South, and for many decades thereafter, there were essentially two choices: You could be a schoolteacher or a nurse. Florella chose the latter.

She went to high school and college at Claflin. In the house, I found a crumbling photograph of her with her classmates, posed on the steps of one of the campus buildings. In Orangeburg, that was as far as she could go toward her goal; Claflin didn't have a nursing school. But another Black college did: Hampton Institute, founded in 1868 across the busy Hampton Roads Harbor from Norfolk, Virginia. So, Major Fordham sent his daughter there, hundreds of miles away, to complete her education. In 1903, Florella came home as the first formally trained and qualified nurse, of any race, in Orangeburg County.

Almost immediately she became a key figure in Orangeburg's rudimentary health care system. The city had a few doctors but no hospital, so she spent her days and many of her nights making house calls, taking along her leather bag full of medicines and instruments. When her expertise was needed, the color line was conveniently ignored; the white citizens of Orangeburg had no problem accepting care and following instructions from a short, stout, imperious Black woman who might salve their pain or save their lives. In the years before the city finally got its hospital, which happened in 1919, Aunt Doc delivered more than five hundred babies.

It turns out, evidently, that she also had one of her own. Aunt Doc never married, and by the time I was born, she was in her seventies, well beyond courting age. I grew up thinking she was childless. From all evidence, I appear to have been wrong.

In retrospect, this was something the adults in my family were careful never to talk about, at least not in front of the children. My mother was an only child, but she had a host of first cousins, sons and daughters of my grandmother Sadie's siblings. Most of these cousins had been born in Orangeburg or had at least spent considerable time there, and they often came to the family's homeplace to visit. To Ellen and me, they were "Aunt This" and "Uncle That." When any of them arrived, my mother and grandmother would patiently explain who was who. For example, there were Aunts Fannie and Flora, who lived in Upstate New York and who were our great-uncle George's daughters. There was Aunt Dorothy, who lived in Washington, D.C., and was one of Great-Uncle Marion's children. There were Aunts Tish and Grace, both from Cincinnati, who were Great-Aunt Grace's daughters.

But then there was the relative from New York City who came only occasionally, a woman my mother called Cousin Rosalee. Whenever I asked how she was family, I got a lot of hemming and hawing but never a straight answer. I distinctly remember one time, when I persisted with the question of how Cousin Rosalee was related, and my mother abruptly ended the conversation by saying, "We don't know." I was probably no older than seven or eight, but I knew that what my mother had said couldn't possibly be true; my family lived and breathed its history. She had to know; all the adults in the house had to know—but for some reason, they wouldn't tell me.

More than three decades passed before someone offered an answer. Aunt Grace, my mother's Cincinnati cousin who had become absorbed in our family's genealogy, sent to all Major Fordham's descendants a detailed family tree she had drawn from research and deduction. Next to Aunt Doc's name and dates—"Flora Ella Fordham (11/25/80—3/2/73)"—she had left blank the line for the name and dates of a husband. Below, though, she had listed a daughter, "Rosa Lee Green (1895–1987)." When Aunt Grace's research arrived at Boulevard and Oak, my mother was offended that Grace would have accused Aunt Doc, by then long deceased, of having had a child out of wedlock. But my mother never offered an alternative version of events.

The 1950 census lists the first name of the woman in question as "Rosalee" and her birth year as 1896. She is listed as then living on 146th Street in Harlem with her husband, John C. Chadwick, who was working as an elevator porter. At the time, apparently, the Chadwicks had taken in a lodger to help make ends meet. The only other record I managed to find shows that Rosalee is buried in a cemetery in suburban Westchester County.

For me, seeing that entry on Aunt Grace's tree was one of those forehead-smacking moments when you see something that should have been obvious all along. Cousin Rosalee was the spitting image of Aunt Doc—younger, of course, and a good deal taller, but with the same skin tone, the same round face, the same features, the same broad smile. And whenever Cousin Rosalee visited, she spent most of her time with Aunt Doc. They would laugh and talk for long hours in Aunt Doc's room or out on the front porch, just the two of them. During one visit late in Aunt Doc's long life, when she was suffering from dementia, I remember Cousin Rosalee mostly just sitting with her in silence.

Aunt Doc would have been sixteen when Rosalee was born—the same age her mother, Louisa, was when she married Major Fordham. I have searched in vain for documents that could tell me more; everyone with firsthand or even secondhand knowledge is gone now. I have no reason to believe Aunt Grace was wrong in her assertion; she may have been an amateur sleuth, and I've found that she missed a couple of dates on the family tree by a year or two, but she did a remarkably thorough job. All her other lines of descent check out. My assumption has to be that she was correct that Cousin Rosalee's father's name was Green, but I've been able to learn nothing else about him. I'm left to imagine a pretty young lass, a handsome young swain, and nature taking its course. At the same time, I am mindful of how vulnerable women of Aunt Doc's era were to sexual assault, including rape.

It is safe to say that Major Fordham, who believed so deeply in propriety and appearances, would not have been pleased at the news of his daughter's condition. Yet there was no shotgun wedding. And there was no rupture with Florella, whose judgment he trusted enough to give her the principal role in settling his estate. Ellen and I agree that the Major and Louisa likely would have sent Florella away for the child's birth, perhaps to the relative anonymity of Charleston or Columbia, perhaps even farther, to someplace where the name Fordham rang no bells. In any event, because Rosalee was an acknowledged and cherished member of the family all her life, as an infant she must have been welcomed into the household. Marion, the youngest of the Fordham brood, was just five when she was born; to him, Rosalee would have been more like a baby sister than a niece.

All this makes me even more in awe of Aunt Doc; what a remarkable woman she was. She refused to be detoured or even slowed down, finishing at Claflin and then going away to far-off Hampton for her nursing degree. Back in Orangeburg, with its dearth of health care, she was less a nurse than a de facto country doctor, performing a physician's duties. Like her father, she devoted time and energy to working for the betterment of the race. Papers I found at the house show that she was active in the National Association of Colored Graduate Nurses, a Black nurses' organization headquartered in New York, and served as secretary of the group, attending the association's national convention in Richmond in 1912. She and the organization worked to obtain pensions and establish retirement homes for Black nurses at the end of their careers. And she would have done all this as a single parent—doubtless with the help of other adults in the Fordham household, including her mother, who must have been taking care of little Rosalee when Aunt Doc was away.

In 1932, Aunt Doc agreed to become the head nurse, the chief medical officer, at South Carolina State. She held that job until retiring in 1952, at age seventy-two. Indolence did not suit her, however, and just a few months later, she was persuaded to step into the head nurse role at Claflin. That's how I remember her when I was little, presiding over the Claflin infirmary, a small freestanding building in the middle of the campus with a mulberry tree in front. She always wore her crisp, white nurse's uniform and cap when she was working. Whenever I was there, she would let me play with her stethoscope but would warn me to leave the other instruments alone. I remember painfully clamping my finger in a pair of her forceps. She would have been nearly eighty when she finally retired for good.

Whenever I got a bad cold or the flu, the first responder was Aunt Doc, who would take my temperature, ask about my symptoms, and rummage in her bag of potions. I remember that she would say to my mother, "Here, Louisa, let me give him a little paregoric," and then have me slurp a small dose of clear liquid from a spoon. It wasn't until a few years ago that I looked it up and learned that paregoric is "a camphorated tincture of opium"—liquid smack, essentially, at the time widely used to treat diarrhea. No wonder it always made me feel so very much better.

MAJOR FORDHAM COULD BE patient with Florella, Grace, and Sadie, but he was less tolerant with his sons, George, Harry, and Marion. There was hell to pay when the boys failed to live up to his expectations. Among the Major's papers, I found a scathing letter he wrote to one of them, who had committed the mortal sin of bouncing a check. The

Major wrote that he had been contacted by the victim, a local businessman, and had covered the check and offered his and the son's deepest apologies—all of which was embarrassing and none of which should have been necessary. He recounted the young man's past sins in detail, expressed his utter exasperation, and ended by all but calling his son an incorrigible wastrel. It is not clear which young man he was addressing; the miscreant is referred to only as "my son."

It is also unclear why that letter was there for me to find in the Major's safe. Perhaps he realized he was being overly harsh and had thought better of sending it. If he was a tough-love parent, it worked: His sons grew into successful, responsible adults who were respected in their communities. And the youngest—on whom the Major was often toughest—was a war hero.

The headstone on Marion Fordham's grave in Orangeburg Cemetery bears his name, his dates, and the inscription "World War I." I always knew that my great-uncle, who died before I was born, had been one of the hundreds of thousands of Black patriots who fought for their country in the Great War. What I did not know, until I began researching his wartime service, was what he and his fellow Black soldiers had experienced and endured.

At the age of twenty-seven, more fit for duty than his older brothers, Marion was drafted on February 17, 1918, and sent halfway across the country for basic training. He had responsibilities he was forced to leave behind. He had already completed his education as a pharmacist and opened a druggist's shop, which family members would have to manage in his absence. More important, and painful, was the fact that his mother was unwell. Two months later, when Louisa Fordham passed away, the baby of her family would be far from home.

According to U.S. Army records, Marion trained at Camp Funston, part of the sprawling Fort Riley military complex near Manhattan, Kansas. He was joining the racially segregated army's Ninety-Second Infantry Division—one of two Black units, along with the Tenth Cavalry, that had collectively inherited the nickname Buffalo Soldiers. Quarters and facilities for Black inductees were in a separate "Negro zone" at the camp, which spared white trainees the indignity of doing their calisthenics, taking their meals, or laying their heads down alongside African Americans. By day, the new soldiers drilled, hiked, practiced with weapons, and learned to follow orders. In the evenings, they could socialize at the "Colored" recreation hall, an amenity that had been erected by Black draftees. And if they earned the privilege, they might be allowed to leave the confines of the post and enjoy what nightlife there was for young Black men in the towns of Manhattan and Junction City.

On June 19, 1918, Marion embarked from Hoboken, New Jersey, for the Atlantic crossing to France on the SS *Great Northern*. The passage took seven days. He and his unit landed in the French port city of Brest and were sent to a U.S. camp in Tours. After a few days' orientation, they were ordered forward to the trenches of the Western Front.

Given his training as a pharmacist, Marion had been assigned to a medical unit, Field Hospital 367 of the 317th Sanitary Train, one of the ambulance companies whose duty was tending to the Ninety-Second Infantry's wounded. Some of the ambulances were motorized, but Marion's was mule-drawn, which made his job one of the most dangerous that medics in the Great War faced: While the trucks were confined to passable roads, mules could pull wagons across muddy fields and get right up to the actual front, where injured soldiers were triaged and given first aid. The mule-drawn ambulances then took the casualties to motorized vehicles for transport to field hospitals. Marion and his unit spent a week with the French medical corps they were relieving, learning their way around the sector. Other than that, they had no real training for operating—and somehow surviving—amid the dreadful, chaotic, horrifying, agonizing birth of modern industrialized total warfare. When the French medics departed, Marion and his cohort of Black healers were left on their own for the duration.

The Ninety-Second Infantry fought alongside the French in the Meuse-Argonne campaign from September 1918 until Armistice Day. That thrust was part of the mammoth Allied offensive that finally ended the war, and it was by far the biggest and bloodiest battle for the American Expeditionary Forces. More than a million U.S. troops were involved in the forty-seven-day battle, and more than twenty-six thousand of them were killed. The Ninety-Second was one of the American units that fought under French, not American, command.

The Buffalo Soldiers had to quickly become inured to the constant threat from enemy shells and mustard gas. Military aviation—the terrifying new reality of death raining down from the sky—was in its infancy, but soon Marion and his unit rarely even bothered to look up when they heard the drone of aircraft overhead. The most unceasing torment came from "cooties," which is what soldiers called the body lice that plagued victims night and day with itching. The cooties were ubiquitous in the trenches, compounding every soldier's misery, and they found their way into the Ninety-Second Infantry's ambulances on the clothing of the wounded. Each night before bedding down, Marion would have to carefully "read his shirt"—inspect the garment inch by inch to pick off every single louse, one by one.

Unseen and unheard was the deadliest threat of all: the devastating second wave of the worst influenza epidemic in recorded history, the so-called Spanish flu, which killed an estimated fifty million people worldwide and ravaged the Allied and German lines. The United States, like the other combatant nations, lost more soldiers to the flu than to enemy fire. Marion somehow dodged that microbial bullet, just as he dodged the many other bullets fired in his direction.

The base hospital for Marion's unit was near a small town called Toul, not far from Nancy, where there was a large Allied airfield. One salient circumstance, from the point of view of Marion's crew, was that the compound also housed a large ammunition depot. The Germans knew about the arsenal, which meant there was a constant threat that they would try to bomb it, potentially blowing the munitions—and my great-uncle—to smithereens. The medics had to work as if this danger did not exist. Soldiers with minor injuries were patched up and quickly sent back to the front. Those with more serious wounds remained at the hospital for treatment until they were well enough to return to the trenches. For any soldier who had lost an arm or a leg, the war was over. Amputees were transported to Brest to be shipped home.

Forty-five soldiers from the Ninety-Second Infantry were killed in the Meuse-Argonne campaign, and 259 were wounded. Another 51 were killed and nearly 700 wounded in other battles.

The soldiers of the Ninety-Second had a novel experience when they encountered the French people: They were treated not as Black men but simply as men. Not for the last time, the French welcomed Americans as liberators, irrespective of their race. Marion's ambulance unit regularly ministered to French soldiers on the battlefield; they and their officers, too, seemed ignorant of the color line that had defined the Black medics' lives at home.

White American soldiers, however, behaved according to the familiar American script. Even in the middle of an apocalyptic war, even with a common enemy and a shared mission, even in countries where they were foreigners and compatriots, they still insisted on treating African Americans as despised members of a lower caste. At U.S. installations, just as back home in the South, there were separate sleeping quarters, separate drinking fountains, and even separate latrines. The Ninety-Second's interactions with white units were brief, but they left an impression.

William Knox, a Black veteran who drove one of the motorized ambulances in Marion's unit, gave an interview in 1980—archived by the National WWI Museum and Memorial collections database—in which he recounted an incident that did not end quite the way the army might have intended:

> A colored soldier . . . came up to the watering trough with these four horses to get watered. A white soldier out of the Rainbow Division came up with four horses to drink. He said, "Pull over there, nigger, and let my horses drink." [The Black soldier] said, "I was here first," and this white soldier upped with his gun like that, and this colored

fellow shot his eye out. He was just quicker. When you do something over there, they send you to the front. The officer in charge will send you over the top that night—if you get back, you were justified. If you don't get back, you were convicted. They sent this colored soldier to the front, the officer in charge sent him over. Next morning, he came back with forty-one Germans marching in front of him, hollering "Kamerad!" You see, that was because they were hungry. [The French] took him to Paris and banqueted him, give him the Croix de Guerre and everything.

Marion was in France for Armistice Day, November 11, 1918, and the glorious celebration of the end of the "war to end all wars." Every soldier's first thought, of course, was of going home. But it took months for Marion's unit to find a place on a transport, which meant he spent Christmas and New Year's Eve in Europe. Finally, on February 17, he was given a berth on the ship *Olympic*, out of Brest, and on February 24, he landed in New York.

A long, happy train ride brought him home to his family and business in Orangeburg, with many stories to tell.

SADIE, THE YOUNGEST OF the Major's daughters, was so full of life and elegance that I wonder if she ever had a bad day.

My grandmother was tall and dark, with her father's cocoa-brown skin and high cheekbones, and she carried herself with the Major's regal bearing. There was nothing unapproachable about her, though. She loved people, and she had a magnetism that made people love her. Her sparkling wit could be sharp but was not mean-spirited, and she saw the humor in every situation. "Just as well to laugh as to cry," she used to say after some mishap, disappointment, or minor disaster. "Laugh, and the world laughs with you. Cry, and the world laughs *at* you."

When Ellen and I were growing up, there were three divas in the house. Our mother and Aunt Doc were powerful and opinionated women, but Miss Sadie—which was what the outside world called her—was the prima donna. Her rule in the kitchen was so absolute, and her food was so good, that my mother never really bothered to master her recipes and techniques; my father was the one who assumed many of the cooking duties as Sadie grew old. Whenever the doorbell rang, which was quite often, Sadie would make a great show of complaining: "People! Shoot. I get so tired of people, I don't know what to do. And you know if they sit down, they'll *never* leave." But then she would unfailingly greet those uninvited guests warmly and insist they have a seat. The truth was that she *needed* people and couldn't have gone more than a day or two without visitors if she'd tried. She always had something to serve them—a slice of her perfect pound cake, a piece of her addictive gingerbread, a few sugared pecans from the trees in the backyard, a full meal if they admitted to being hungry. And she could talk and laugh, thoroughly enjoying the conversation, for as long as the least considerate guests cared to stay.

My parents rarely drank alcohol, except a glass of spiked eggnog on Christmas Eve, and neither did Aunt Doc, as far as I can recall. But sometime in the middle of every day, usually early in the afternoon, Sadie would have a single can of beer—always Schlitz, her favorite brand. And at night, as she went to bed in the big first-floor room that had once belonged to her parents, she'd call Ellen or me and say, "Go to my wardrobe and bring me my medicine." We'd scurry to do as she asked. It took me years to realize that what we believed to be some urgently needed medicinal elixir was actually a bottle of bourbon, from which she religiously took a bedtime swig. Sadie ate whatever she wanted, and she cooked the old-fashioned way, with real butter and cream. We were never without a big can of Crisco, which she used liberally. Next to the stove was a canister where she collected bacon grease, which she used for frying. If anyone had ever suggested that she exercise—physical exertion for the sake of physical exertion—she would have laughed for days. Sadie lived to be ninety-eight.

She was the musical one of Major Fordham's daughters, having learned her scales and chords on the big black piano in the sitting room. Like her brothers and sisters, she was educated at Claflin. By 1913, she was teaching first grade at Claflin's grammar school and giving music lessons.

Unlike her mother, who had married as a teen, Sadie was in no hurry to settle down. She was twenty-nine when she wed a handsome brick-mason named Eugene James Smith on April 15, 1916. The family Bible does not record where the ceremony took place, but it must have been either at the Fordham house or at Trinity Methodist Church, down the street. The Bible does note that the wedding was performed by "several ministers," which does not surprise me. Sadie's wedding would have had to be an elaborate production.

The bridegroom—for whom I am named—was the grandson of Francis A. Smith, the antebellum free person of color in Charleston who voted to end color prejudice at his "Brown" social club. Eugene Smith's father, Francis D. Smith, had moved his family to Orangeburg, just as Sadie's father had done. Eugene studied at Claflin, too, in the college department that taught the practical trades. He and his brother Alonzo both learned bricklaying, and Alonzo went on to become an instructor in the program.

Claflin is affiliated with the Methodist Church, which was an important institution in the Fordham family's life. They were in the pews at Trinity every week—except Sadie, who was behind the preacher with the choir, playing the piano. By the time I was old enough to remember, arthritis and age had forced her to give up that role. She seldom played the big black piano at home anymore.

Sadie was famed far and wide for her cooking, and fiercely proud of that reputation. One of the old photographs my mother kept shows a long line of people at our front door, queued as if for a soup kitchen. I wondered if the shot had been taken during the Depression. My mother didn't know the date of the image, but she knew that the backstory had nothing to do with the state of the economy. The pastor at Trinity was hosting some big church event, and attendees would be coming from across the state. Rather than ask Sadie to organize and prepare food for these visitors, as Trinity pastors always did, this reverend had the nerve to get someone else to do it. Sadie was so offended that she prepared a rival spread, inviting the visiting church people to walk the few blocks to our house and dine with her instead. My guess is that at least some of them ate dinner twice that day and that Sadie's meal was superior to the other.

She made grits every morning for breakfast—I am the only person in my family, and apparently the only person from the South, who does not like grits—and rice every day with dinner. She cooked vegetables slowly until they melted in your mouth—string beans or butter beans or black-eyed peas, with cured meat like country ham as seasoning. She also made what I would have said were Great Northern beans, but she called them "Fordham beans," either because they were somehow different or because of her preparation. Sadie's fried chicken was to die for. She liked her meat well done and tender, her pork chops and beef roasts almost as if they had been braised. When it was in season, she would make fried corn, which involved cutting the sweet kernels off the cob and sautéing them in some of that bacon grease she had saved up. I would eat as much of that dish as she cared to prepare, especially if she served it on days when she also made fried fish, my favorite. Our next-door neighbor George Green—whose house was on land that had once belonged to the Fordhams—loved to go fishing on nearby Lake Marion. When he came back in the afternoon, he would stop by with a share of his catch for Miss Sadie. My father didn't particularly like fish, for some reason, which meant a double portion for me.

And then there was Sadie's baking. She always made something to go with dinner—corn bread, biscuits, a loaf of homemade bread, hot rolls. There would be gingerbread or pound cake in the pantry for all-day consumption. For dessert, sometimes we would have ambrosia, a southern dish that involved orange sections and shredded coconut. Ellen has, and still uses, many of Sadie's old pots and pans, some of which we believe were passed down to her by Louisa Fordham. In one of my kitchen cabinets, I have the big beige ceramic bowl in which Sadie mixed her gingerbread batter. She would let me lick that bowl clean if I promised to behave.

Sadie's domain, the kitchen, is a large room in the southwest corner of the house, with windows overlooking Oak Street and the backyard. By the time Ellen and I came along, Sadie had effectively been the mistress of the house her father built for decades—ever since Louisa Fordham's death in 1918. Even before that, she had established herself as one of the leading ladies of Orangeburg's Black community.

In 1910, along with Florella and twenty-eight of their friends, Sadie was one of the founding members of the Sunlight Club, an organization that continues today. It was affiliated with the National Association of Colored Women's Clubs, a broad movement by African American women across the country who wanted to play a constructive role in the betterment of their communities. Over the years, the Sunlight Club has provided food and clothing to the needy, given Christmas gifts to children whose parents were poor, run a nursery school, supported a camp for tuberculosis patients and an orphanage, established a school for adults during the Depression, and organized Orangeburg's first Girl Scout troop for African Americans—more than a century's worth of good works over four generations.

I remember Sadie attending monthly meetings at the Sunlight Club's headquarters, a house on Treadwell Street that the organization acquired in the 1930s and still uses. My father or mother would drop her off and pick her up; the club was only a couple of blocks away, near where some of Eugene Smith's relatives lived, but it was too far to walk at her age. I was her chauffeur a few times after I got my driver's license. When she came home from a meeting, she would report to my mother and Aunt Doc about who had been there, who had not, what had been talked about, and which absent member's ears should have been burning.

One of the other Sunlight Club founders was Sadie's dearest friend, Bessie Sulton. Hardly a week went by without "Aunt" Bessie coming to our house for a visit or our family going over to the Sultons' house on Russell Street so that Sadie could sit with Bessie. Aunt Bessie's husband, McDuffie Sulton—Uncle Mac, as we knew him—descended from a long-established Orangeburg Black family, one that had been every bit as prominent as the Fordhams. I was offered a clue to the Sultons' history and heritage whenever I shook Uncle Mac's hand: He was missing a thumb.

An ancestor of his named John Sulton, the son of a Turkish immigrant, married a free Black woman and, in 1825, founded a sawmill near Columbia. At his death, the business passed down to his son Dennis, who was classified as "Colored," which placed the family definitively on the Black side of the wall that divided American society by color. In 1903, Dennis's son, J.J. Sulton, moved the sawmill to Orangeburg, where it became such a thriving enterprise that the mill had its own private railroad siding for bringing in logs and taking away finished boards and timbers. By then J.J.'s two sons, McDuffie and J.J. Jr., were involved in running the business, having both been educated at Claflin. The J.J. Sulton and Sons lumberyard sprawled across ten acres on the south side of Orangeburg, included drying kilns and a planing mill, and produced up to seven million feet of finished lumber annually. The Sulton sawmill survived for more than half a century. In 1931, a trade magazine, *Southern Lumberman*, described the business—wholly owned and operated by African Americans—as "the oldest continuous lumber manufacturing operation under one name in the South."

Like the Fordham family, with their contiguous properties, the Sultons lived in what could be thought of as a compound. The old man, J.J. Sulton, built a house for himself and his family on Russell Street and, using a different design, twin houses for his sons, McDuffie and J.J. Jr., on the next two lots. One of McDuffie's daughters, Maxine, lived in a house around the corner (and was the principal of my elementary school). A Sunday-afternoon visit to see Aunt Bessie and Uncle Mac meant at least brief stops at three or four different houses. Ellen and

I would join the Sulton cousins of our generation in games of tag that ranged across all the adjacent Sulton backyards.

At Trinity Methodist Church on Sundays, in the years after Sadie stopped playing the piano for the choir, Sadie and Florella sat together along the right side of the nave, near the front, where their family had always sat. Aunt Bessie and some of the Sultons sat in that same area. There were no officially assigned pews, but everybody knew which seats were reserved for whom. Our parents always sat some distance away from Sadie and Florella, in the right wing of the transept; Ellen and I sat with them unless we had duties that required we sit elsewhere, such as singing in the youth choir. For a while when I was ten or so, I sat away from the family, in the opposite wing of the transept, with friends who were my age. We were in my grandmother's line of sight, and I could feel her glare when we misbehaved. After the service, it felt as if it took an eternity to leave the sanctuary—so many of our family's friends had to be spoken to and visited with. Later, at home, Sadie would give her review of the pastor's sermon—had he gone on too long, had he been too fiery or too bland—and critique the hymn selection and the choir's performance. Then we would sit down to the sumptuous meal she had prepared, eating together at the dining room table, not the smaller kitchen table where we had breakfasts and suppers.

The point of all this is that my sister, Ellen, and I grew up in Sadie's world, which was a world of history—her own history, her family's history, her friends' history, her city's history. More than any of her siblings, more even than her older sister Florella, Sadie was the center of the Fordham universe, the hub around which everyone and everything else revolved. After her mother's death, the house Major Fordham had built became the house where Miss Sadie lived. She was the hostess, the griot, the custodian and curator of the Fordham legacy. She was the Major's natural heir, sharing her father's self-confidence and pride. She strutted when she walked, and she held her head high.

WHEN HIS YOUNGEST SON, Marion, came home from the Great War, Major Fordham was still occupied with the practical implications of Louisa's death. The Fordhams' real estate holdings traced a familiar arc. When opportunity allowed African Americans to rise, their portfolio of land grew. But as Jim Crow reapplied the white knee to the Black neck, growth petered out into stasis, then gradually slid into decline. Our family was fortunate in having acquired enough land in the good years to be able to weather the bad by selling it off, little by little. In 1920, the Major conducted a flurry of property sales that he kept track of in a tiny notebook. The lots he owned down Oak Street went one by one, as did the lots he owned a quarter mile away, off Goff Avenue. The Fordham lots stretching north on Boulevard had by then been parceled out to the Fordham sons as they reached maturity; the house where Marion lived, now in others' hands, is still standing. The Major made only one substantial purchase during this period that I can find: In early 1921, he bought fourteen lots, out on the edge of town, for $2,500—a nest egg in property that would keep the family afloat during lean years.

Also, in February 1921, the Major made a minor purchase that means a lot to me: He bought two of the six pecan trees that still stand today on our property. One of the autumn chores Ellen and I performed when we were little was to go out back with a bucket and collect the ripe nuts that had fallen overnight. Some of the trees produced the paper shell variety, which was my favorite—the nuts were big and easy to crack. A couple of our trees produced a smaller nut with a thicker shell, and my mother thought those had more flavor.

The exercise of settling Louisa's estate must have made the Major acutely aware of his own mortality, because in September 1922, he sat down and wrote a will. The will directed that all outstanding debts be paid first. Then, from the death benefit of a Metropolitan Insurance Company life policy and any remaining cash in his bank accounts, he left one thousand dollars each to his sons, George, Harry, and Marion. He made his daughters, Florella, Grace, and Sadie, the co-executors of his estate and left the family home, and all other property not specifically assigned, to them. As they sold parcels of real estate, one-tenth of the proceeds were to be deposited in the Farmers and Merchants Bank "for use in helping to care for the poor and needy and to help spread the Gospel."

He appointed Sadie to take his place as business partner with a man named Lyons in a separate real estate venture, with the understanding that if the partnership were dissolved and the assets sold, the proceeds would be divided equally among his six children—with one-tenth going to helping the poor.

Two months after finishing the will, he fell ill with bronchitis and pneumonia. On December 4, 1922, surrounded by family at the home he was so proud of, Major John Hammond Fordham died.

He had been born five years before the beginning of the Civil War. When he died, the Roaring Twenties were in full swing. Warren G. Harding had recently become the first president to install a radio in the White House. Benito Mussolini was the new prime minister of Italy. British archaeologist Howard Carter had just discovered the treasure-filled tomb of the Egyptian pharaoh whose name headline writers shortened to King Tut.

African Americans' lives were constrained by racism in the North and suffocated by Jim Crow in the South. Still, somehow, they were managing to generate a great cultural flowering. The Harlem Renaissance, which would go on to produce some of the greatest art and literature of the century, was getting started. And Black musicians in New Orleans, such as Jelly Roll Morton and Louis Armstrong, were mixing African and European traditions into the greatest and most original American contribution to world music: jazz.

The more time I have spent immersed in the Major's life, the prouder I am of the man and the life he lived. All of us who are his progeny stand on his broad shoulders. I include Ellen and myself, of course, but also our mother, with her two master's degrees; our Aunt Dorothy, Marion Fordham's daughter, who had a brilliant career in the U.S.

military; Kara Walker, one of Grace Fordham's great-granddaughters, who is acclaimed as one of the most important artists of our time; and scores of other cousins once or twice removed who have succeeded in academia or business or the professions. Major Fordham set an uncompromising standard that we all feel obliged to meet. He saw opportunity at twelve years old, walking up the steps of the Avery Institute for the first time, and he never looked backward, always forward. His mission in life was not just to rise but to see African Americans rise with him, as a race and as a people for whom nothing was impossible, a people who needed only to be given the chance to climb and build and soar.

His was truly a great life. But I can't help asking myself: What if?

What if Reconstruction had not been cut short by the Hayes-Tilden Compromise of 1877? Would the Republican Party have maintained its brief dominance across the South? Would the Major have been able to use his position as coroner of Orangeburg County as a springboard to higher elective office? Would his political skills have taken him to the state legislature? To the governor's mansion? All the way to Washington? How far could he have risen?

What if that Confederate monument in the middle of town had never been built? What if the Lost Cause myth had righteously been snuffed out as treason, which is clearly what it was? Whose statue would have gone up instead? What story would it tell, and what values would it celebrate?

What if the Jim Crow regime had never been imposed by legislation and enforced through terror? How extensive might the Major's real estate holdings have become? How much more land would he have owned to pass on to his children? What other worlds could he have conquered? At a time when the national economy was growing by leaps and bounds, and Gilded Age barons were amassing vast generational wealth, why wasn't Major Fordham—their equal in brains and ambition—among their ranks?

The Major never would have thought of himself as a victim, but that is what he was. He created opportunity for himself, his family, and his descendants. He never complained. But he could have done more, could have been more, if America had simply let him. And in keeping Major Fordham down, America limited its own potential. America made itself a lesser nation.

Chapter Eight

THE ROBINSONS MAKE THE GREAT MIGRATION

Growing up in the house my great-grandfather built, I knew that Major Fordham's saga was uncommon: a Black man in the South, born free before the Civil War, who had slipped through a crack that was briefly opened by Reconstruction and who managed to build a comfortable life for himself and his family. And I knew that the ancestors of my father, Harold Irwin Robinson, had a story more typical of the African American experience.

Beyond the sketchiest outlines, though, I knew very little in detail about my Robinson forebears. It was like squeezing blood from a rock to get my father to open up about his family history. He was not a taciturn man; Ellen and I could talk to him about any other subject, and he'd instantly pull up facts and figures from what seemed like an inexhaustible well. He would talk about his mother, his brothers, and his sister, and occasionally he would mention some cousin or another, but that was about it. From what our mother told us, it seemed clear that he had unresolved issues with his own father, who was divorced from my Grandma Robinson when my dad was a young boy. My father wouldn't be drawn out on the subject; he was of a generation to whom the concept of sharing innermost feelings was alien.

I know now that my father's American history began in the states along the Gulf Coast where industrial-scale slavery, in the service of King Cotton, reached its brutal apotheosis. From there the story progressed along the path of the exodus of African Americans seeking freedom and opportunity in the North. Then my father's story diverged from the expected, when he chose to move back to the South and the struggle.

Just to be able to write that brief summary paragraph with authority required a stroke of fortune. In August 2022, my wife, Avis, had a show of her paintings and quilted fabric artworks at the Columbus (Ohio) Museum of Art. I told her I was excited about going to the opening, because I knew that my father's father, K.W. Robinson, had lived in Columbus at some point after leaving the family, had preached at a church there, and was buried at Green Lawn Cemetery; I hoped I might use the trip to Columbus to find out more about him. Avis mentioned this connection to the curator of her museum show, who offered to put me in touch with researchers at the Columbus Metropolitan Library. I called the library, laid out what little I knew about my Grandfather Robinson—who died before I was born—and made an appointment to drop by when I was in town.

Never underestimate librarians. Standing proudly a few blocks east of the Ohio Statehouse, the Main Library building has an imposing neoclassical facade that belies an open, airy, light-filled interior. My hosts led me upstairs and showed me to a long table on which sat a neat stack of papers. I had arrived hoping for a few new facts about my grandfather's time in Columbus—places he might have lived, jobs he might have held. I got much, much more: A staff genealogist had researched the origins of both of my Robinson grandparents, and she spent the next hour walking me through her findings.

My paternal grandfather, K.W. Robinson, was born on May 10, 1881, in Franklin County, Georgia. His birthplace is in the northeastern corner of the state, between Atlanta and the Savannah River, and, like Orangeburg, is also in the Cotton Belt, a thousand-mile Nike swoosh of land across the South with soil that is ideal for growing cotton. The lucrative crop that once ruled as King Cotton and the brutal, industrial-scale slavery required to produce it were the forces that shaped my father's family tree, much as Charleston's differentiated economy and racial caste system shaped my mother's.

The story of my Robinson lineage hews more closely to the way the Black American experience is usually rendered. In a sense, it begins a hundred million years ago: During the Cretaceous period, the time of the dinosaurs, much of the southeastern United States lay submerged beneath a shallow sea. All of Florida, even the Panhandle, was underwater; the Atlantic coastline traced an arc through what is now North Carolina, South Carolina, and Georgia, roughly a hundred miles inland from today's beaches. In what is now Alabama, the coastline curved sharply northwest, then plunged southward again through what we know as the Mississippi Delta. The warm waters off that ancient shore were an ideal habitat for tiny marine plankton, which left behind their carbonate shells over millions of years, creating a deposit of organic material that amounted to a thick bed of fertilizer. When the seas receded, that ancient, now-invisible coastline became the northern limit of a wide, curving band of rich soil that turned out to be perfect for growing cotton—much better than the hilly land to the north or the present-day littoral to the east and south.

Eli Whitney's cotton gin, patented in 1794, automated the laborious task of separating cotton's fibers from its seeds. That made the crop vastly more profitable. Demand from the newly mechanized textile mills of Europe, and soon of New England, was essentially unlimited, so supply rose to meet it. More and more land was planted in cotton—which, in turn, meant the need for more slave labor to plant, tend, pick, and process the crop. That is how K.W. Robinson's parents, Bill and Sally, came to live in Franklin County.

I have found no record of William Robinson or Sarah (Sally) Kees until after the Civil War. They first show up on July 26, 1873, when they were granted a marriage license by a Franklin County official named S. J. Harris. The following day, they were married by a man named William Owen, whose authority to perform the ceremony appears to have been civil, not religious. Sarah was twenty-one; Bill's age is not given, but I believe he was a few years older.

By the time they formalized their union, the couple already had a young son—Thomas Prather Robinson, born in 1872. They went on to have five more boys: Claud, who eventually became a prominent minister in Atlanta; Tugalo, who moved to Chattanooga, Tennessee, and worked as a laborer; Jesse, who ended up in Columbus, Ohio, and was music director at the church he attended; William, whom I know little about; and K.W., my grandfather, who died before my sister and I had the chance to meet him—and whom my father and his siblings stubbornly refused to talk much about.

K.W.'s first name was Kadozier. I have no idea why the Robinsons gave three of their boys pure-vanilla Anglo names and saddled the other two with exotica. Tugalo was likely named after Tougaloo College, a historically Black school founded in 1869 in Jackson, Mississippi; the name comes from a Choctaw word meaning "the place where two streams cross." As for Kadozier, the Robinsons either invented a name or chose one whose derivation is long lost. As an adult, my grandfather rarely used his given name. One of the few things all sources agree on is that everyone called him K.W.

I don't know anything specific about Kadozier Walker Robinson's early years in Franklin County. I do know that while he was coming of age, the iron fist of Jim Crow was coming down. Perhaps because opportunity was scarce at home, or perhaps because of the peripatetic nature that became evident later in his life, he had already left home by the time he was twenty-five. On May 19, 1906, he was two states away, in Aberdeen, Mississippi, where he married Hattie Myrtle Vails, our Grandma Robinson.

Hattie was born in 1886 in Vernon, Alabama, and grew up a few miles away, across the Mississippi state line, in Aberdeen. Her parents, Sam and Martha Vails, had moved there to find work. Like Franklin County, Georgia, the counties in Alabama and Mississippi flanking the border and the Tombigbee River are blessed, or cursed, with that rich, black Cotton Belt soil. Like Bill and Sally Robinson, Hattie Vails's parents were born before the Civil War. They would have been children when the fighting began and enslaved until it ended.

Black victims of slavery lived in well-justified dread of being "sold down the river" to the Gulf Coast states. To the extent that there may have been any latitude in a crowded and complicated urban space like Charleston, any room for life beyond ceaseless, soul-crushing labor, there was none of that in the parts of Mississippi and Georgia where the Vails and Robinson families lived. They and their kin would have been treated as creatures who existed only to work as commanded by their white captors, to pick a bale of cotton and then another bale and then another, to cook and sweep and clean, to be raped at white men's pleasure. The enslaved were housed in teeming shacks and allotted enough food to have the strength and energy to continue working. They were whipped for insubordination, punished for failing to work hard enough, maimed for trying to escape. On Sundays, unless they had displeased those who imprisoned and tortured them, perhaps they were allowed to sing and pray.

In 1864—after Emancipation but before freedom—the Battle of Okolona was fought near where the Vails family lived following the war. The clash ended in a minor but bloody victory for Confederate forces under General Nathan Bedford Forrest, one of the most heinous war criminals in U.S. history.

Forrest took pleasure in massacring Union troops, especially Black soldiers, who were trying to surrender, most famously at the Battle of Fort Pillow, in Tennessee, where hundreds were killed in cold blood.

That atrocity was condemned in the North as a war crime, but Forrest was staunchly defended and even lionized in the South. Not surprisingly, he was never punished after the war; quite the contrary, he was made into a folk hero by white revanchists during their successful crusade to bring Reconstruction to an end and take back the freedom it had allowed African Americans to seize. After the war, Forrest went on to serve as the first grand wizard of the Ku Klux Klan. An equestrian statue honoring him stood, in pride rather than shame, at Forrest Park in Memphis for more than a century, from 1905 to 2017, before finally being taken down. His name has since been stripped from the park.

In Aberdeen itself, there was a minor battle between Union and Confederate troops during the Civil War. At the time, Aberdeen was the second-largest city in Mississippi and served as a major cotton port—the precious cargo was shipped down the Tombigbee, which flows south into the Alabama River and Mobile Bay. On February 18, 1864, Union forces from the Ninth Illinois Cavalry clashed with rebel militias and seized control of the town, destroying Confederate supplies and war matériel and taking eighteen prisoners of war.

To the extent that either the Robinson or Vails family obtained any measure of liberty before Appomattox, they had to seize it for themselves in the chaos of the war. Some enslaved workers fled the plantations where they had been jailed and found their way to refuge in the Union lines. When a military clash seemed likely nearby, plantation owners sometimes moved their enslaved workers away, to keep them from being freed by Yankee invaders. Some enslaved Black men and women refused to work; some negotiated new terms and conditions. Many, however, were even more cruelly oppressed than before because of fears that the chaos of war could spark a blood-soaked general uprising. Many of the enslaved were locked down ever more tightly, their movements severely restricted and their every word or gesture measured for any hint of sedition, for as long as the soon-to-be-former "masters" could keep the system from buckling under Union pressure.

Eventually—for Bill and Sally, in Georgia, as Sherman's army plowed through on its scorched-earth march; for Sam and Martha, in Mississippi, as Union columns squeezed supply lines—things fell apart, first on a few plantations here and there and then more widely across the Deep South. Emancipation finally came, and my father's grandparents were enslaved no more.

THROUGH COMPREHENSIVE DESIGN AND relentless application, the regime of racial stratification in the South was hardened into a system that is encapsulated by a foreign-language word from half a world away: *apartheid*.

There was total white control of political and police power. There were laws that mandated segregation in schools and other public spaces; when I was growing up in Orangeburg, for example, every year we had two county fairs on two separate fairgrounds, one designated "White" and the other "Colored." There was the assumption in the workplace, as if it were God's plan, that whiteness equaled "professional" and Blackness equaled "menial," though this was subverted in Orangeburg by the two colleges and the fact that the lion's share of PhDs in town were held by African Americans. There were white neighborhoods and Black neighborhoods, of course, with vast disparities in municipal services and amenities. We would drive through the prettiest white neighborhood sometimes, but never think of stopping our car there, much less getting out and taking a walk. Black people had no business in white neighborhoods except as servants or tradesmen.

I was born into this reality in the 1950s, at a time when things were beginning to change, when the jaws of the Jim Crow vise were being forced open. But in the early years of the century, the vise was still being tightened. African Americans in the former Confederacy faced a choice that would shape the rest of their lives: Should they stay and make the best of it? Or should they leave their homes and set out for distant, cold, unfamiliar places to try to make a better life? In wave after wave, millions packed their bags and headed north in the exodus we now know as the Great Migration. Kadozier and Hattie Robinson, my father's parents, were among them.

Their marriage license gives my grandfather's occupation as "farmer." In Mississippi in 1906, that almost surely meant he was working the fertile and productive Cotton Belt fields as a sharecropper. By definition, then, he would have had more of a subsistence than a life.

For African Americans, sharecropping was one modality of the massive theft of Black labor that the author Douglas A. Blackmon documents in his Pulitzer Prize–winning opus, *Slavery by Another Name.* Farmers leased acreage from white landowners, paying the rent with a portion of the crops they grew. By the time they had also paid the landlord for seed and fertilizer, and covered other added costs, they were left with barely enough to keep their families fed and clothed—but not enough to put aside savings, purchase their own land, and break the cycle. And as we saw with the Elaine Massacre in Arkansas, efforts by Black farmers, including those who did own a patch of land, to band together to demand fairer economic arrangements—the right to keep more of the fruits of their own toil and sweat, the right to be paid a fair price for what they grew—were met with terror and even mass murder, condoned if not encouraged by the state. It was possible to survive as a farmer or sharecropper in the South, but it was a mean survival, and it was not the kind of life K.W. and Hattie were determined to make for themselves and their family.

They went first to Texas, where, later in 1906, their first child was born—a daughter named Primrose. I'm not sure exactly where in Texas they were or what they were doing, but in any event, they did not stay long: By 1911, they were back in Mississippi, just a few miles from Aberdeen. That year, in Okolona, their first son, Lowell, was born. They also had a second daughter, Roberta, who died young in 1919 of the Spanish flu.

After a stay of just a few years, the peripatetic Robinsons moved back to Franklin County, Georgia—William and Sarah Robinson's home-place, where K.W. had grown up. The racial, social, and economic facts of life there, in a little town called Canon, would have been the same as they were a few hundred miles west in Okolona. Hattie and K.W. stayed put, surrounded by the extended Robinson family, long enough for their second son, Francis—my uncle Franz—to be born in 1913. And they stayed long enough for the third, Harold—my father—to arrive on March 15, 1916.

By then K.W. had found his calling as a preacher, though he also took other jobs to support the family. I know that he and Hattie were still in Canon as late as 1918, because that is where K.W. registered for the World War I draft. He gave his occupation as "farmer," which meant that, once again, he knew the hardship and unfairness of agriculture under Jim Crow. His parents apparently did own some land, since Sarah eventually donated a piece of property for the building of a church, Fairview Baptist. But that life still wasn't what K.W. wanted. He had not fared better by going west to Mississippi and Texas. Now he and Hattie set out to build their family's future in the North.

The epic exodus of millions called the Great Migration, chronicled eloquently in Isabel Wilkerson's magisterial book *The Warmth of Other Suns*, is one of the most stirring of American stories. It encompasses all of what this nation sees as its most admirable and essential characteristics: ambition, drive, pioneering fearlessness, hunger for hard work, thirst for freedom, undaunted optimism. Here is my favorite example of how the exodus shaped America: A few years before my grandparents went north, a Black family named Shields, from Alabama, and another Black family named Robinson (no relation to me), from South Carolina, separately moved to Chicago. Both families were leaving the places where their ancestors had been enslaved, places that subsequently had been seized by Jim Crow. A daughter of the Shields family and a son of that Robinson family—both born in Chicago—fell in love and got married; he worked at the city water plant, despite struggling with multiple sclerosis, while she worked as a secretary. Their son, named Craig, graduated from Princeton University and earned an MBA at the University of Chicago. Their daughter, named Michelle, also graduated from Princeton and went on to Harvard Law School. Michelle eventually married another Black and brilliant Harvard Law graduate, named Barack Obama. This granddaughter of the Great Migration became First Lady of the United States.

Why did K.W. and Hattie decide that was the moment to leave? The bloody wave of white-supremacist terror had to be a factor. In 1918, Georgia led the nation in lynchings; and in 1919, the year of the Red Summer, there were anti-Black riots and killings across the state. There was no realistic prospect of progress toward safety and opportunity in the former Confederacy, which meant that every Black family had the same decision to make. Major Fordham was too old, too rooted, and far too stubborn to pick up and start all over again, but his sons Marion and Harry at least explored life away from home, and their sister Grace and her husband moved north to Cincinnati. William and Sarah Robinson must not have been of a mind to relocate, but their adult children had the youth and energy to join the diaspora. K.W., in particular, was infected by a wanderlust that shaped his entire life. He and Hattie would have known that if brighter prospects for their children were out there to be found, it was useless to seek them in Franklin County.

They made their first stop in Chattanooga, where K.W.'s brother Tugalo already lived. That was the way the Great Migration worked: Families went where relatives or acquaintances, folks from back home, had established a foothold. Sometimes they stayed at that first stop permanently; often, as with the Robinsons, they were there just long enough to get their bearings and prepare for the next onward push.

K.W. and Hattie made another stop, in Columbus, Ohio, where another Robinson brother, Jesse, had already settled. I'm not sure exactly how long they stayed in either of those places; I believe they spent longer in Columbus than in Chattanooga. But I do know that by 1922—when the last of my father's siblings, a boy named Roy, was born—the family had already forged ahead. My cousin Theresa tells me that they landed briefly in Flint, Michigan, where the company that became General Motors had been founded, a boomtown where work could be had. But soon they made their last move, as a family, to the place that would become home, the place where Roy's birth was recorded: the leafy, liberal college town of Ann Arbor, Michigan.

What drew them there was the dynamic, smoke-belching, fast-growing metropolis thirty-five miles to the east. By the time my Robinson grandparents arrived in Michigan, Detroit was well on its way to becoming one of the biggest and most important manufacturing centers in the world—the city whose factories, two decades later, would empower the United States to serve as the Allies' great "arsenal of democracy" in World War II.

From the 1920s through the 1950s, Detroit was one of the nation's and the world's most powerful magnets for people, of any race or creed, who wanted to flee oppression and privation in search of a chance to make a better life for themselves and their children. Black Americans, like white Americans, came to work in the burgeoning automobile industry that tycoons such as Henry Ford, Ransom Olds, the Dodge brothers, Walter Chrysler, Henry Durant, and Charles Stewart Mott were building in the city that sprawled outward from the banks of the Detroit River. In the early decades of the century, Detroit's explosive growth seemed to be happening in real time. It was said that you could drive past an open field one day, then go by that same spot a week later and see a new factory.

The biggest of all, by far, was Ford's vast River Rouge plant, which was under construction when the Robinsons arrived in Michigan. Within a few years, it became the greatest vertically integrated factory in the world. River Rouge was a universe apart, self-contained, and virtually autonomous. The complex spread across an area along the river, southwest of the city center, that measured nearly two square miles. River Rouge had its own steel mill, its own electricity plant, its own glassworks, its own docks, and a hundred miles of railroad tracks to shuttle materials and components among structures. It encompassed hundreds of buildings, some of them designed by one of the most acclaimed architects of the time, Albert Kahn, who incorporated new "scientific" principles involving natural light and the era's version of ergonomics. A steady parade of train cars, barges, and trucks arrived at the Rouge plant laden with raw materials such as iron ore and sand. Another parade left the complex carrying finished Model T and Model A sedans destined for showrooms across the country. At its peak, River Rouge employed more than a hundred thousand workers.

Henry Ford was an anti-Semite and a racist. At his first big plant in Highland Park—an enclave city surrounded by Detroit—he hired Black workers only as janitors. But when he built River Rouge, with its insatiable need for labor, he set aside any qualms about hiring African Americans for his assembly lines. He didn't just accept them; he wanted them: The European immigrants in his workforce, who had European ideas about labor solidarity, were agitating for a union shop. Ford found that white migrants from the South were less demanding—and that African Americans from the South gave him the least trouble of all, as the unions did not welcome Black members. Ford Motor Company began rapidly hiring Black workers, to whom it offered a steady job and the fair wage of five dollars a day.

Many white workers at the Rouge plant lived in the nearby Detroit suburb of Dearborn, where Blacks were excluded; and many African Americans settled in another suburb, called Inkster. (I've been told by Detroiters that those names referred to white supremacy and despised skin color, respectively, reflecting Henry Ford's racism. In fact, however, the names come from a Revolutionary War general named Dearborn and a Victorian-era sawmill owner named Inkster.) By 1930, ten thousand African Americans worked for Ford at the Rouge plant—more than worked for all the other automakers combined. For many Black newcomers, it was a career, a long-term ladder to the middle class. For some others, like the Robinsons, clocking in at the Rouge Plant was a temporary expedient that could help the family through tough times, generate savings for college, and perhaps pay for luxuries they could not otherwise afford.

At various times, my father and all my uncles did stints working there. My dad's experience was memorable, but not in a good way. According to the Henry Ford Museum, dedicated to the industrialist and the company he founded, many Black workers at the Rouge plant were consigned to "lower paying, dirty, dangerous, and unhealthy jobs." One place where African Americans predominated, for example, was the Rouge plant's Cyanide Foundry, where workers processed deadly potassium cyanide for use in hardening steel.

The great boxer Joe Louis, who grew up in Detroit, was one of the many Black men who worked for Ford. Frustrated after an early defeat in the ring, Louis decided to hang up his gloves and take a full-time job at the Rouge plant—but only for a few months. "Eventually, I couldn't stand it anymore," he recalled in his autobiography. "I figured, if I'm going to hurt that much for twenty-five dollars a week, I might as well go back and try fighting again."

As for my father, for the rest of his life he insisted on exclusively buying cars made by GM—always used cars, even when he could afford to buy new. And he refused even to consider driving anything made by Ford.

WHEN THE ROBINSONS ARRIVED, Ann Arbor was about as different from their starting point of Canon, Georgia, as any place in the United States could be. Home to the University of Michigan, it offered a different kind of opportunity from what others sought and found in the conurbations of Detroit or Chicago or Cleveland: Then, as now, Ann Arbor was a quintessential midwestern college town.

The Robinsons settled south of the business district and the U-M campus, a few blocks from the site where, shortly after they arrived, "the Big House" would be built—Michigan Stadium, the largest-capacity stadium in the country and the third-biggest in the world. My father told me he remembered the noise and bustle of construction in the neighborhood; he would have been eleven when the famous venue opened in 1927.

In the Roaring Twenties, Ann Arbor was hardly a place without racial discrimination. Informal redlining had already begun to establish residential zones. There was a mostly Black neighborhood called Kerrytown, north of downtown, near the train station and the Huron River. Black-owned businesses lined Ann Street. Children from the neighborhood went to Jones School, which served as a focal point for the community.

But when my father and his brothers—Lowell, Francis, and Roy—were growing up, there was no legally mandated segregation in Michigan. There were no separate water fountains and playgrounds, no rules about who had to sit where on buses, no separate schools, no rules of etiquette requiring Black people to give way to white people on the sidewalk. My father and my uncles were the only Black men of their generation I knew who went to integrated schools. All of them graduated from Ann Arbor High, which occupied a huge neoclassical structure at the corner of Huron and State Streets that one newspaper had proclaimed "the finest public school building in Michigan, if not in the United States."

In the 1923 Ann Arbor city directory, K.W. Robinson is listed as living with his family at 809 Greene Street and working as a porter at the University of Michigan Hospital. According to the family's oral history, he also worked as a railroad porter at the train station across town. The Robinsons were just getting settled, but my grandparents' marriage was already in serious trouble: On February 21 of that year, Hattie Robinson filed papers to divorce her husband. My father was in grade school, about to turn seven—a tough age to see his family break apart.

Everything else I know about K.W., my paternal grandfather, has come from digging through archives and exchanging bits and pieces of information with my cousins Theresa and Charles, who are Uncle Lowell's daughter and son. Our fathers hardly ever talked about their father, K.W., and neither did Uncle Franz. I don't recall ever hearing Grandma Robinson speak his name. I haven't even been able to track down a photograph. I have to conjure him. The three sons of K.W. whom I knew—Lowell, Franz, and Harold—resembled one another so strikingly that anyone who saw them together would instantly know they were siblings; and I have seen a photo of K.W.'s brother Claud, who looked like his nephews Lowell, Franz, and Harold, and Theresa remembers from photographs she has seen that our grandfather "looked like they all look." The fuzzy mental image I extrapolate from all these clues is the only picture of my grandfather that I have.

Why did the family he left behind in Ann Arbor erase him so completely, almost as if he had never existed? Why couldn't his sons be coaxed into talking about him? Why, when K.W. died in 1947, was my father the only one of the siblings to attend the funeral? And why, according to my mother, did he have to be persuaded that going to the services was the right thing to do?

Again, snippets of information and leaps of imagination are all I have. "Desertion" is the offense Hattie cites in her divorce petition, so it is possible that his sons resented the fact that K.W. had left them and their mother to fend for themselves. I know that in his absence, the family did struggle to meet expenses. Another plausible reason is that K.W. could have been a womanizer; though he worked to make money as a porter, he was a Baptist preacher by calling, and that implies a certain charisma and presence. He would hardly have been the first silver-tongued pastor to take a special interest in the salvation of female members of his flock.

But would any of that be enough to explain the intensity of the feelings the Robinson men harbored about their father? I have to wonder if K.W. was abusive in some way, physically or psychologically. I have to wonder if he did something, committed some act or some sin, that the family found unforgivable. Franz never had children; both Lowell and Harold were gentle fathers. All were dedicated husbands who enjoyed long, stable marriages. And you could have known any of them for many years without an inkling that a man named K.W. Robinson had ever walked the earth.

I know that K.W. was in touch with the family for at least a few more years after the divorce filing. In 1926, according to a notice in *The Ann Arbor News*, he transferred a small piece of property to Hattie. On November 25, 1929, the Robinsons' divorce was made final, and Hattie was awarded alimony, which I assume K.W. must have paid. Hattie was a no-nonsense woman who, as the saying goes, "put up with no mess." There would likely be more court records if she'd had to pursue K.W. to honor his obligations.

After the divorce, I lose track of K.W. for a decade. I believe he spent some of that time in Columbus with his brother Jesse. In the early 1940s, he turns up far away, in Topeka, Kansas, working at a quarry—and, presumably, also pursuing his vocation as a minister. What drew him there, of all places? I assume it was not the privilege of spending eight or ten hours a day breaking rocks in the hot Kansas sun. Perhaps the lure was an opportunity to preach in some Baptist church. Topeka is where K.W. signed up for the World War II draft—even though he was sixty years old and hardly fit for combat—and from that registration card, I get the fullest description of my grandfather I've been able to find. He was five feet, eight inches tall and weighed 152 pounds; he had brown eyes, black hair, and dark brown skin; and he had a "vivid scar on head, left side."

Within a couple of years, he was back in Columbus, where I know he finally found a clerical job, as associate pastor of the Hosack Street Baptist Church, a thriving Black congregation on the city's South Side. He was introduced to that church by his brother Jesse, who was already a stalwart at Hosack Street Baptist, serving for many years as director of the choir—and perhaps its finest voice, making use of a Robinson family trait, good vocal pipes. Jesse and his wife had eleven children, ten of whom lived to adulthood. My father stayed in touch with various of Jesse's sons and daughters—he seemed pretty close to his multitudinous Columbus cousins—and I can't imagine how he could have avoided some contact over the years with K.W. The truth is that I simply don't know. Our father wanted Ellen and me to know all about our relatives in Michigan and Ohio. But like a ruthless, cold-eyed editor, he deleted his father from the story.

Chapter Nine

JIM CROW AND HARD TIMES

After Major Fordham's death, my grandfather Eugene Smith became the de facto patriarch of the family. He would bear that distinction, and that burden, through hard times.

He and Sadie had their only child on November 4, 1921, a year before the Major's death: a daughter—my mother—named Louisa Gertrude after her grandmother. Sadie had just a one-third share in the house at Boulevard and Oak, as per the Major's will, which left the property to all three daughters equally. But the middle daughter, Grace, had married and migrated with her husband to Cincinnati. The eldest, Florella, remained single and lived right there her entire long life. Sadie was charismatic and full of sparkle, and she resembled the Major, with her dark skin, her piercing eyes, and her wicked sense of humor. She was still at the house the Major had built, and now she had a husband and an heir. She was the natural keeper of the Fordham flame.

The Major's sons had scattered, as can be traced by land documents. Left with more real estate than they wanted to manage, the Fordham sisters decided to sell the Oak Street lot next to the main property for sixteen hundred dollars. They had to make sure they had clear title, however, because the Major's will was ambiguous—at one point, it leaves "all other property not specifically assigned" to his daughters, but elsewhere it instructs that proceeds from the sale of some real estate go to all six of his children equally. In February 1924, to clear things up, each of the Fordham men formally signed away any interest in the Oak Street lot in exchange for the token sum of one dollar. George signed his quitclaim document and had it notarized in Newberry, about eighty miles northwest of Orangeburg; Harry had his papers notarized in Jacksonville, Florida; and Marion had his surrender of property rights made official by a notary in Pittsburgh, Pennsylvania.

This amicable way of settling what might have been contentious property disputes became a new family tradition. Major Fordham, you recall, had gone so far as to sue his own mother in court—unsuccessfully, in the end—over real estate in Charleston. Perhaps that bitter example had led his sons and daughters to take the diametrically opposite approach. Later, the daughters would consolidate ownership of the family house and grounds in Florella's hands and then transfer the properties to Eugene Smith for a token sum; and later still, Sadie would transfer ownership to my father in the same manner.

I never met Eugene James Smith. He died in January 1954 of coronary occlusion at the age of seventy-two; I was born two months later. In addition to suffering from heart disease, he had diabetes and injected himself with insulin daily. But photographs show him as muscular and robust, the result of a lifetime spent working with his hands as well as his mind: He was a brickmason, and apparently a good one.

Eugene was one of nine siblings, only a couple of whom I remember well: Aunt Maggie, who lived a few blocks away on Treadwell Street; and Uncle Alonzo, who lived even closer, around the corner, on Peasley Street. I remember my mother talking about her uncle Milton and her uncle Cornelius, but I have no recollection of the times they came to visit us or we went to visit them. Aunt Maggie's son, Gene Montgomery—yes, another Eugene in the family—was the relative on my grandfather's side whom I knew best. He and my mother, first cousins, had grown up together and were close; and he and my father became good friends. Rarely did a week go by when we didn't see Uncle Gene in church or he didn't stop by after work to sit a spell. My grandmother was especially fond of him, and he of her.

My grandfather was light-skinned—a legacy from *his* grandfather Francis A. Smith, the "mulatto" in Charleston who was listed in the city's Free Negro Book years before Henry Fordham bought his way in. I mention skin color only because one branch of Francis Smith's progeny was so "fair," with such "good" hair, that they decided to leave the African American world and pass for white, according to my mother. I never met them; as "white people," they probably wouldn't have deigned to have much to do with us; nor would we have bothered with them. But my mother did have an old photograph of some of those Black-no-more Smiths, and they could have fooled anyone about their heritage. A wide range of skin tones is not uncommon in African American families; my grandfather's sister Maggie was caramel-brown, while his brother Alonzo's color was more like cocoa.

First Alonzo, who was the elder by three years, and then Eugene studied at Claflin, which at the turn of the century was more than a college. It was also a grammar school and preparatory school, which all the Fordhams and at least some of the Smiths attended; and also a trade school, where young men and women learned skills such as architectural drawing, blacksmithing, carpentry, cooking, dressmaking, and shoemaking. Alonzo and Eugene learned bricklaying. For them, the art and craft of masonry became a career. Alonzo went on to become an instructor in the Claflin bricklaying program, where students learned the process from start to finish—beginning with the making of the bricks. A few of those old bricks and an ancient wheelbarrow the Smith brothers used are still in the backyard at Boulevard and Oak.

We have fewer records from Eugene Smith's tenure as patriarch than from before or after. But there are enough to show that there were some tough times for the family—mortgages taken out on the house, periods when it was apparently hard to keep up with the payments, sales of more bits and pieces of property. My grandfather's income tax forms do not show a lot of money coming into the household, but that is an incomplete picture. Aunt Doc was earning an income too, from her work as a nurse. And because there was extra room in the house, Sadie could sometimes take in boarders—mostly students from out of town who came to attend Claflin or South Carolina State—to help make ends meet.

One of those boarders became a member of the family in all but blood. To Sadie, he was like a son; to my mother, like an older brother. To me, he was my godfather. And by the end of his life, to generations of young people in his rural hometown, he was an educator, a role model, a mentor, and a lifelong inspiration.

Charles Edward Murray, whom we all knew as Edward, was born in 1910 in Greeleyville, a speck of a town in Williamsburg County to the east of Orangeburg, on the other side of Lake Marion. That part of the state, smack in the Cotton Belt, is heavily Black and poor. Edward was born both. When he was twelve, his father died, and he was left an orphan. A childless and relatively well-off Black couple, Edward and Margaret McCollum, took him in as a foster son and raised him in the grandest house in town. The McCollums specified in their wills that Edward would have the right to live in the house for the rest of his life.

Edward was a prodigy. In 1925, at fifteen, he came to Orangeburg for college at South Carolina State—and boarded at our house. There were dormitories on campus, but I believe the McCollums knew my grandmother through a Methodist Church connection and wanted young Edward to live in a proper home, with structure and rules. He arrived at the Fordham house and never left our family. My mother, Louisa, was four when he first walked through the door, and she immediately became the little sister he never had. He sometimes opened letters to my grandmother Sadie with "Dear Other Mother." And as for my grandfather, I found one letter Edward wrote home from Iran—where he was stationed during World War II—in which he reminisced that when he first came to live at our house, he had hesitated to unpack his trunk "for some time during my process of trying to figure Mr. Smith out."

The figuring out was mutual. Edward was what the era called a "confirmed bachelor." No one in our family ever discussed that fact. Ever. I remember one time, when we were visiting for Sunday dinner at the big house in Greeleyville where Edward lived alone, one of the ladies from his church dropped by with some food she had cooked for him. My father joked that the lady seemed sweet on him and that maybe, at long last, he would finally get married. Everybody had a chuckle, including Edward, and then they moved on to talk about something else. Edward was in his fifties at the time, and I was maybe ten, and I remember thinking that, no, Edward definitely was never going to marry that lady. I knew on some level that he was a gay man well before I had any idea that such a thing as a gay man existed.

Throughout his life, he never accepted any label. But he also never pretended to be anyone other than who he was. In World War II, he served in the army with the all-Black 352nd Engineer General Service Regiment, which was assigned to the Persian Gulf Command. The unit sailed out of San Francisco on January 4, 1943, on the converted British ocean liner *Mauretania*. The ship made refueling stops at Pearl Harbor, still scarred from the Japanese attack; at Wellington, New Zealand; at Fremantle, Australia; and at Bombay, now Mumbai. There, the regiment was transferred to a British troop transport ship for the last leg to Khorramshahr, Iran. The mission assigned to the 352nd was to maintain and operate the long corridor across Iran, to Tehran and beyond, through which the Allies were supplying weapons to the Soviet Union for the battle against the Nazis on the Eastern Front.

Edward's duties in Iran were administrative, performed in offices and not on battlefields. That was a good thing, both for him and for the war effort. He said he was assigned to office work from his first day in the army, at Fort Benning, in Georgia, and never even went through a full course of basic training. I remember how he joked about his incompetence with a rifle, showing us what a ridiculous spectacle he had been trying to shoulder and fire his weapon. His demonstration looked, frankly, like a bigoted homophobe's pantomime of effeminacy. But to Edward, there was no hint of embarrassment involved. He found his own incompetence at modeling machismo genuinely amusing.

The army didn't need his brawn, however. It needed, and used, his brain—his analytical and organizational skills. I wonder if he might have been hazed, ridiculed, even tormented by his fellow soldiers, but there is no sign of that in the good-natured letters he sent home to my grandmother. The closest thing is one passage in a letter, typed on the gossamer paper called onionskin, that he sent home in August 1944 from a base in Iran, after having been overseas for eighteen months: "I must tell you about a little episode that occurred on the ship when we were coming over, but I will have to tell you when I get home. I know Mr. Smith will laugh until he cries. I laugh now when I think of it. I will say this much. *I have always been taught that a good run is better than a bad stand.*"

I remember times when I heard my mother or grandmother mention that we wouldn't be going to Greeleyville on some given weekend because one of Edward's friends from out of town was visiting. They would say the word *friends* with a certain emphasis. These men might have known Edward from his army days, or they might have been from the time he had spent in Philadelphia doing graduate studies at the University of Pennsylvania. Or maybe they were from another sojourn away from home. I never met any of Edward's friends. In retrospect, I wonder if any were lovers, past or present, and if that might be the reason we always steered clear.

I would love to know what it was like for Eugene Smith and Charles Edward Murray to accept each other and ultimately become like father and son. Somehow they managed to come to agreement on a definition of manhood broad enough to encompass them both. "Enclosed you will find a small money order from the son," Edward wrote in one of his letters to my grandmother from Iran. "Please give Mr. Smith a few cigars for me."

Black America writ large, like the rest of America, was structurally and systemically homophobic. The reality on a personal level, however, was more like an extreme version of Don't Ask, Don't Tell. I have known Black pastors who would preach a fiery sermon against homosexuality as being unnatural and against God's will—and then proudly introduce a selection by the choir led by a music director whom everyone in the congregation, including the pastor, knew to be gay. As it happened, Edward was the longtime director of the senior choir and coordinator of music at Mount Zion United Methodist Church in nearby Kingstree, a somewhat larger town that was the Williamsburg County seat.

No one in Greeleyville or environs could have imagined that Edward was anything but gay. The same was true for his Black fellow students at SC State, the Black soldiers he served with during the war, and every adult in our Black family. There must have been times when his life was complicated, difficult, painful. Walking the thin line between intolerance and acceptance must have been precarious, but he walked it with skill and grace.

EDWARD'S GESTURE OF SENDING a money order home from the war was born of more than thoughtfulness. The 1930s and '40s were lean times for the Fordham household, as for the nation and much of the world.

My grandfather left behind the deposit book for an account he had at the Edisto National Bank of Orangeburg. The story it tells is that money was not in surplus during the decade after Major Fordham's death. There were months when Eugene Smith was able to make regular weekly deposits of ten or fifteen dollars, but there were also long stretches when he made no deposits at all. The account's balance, as recorded, never exceeded eight hundred dollars. That was a decent amount of money in a small South Carolina town back then, but hardly a fortune. Aunt Doc brought income into the household, too, though, and Sadie was entrepreneurial with her piano lessons and her cooking. There was also the cash the Major had left behind, and anything over and above the one thousand dollars he left to each of his sons went to the daughters. Sadie and Aunt Doc each would have received a one-third share.

And the family had land. They mortgaged bits and pieces, then sold them when it was necessary. At one point, in 1923, a mortgage that Major Fordham had taken out on the family home became delinquent, and the lienholder filed suit, but the debt was satisfied with funds from the sale of some other lots the Fordham sisters owned; Sadie and Aunt Doc needed a signature from Grace, who was in Cincinnati, to complete the transaction. The family was certainly not wealthy but certainly not poor—and there was enough money to treat the Smiths' only daughter, Louisa, like the proper princess she was.

An only child, born relatively late in her parents' lives—Sadie was thirty-five, Eugene was forty—my mother was spoiled rotten. There are pictures of her as a baby in an elaborate English-style pram, pictures of her as a young girl in a crisp white pinafore, and formal studio photograph after studio photograph of Louisa beginning when she was a preteen in pigtails. She was indeed a beautiful child who grew into a beautiful woman, chocolate-skinned and slender, with a model's triangular face, piercing dark eyes, and visible confidence: She strolled when she walked as if she owned the sidewalk. Our family valued brains over beauty, though, and she was whip-smart, an A student. She kept some of her schoolwork, and I can see that from an early age, she was a clear, confident writer.

Louisa was just turning eight when, in 1929, the regular deposits Eugene Smith had been making at the Edisto National Bank slowed down and became smaller. In July 1932, when my mother was about to turn eleven, the deposits stopped for good. The Great Depression had the nation in its long, strangling grip.

There was no money to tuck away for a rainy day, not in the middle of an economic monsoon. Even if there *had* been extra money, soon there would be nowhere to put it: Bank runs by desperate depositors had devastated the banking system, and in an attempt to save what was left of it, President Franklin Delano Roosevelt declared a weeklong nationwide bank holiday on March 6, 1933. Despite Roosevelt's promise to seek a national guarantee of bank deposits—which led, three months later, to the creation of the Federal Deposit Insurance Corporation—the local bank where Eugene Smith had his account, Edisto National, was one of the many financial institutions that never reopened after the bank holiday. A year earlier, another local bank, Orangeburg National, had failed, and Edisto National had been appointed to take over its assets and liabilities. Now it, too, was gone as the city's banks fell like dominoes.

Much of the South was already in trouble before the 1929 stock market crash; cotton prices had plunged in 1926, depriving the regional economy of its fuel. As the Depression set in, there was less and less work for tradesmen like Eugene Smith, until finally there was none. Among the building projects that abruptly halted was construction of the new sanctuary to house Trinity Methodist Church, the brick building with gorgeous stained-glass windows where I spent so many Sundays. Eugene and Alonzo Smith, two of the best bricklayers in town, were suddenly deprived of that and other sources of work.

Once the Depression reached its nadir, few in Orangeburg had any work to speak of. As happened in small towns across the country, people resorted to an atavistic, pre-money system of barter—eggs from my chickens in exchange for meat from the hog you've just butchered; fish that a Claflin professor caught this morning in exchange for the plumbing job a Claflin maintenance worker knew how to perform. Eugene Smith could lay bricks; Sadie could teach piano and cook; Aunt Doc had her medical knowledge and her potions. They had tradeable skills.

The dearth of income was bad enough that my grandparents and great-aunt fell behind on mortgages they had taken out on the house at Boulevard and Oak. But in 1935, they were able to refinance all that debt and more—a total of twelve hundred dollars—with the Home Owners' Loan Corporation, a government-sponsored lender that the Roosevelt administration established as part of the New Deal. The HOLC was a godsend to our family and countless others—at least at first. But for

Black America writ large, the lender's long-term impact was a theft of equity that persists today. HOLC essentially invented redlining.

In 1935, to manage its huge and ballooning portfolio of risk, the corporation began a City Survey project that produced maps classifying neighborhoods according to the creditworthiness of their residents, with the riskiest neighborhoods shaded red. Those "redlined" neighborhoods were disproportionately African American. Long after the Depression had ended, the impact of those maps endured. Private lenders—acting on government advice—charged higher interest rates in redlined neighborhoods or simply refused to make loans there. That launched a self-perpetuating cycle of undercapitalization. Those neighborhoods became poorer, more run-down, more racially segregated. Almost two-thirds of the neighborhoods redlined by HOLC in the late 1930s are minority neighborhoods today. A New Deal program that was established with the best of intentions—and that saved the homes of millions of Americans, Black and white—also ended up denying millions of Black Americans the opportunity to build generational wealth.

In the 1936 Orangeburg map, a narrow strip along Boulevard—including our house and most, but not all, of our backyard—is classified "wholesale," perhaps because of a warehouse that stood a block and a half south, between Peasley and Amelia Streets. The rest of our yard, all the houses stretching down Oak Street, and the rest of our neighborhood to the west are listed as "blighted," with the annotation "colored." White neighborhoods are classified as "best residential," and slivers of a couple of Black neighborhoods, including the two blocks along Russell Street where the Sulton family lived, are deemed "best colored." Property values, lending risk, and insurance rates throughout the city would have been set accordingly.

My grandmother seldom talked about the Depression, except to say that those were very tough times. People who lived through those years of privation talk mostly about food. A few years ago, the Orangeburg *Times and Democrat* interviewed local Depression survivors as part of a series of articles about the city's past. Said one woman, "At the time, things were really cheap. You could buy a two-pound round steak for fifty cents or a ten-pound pork roast for a dollar, but getting that dollar! That was another story. You couldn't buy a job in those days." Said another Orangeburg old-timer, "A typical meal for a family of four was a hot pot of grits, a small can of salmon from the A&P and a dash or two of catsup—if you were lucky enough to have catsup. A family of seven could be fed on a soup bone and vegetables for fifty cents. . . . We had chickens behind a fence, and people would jump over the fence and steal them."

I've always thought the experience of growing up during the Depression was responsible for both my parents' extreme thrift with food. When the family had finished eating dinner—the midday meal—or supper, my mother always saved the leftovers, even if they consisted of just two or three mouthfuls. Larger portions would go into the standalone freezer, which she kept well stocked, faithfully annotating each item with its date. Her thorough and systematic method of food storage stemmed partly from the insecurity of her Depression youth, when wasting a precious morsel was not an option, and partly from her training and experience as a librarian, which had instilled the reflex to keep, label, and categorize.

For my father's family, too, the Depression was an ordeal. Hattie Robinson had five children—the youngest, Roy, was seven when the stock market crashed in 1929—and no husband. Because of the dominance and sudden collapse of the auto industry, Michigan suffered unemployment of 34 percent between 1930 and 1933, compared with 25 percent for the nation as a whole. The University of Michigan was Ann Arbor's economic engine, and it kept functioning, although there were many students who had to go home; the pretty little college town fared better than nearby Detroit or its satellite factory towns. But "better" simply meant economic devastation to a somewhat lesser degree. Banks failed there, too. Construction came to a halt, at least until New Deal projects got under way. Local governments in Ann Arbor and next-door Ypsilanti had such profound revenue shortfalls that they began paying municipal workers and creditors in scrip, which was accepted by local merchants for goods and services. Because nobody had any money, cities across the country had to make their own.

An author named Edmund G. Love, who was born in Flint and went to U-M during the Depression, wrote a memoir of those long years that he titled *Hanging On, or How to Get Through a Depression and Enjoy Life*. He recalled, "No one that I knew ever thought that things would stay bad forever. . . . People talked about the upturn that would come the next spring. The next spring people would talk about the upturn that would come in the summer, and so on. The thing is that people really believed this. They had a blind faith in it. And because they did, they set up a pattern of living. It was called 'hanging on.'"

The great playwright Arthur Miller spent part of the Depression in Ann Arbor. A New Yorker, Miller was determined to go to U-M because of its famous writing competition for students, the Avery Hopwood Awards, known as a literary launching pad. Like most families, Miller's had no money to send him off to college. So he worked menial jobs for two years to save enough for tuition, room, and board—and he won Hopwoods for the first two plays he ever wrote, *No Villain* in 1936 and *Honors at Dawn* in 1937. (I won a Hopwood, too, for an essay I wrote in 1971 called "Recollections of Obscurity." But that episode comes much later in this American history.)

During the Depression, both sides of my family experienced the effects of this nation's general rule: However bad the situation is for white people, it is worse for Black folks. They were prime targets of the "last hired, first fired" rule, which meant that African American workers were first to have their salaries cut, their hours reduced, and ultimately their jobs eliminated. In the unlikely event that some business had an opening, Blacks were automatically shunted to the end of the long line of applicants. The general attitude was that whites should not be unemployed while Blacks were still working, so African Americans were shoved out of their positions as elevator operators, janitors, porters, and trash collectors to make room for white replacements who had lost more prestigious jobs. In 1933, the low point before the New Deal brought some relief, unemployment nationwide reached 25 percent. Among African Americans, the jobless rate was fully 50 percent. In some especially hard-hit big cities, Black unemployment peaked even higher, at 60 percent.

These desperate conditions led African Americans to band together in self-help organizations, formal and informal, as Black communities turned inward for survival. Perhaps the most notable example was the birth of a religious organization whose social and political impact has resonated for decades: The Nation of Islam, which gave American history such consequential figures as Malcolm X and Louis Farrakhan, is a product of the Great Depression.

The group arose in Detroit in 1930, as the city's auto plants were laying off workers—and African Americans were the first let go. A man who called himself Wallace Fard Muhammad and described himself as a biracial Arab from Mecca (but who may have been neither) began attracting attention as he preached an idiosyncratic version of Islam. "More about myself I will not tell you yet, for the time has not yet come," he said in an early message to his growing group of followers. "I am your brother. You have not yet seen me in my royal robes." Some skeptics believe he was an American drifter who fabricated an exotic Middle Eastern heritage; others believe he was of Afghan or Turkish heritage. His background was obscure, but his charisma was undeniable, and he was offering a message that fit the moment.

Migrants who had fled poverty and discrimination in the South found themselves facing poverty and discrimination in the North, but with bitterly cold winters and impatient landlords. Most people were Christians who had no use for Wallace Muhammad's idiosyncratic version of Islam, which was a theology of Black exceptionalism that castigated white people as "devils." But for those who were open to it, the Nation offered a new way of thinking about the injustices that Black men and women were experiencing and a way to leave it all behind. The Nation offered community, dignity, discipline, purpose, self-sufficiency, self-help, and self-worth. Acting collectively at a time when everyone was in need, members could make sure that no family went hungry, that no child went without a winter coat or a pair of shoes.

One of the first loyal members of the Nation was a young man named Elijah Poole, the son of sharecroppers who had left rural Georgia for the factories of Detroit. In keeping with the rule that surnames, or "slave names," had to be discarded, Poole first took the name Elijah Karriem and then, later, as he assumed more of a leadership role as supreme minister of the sect, was renamed Elijah Muhammad. He took charge of the group's 1933 move to Chicago, where its headquarters remains on the South Side, near the University of Chicago. And after Wallace Fard Muhammad disappeared in 1934—some believe he slipped away to Europe; others suspect he was killed by police or internecine rivals—the Honorable Elijah Muhammad, Messenger of Allah, became the Nation of Islam's unquestioned leader. The Great Depression's punishing, soul-sapping hardships sent a steady stream of new members through the Nation's open doors.

President Franklin Delano Roosevelt's massive and unprecedented New Deal programs did make things better. In Orangeburg, the Works Progress Administration and the Public Works Administration funded the construction of a new engineering hall and a new dormitory on the South Carolina State campus, a new hospital and nurses' dormitory for the city, and extensive improvements to the municipal water system—which meant jobs for skilled tradesmen like Eugene Smith as well as unskilled laborers. In Ann Arbor, the PWA paid for construction of six big new buildings at U-M—including West Quadrangle, the Gothic Revival dormitory where I spent my freshman year—as well as a farmers' market and a band shell for the city. All those jobs put money into workers' pockets that they spent for goods and services they previously could not afford, giving new life to retail, transportation, and other moribund sectors of the economy. My parents' families once again could survive, though not thrive. Even at the height of the New Deal, hardly anyone thrived.

What eventually brought the economy back, of course, was World War II. The most devastating conflict in world history changed America, and in many ways changed Black America most of all.

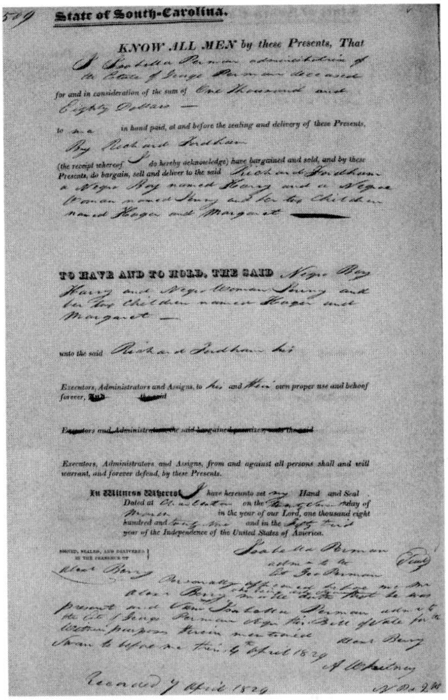

State of South-Carolina.

KNOW ALL MEN by these Presents, That I Isabella Perman administratrix of the Estate of George Perman deceased for and in consideration of the sum of One thousand and Eighty Dollars — to me in hand paid, at and before the sealing and delivery of these Presents, By Richard Fordham (the receipt whereof I do hereby acknowledge) have bargained and sold, and by these Presents, do bargain, sell and deliver to the said Richard Fordham a Negro Boy named Harry and a Negro Woman named Jenny and her two Children named Hager and Margaret

TO HAVE AND TO HOLD, THE SAID Negro Boy Harry and Negro Woman Jenny and her two Children named Hager and Margaret —

unto the said Richard Fordham his

Executors, Administrators and Assigns, to his and their own proper use and behoof forever,

Executors, Administrators and Assigns, from and against all persons shall and will warrant, and forever defend, by these Presents.

In Witness Whereof I have hereunto set my Hand and Seal Dated at Charleston on the day of in the year of our Lord, one thousand eight hundred and and in the year of the Independence of the United States of America.

SIGNED, SEALED, AND DELIVERED IN THE PRESENCE OF

Isabella Perman

Recorded 7 April 1829

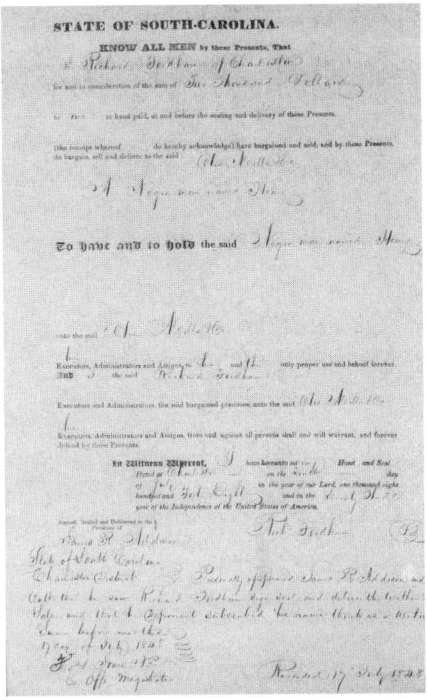

STATE OF SOUTH-CAROLINA.

KNOW ALL MEN by these Presents, That I Richard Fordham of Charleston for and in consideration of the sum of Two Thousand Dollars to me in hand paid, at and before the sealing and delivery of these Presents, (the receipt whereof do hereby acknowledge) have bargained and sold, and by these Presents, do bargain, sell and deliver to the said Otis Mills & Co

A Negro man named Henry

To have and to hold the said Negro man named Henry

unto the said Otis Mills & Co

Executors, Administrators and Assigns to and only proper use and behoof forever. And I the said Richard Fordham

Executors and Administrators, the said bargained premises, unto the said Otis Mills & Co

Executors, Administrators and Assigns, from and against all persons shall and will warrant, and forever defend by these Presents.

In Witness Whereof, I have hereunto set my Hand and Seal Dated at Charleston on the day of July in the year of our Lord, one thousand eight hundred and Forty Eight and in the year of the Independence of the United States of America.

Signed, Sealed and Delivered in the Presence of

Richd Fordham

Recorded 17 July 1848

Left: The record of the 1829 transaction in which Henry Fordham—then a boy known as Harry—was sold to Richard Fordham, the owner of a plantation.

Right: The record of Henry Fordham's 1848 sale to Otis Mills and Co., a Charleston merchandising firm.

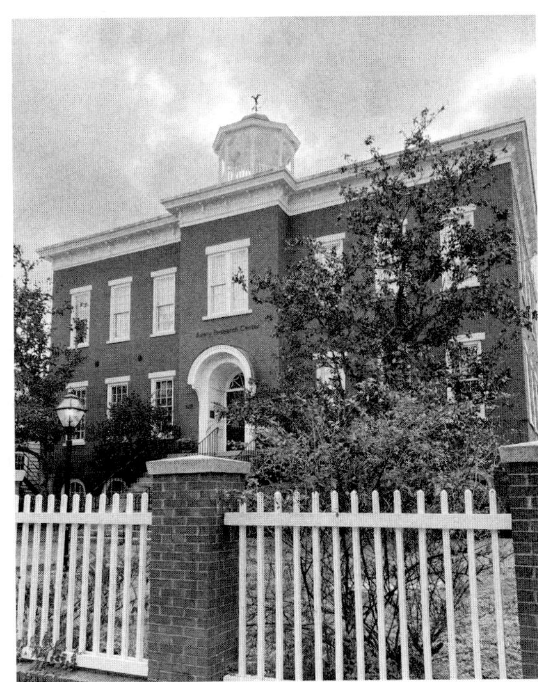

Right: The Avery Institute, the first accredited secondary school for African Americans in Charleston, where John Hammond Fordham enrolled in 1868 at the age of twelve. The building is now a research institute of the College of Charleston.

Left: A classroom at the Avery Institute that has been restored to look as it did in 1868.

Right: Major John Hammond Fordham in his prime. This formal portrait, dating roughly to 1910, hangs prominently in the sitting room of the house he built in Orangeburg, South Carolina.

Left: Louisa Fordham, Major Fordham's wife, as a young bride. She was sixteen when they married; he was nineteen.

Certificate of Marriage.

Sailor, there's hope for thee.

This Certifies, That on the 5th day of August in the year of our Lord one thousand eight hundred and Seventy five

John H Fordham

—and—

Loisa G Smith

were by me united in MARRIAGE, at Charleston according to the Laws of the State of So Ca

Witness.

Wm B Gates
Chaplain

Right:The Fordhams' marriage certificate. The banner curving above the nautical scene counsels, "Sailor, there's hope for thee.

Below: The Custom House in Charleston, where Major Fordham worked as a federal tax official.

Above: A painting by the author's late wife, Avis Collins Robinson, of the house at the corner of Boulevard and Oak in Orangeburg, which Major Fordham built in 1903. The house, still standing, was added to the National Register of Historic Places in 1985.

Below: The author's mother, Louisa (*center*), circa 1945, flanked by her parents, Sadie Fordham Smith and Eugene J. Smith, in the living room of the Fordham home.

Right: Francis D. Smith, Eugene Smith's father.

Right: The author's great-aunt, Florella Fordham, who was known within the family as "Aunt Doc." She was the first certified nurse in Orangeburg, Black or white, and during her long career directed health care services at both South Carolina State and Claflin Universities.

Left: Harold I. Robinson, the author's father, in his World War II army uniform.

Left: Hattie M. Robinson, the author's paternal grandmother, who moved the Robinson family along the route of the Great Migration from rural Georgia to Ann Arbor, Michigan.

Right: The author, at one year old, with his family on the front steps of the home in Orangeburg. The author is being held by his great-aunt, Florella Fordham. In the foreground, left to right, are Harold Robinson, his father; Louisa Robinson, his mother; Sadie Smith and Hattie Robinson, his grandmothers; Charles Edward Murray, his godfather; and a visiting family member from Michigan.

Left: The author (*front row, second from left*) with fellow art students at the Felton Training School on the campus of South Carolina State University. Next to the author, wearing a plaid shirt, is his best friend, Douglas Wells. The teacher is Leo Twiggs, a noted South Carolina artist who was then the head of the SC State art department.

Right: Ellen Robinson, the author's sister, as a young girl.

Right: Sadie Smith (*right*), with her lifelong best friend, Bessie Sulton, in the front yard of the Fordham home.

Left: South Carolina state police officials stand over the bodies of two of the three unarmed Black student demonstrators who were shot dead by state troopers on February 8, 1968. Nearly thirty other African Americans were wounded in the incident, which became known as the Orangeburg Massacre.

Associated Press

Above: Eugene and Avis Robinson and their sons, Lowell and Aaron, in Hawaii in 2019.

Tara Morenfeld, Sky and Reef Photography

ON SEPTEMBER 16, 1940, Roosevelt signed into law the Selective Training and Service Act, which required all American men between the ages of twenty-one and forty-five to register for the first peacetime draft in the nation's history. I should put "peacetime" in quotes, because the rest of the world was already at war. The United States had watched first with unease and then with alarm as Hitler's ground forces made their lightning-fast conquest of continental Europe, capped by the shocking fall of France, and German bombers rained death upon London in the horrifying Blitz. Domestic public opinion favored keeping out of the war, but the hope of neutrality was fading—and Roosevelt was doing everything in his power to prepare his nation for the inevitable.

The following month, on October 16, two of the Robinson men, Lowell and Francis, dutifully registered at a draft board office in Detroit, where they were living together at the time and working for Ford at the River Rouge plant. Harold, my father, registered as well, but he did so in Ann Arbor. The baby of the family, Roy, was just eighteen and not yet required to sign up. My father and all his brothers would serve their country in uniform during the war.

The researchers at the Columbus, Ohio, library who had helped me learn more about my grandfather K.W. Robinson also found a clipping from *The Ann Arbor News* that told me more about the Robinson brothers' military service than I was ever able to pull out of any of them. The clipping was a brief feature story, published on April 7, 1944, about the patriotic local family who had sent three sons to war—and lost the fourth before he could serve his country.

Three Sons Serve

The three sons of Mrs. Hattie M. Robinson, 809 Green [*sic*] St., are all in training at camps within this country but have found that the states of Maryland, Alabama, and Arizona are just far enough apart to break up the family circle.

Capt. Francis L. Robinson, recently promoted at Fort Huachuca,

Ariz., entered the Army in February 1942, and has trained with the cavalry at Fort Riley, Kas., with a medical administration unit at Carlisle, Pa., where he was promoted to second lieutenant, at Fort McClellan, Ala., where he advanced to first lieutenant, and most recently at Fort Huachuca, Ariz.

A graduate of the University [of Michigan] Law College, Capt. Robinson was admitted to the Michigan Bar and practiced with the Bledsoe law firm in Detroit, before entering the Army.

Lt. Harold Robinson, a graduate from the University in chemical engineering, was inducted into the Army in February, 1941, and stationed with the 94th Engineering Battalion at Fort Custer for more than a year. From Custer, he was sent to New Jersey, where he served as provost sergeant, and then was sent to the Edgewood Arsenal, Md., to train in chemical warfare.

Finishing his course in Maryland as lieutenant, he was sent to Camp Sibert, Ala., to Santa Monica, Calif., and back to Camp Sibert, where he is at present.

Mrs. Robinson's third son, Lowell Carlyle, who broke with his family's "Army" tradition and entered the Navy last November, is now stationed at Bainbridge, Md., as a seaman, second class, after taking his basic training at Great Lakes. Lowell, like his other two brothers, received his education in Ann Arbor grade and high schools and at the University.

Another son of Mrs. Robinson, Cpl. Roy Robinson, whom his mother has called "a soldier in the truest sense of the word," died last May at Nichols General Hospital in Louisville, Ky., after being in the Army for six months. He had been sent to Nashville, Tenn., to serve as a technician in the 1008th Quartermaster Unit.

My dad never talked much about his experiences during the war years, except that he never went overseas. But he did once tell me how much he hated being around the noxious chemicals he had to work with, and for that reason would have hated being stuck on that career path, and I assume he must have been talking about the work he did at Edgewood. When he got out of the army, he went to law school and never looked back.

I know that by the end of the war, Francis—my uncle Franz—was in charge of analyzing mortality statistics at a medical division in Livorno, Italy. That made him the only one of the Robinson brothers to serve overseas during the war. I have also learned from army records that Roy was training at an Army Air Forces center in Nashville when he contracted tuberculosis. Taken to the Louisville, Kentucky, hospital for treatment, he died of multiple complications on May 20, 1943.

On my mother's side of the family, my aunt Dorothy—one of my great-uncle Marion's daughters—went into the army and made a distinguished career of it. After the war, she was stationed in Germany and several U.S. posts across Western Europe. She eventually came back to work at the Pentagon, settling into a neat little house near a leafy park in the southeastern quadrant of Washington, across the Anacostia River. Aunt Dorothy never married. She and my mother were close—they were the youngest of the Fordham cousins, almost like sisters—and we visited her often when I was young. I was a bit in awe of her aura of command.

These brief military histories dispel any question anyone might have about the patriotism and sacrifice of African Americans in service to the United States. My grandmother Hattie Robinson sent all four of her boys into the military in wartime. They interrupted their studies and their careers to serve in the still-segregated army and navy, as was their duty. My godfather, Edward Murray, was dispatched all the way to Iran and helped funnel Allied weapons to Stalin's troops. Aunt Dorothy dedicated her life to keeping the nation safe—even though the nation's capital, which was a segregated city, did not welcome her into its finer department stores and restaurants.

In theory, Black World War II veterans were eligible for the college and housing benefits provided by the landmark 1944 G.I. Bill, which is often lauded as the genesis of the American middle class. In practice, however, the fact that the bill distributed its largesse at the local level meant that most African Americans who served in the war were short-changed—and that almost all who lived in the South were simply left out. Segregated universities denied them admission, to no one's surprise, and historically Black colleges could not begin to meet the rush of demand. Mortgage lenders redlined Black neighborhoods, charging prohibitive interest rates or refusing to lend at all. Restrictive covenants in many white neighborhoods mandated that homeowners could not sell their properties to African Americans. For the most part, Black veterans were on their own.

My grandmother Sadie once told me that she was the neighborhood captain for our part of Orangeburg during World War II. She said that her responsibilities included enforcing blackout rules against visible lights, and that she would pull over motorists who were in violation. "Oh yes, and I had a gun, too," she told me.

My mother was skeptical, and so am I. There may indeed have been blackout drills in Orangeburg—they were held in many cities—but there was nothing sustained over any length of time. Ellen remembers that Sadie did have a gun, though—a small antique revolver that looked almost like a toy. Some of my grandmother's stories did take on a measure of embellishment as she got older, and she was in her nineties when she told me about those wartime duties. I'm reminded of what Sadie used to say, with a chuckle, about the process of aging: "When I get old and crazy, just knock me in the head."

IN ORANGEBURG, AS ACROSS the country, the war did abruptly end the Depression. Perhaps the biggest impact was from general stimulation of the agricultural economy, a rising tide that lifted Orangeburg along with other farming centers. Another big boost came from the Hawthorne School of Aeronautics, a civilian flight school five miles south of town that was built under contract with the Army Air Forces as a training center. More than five thousand Allied pilots earned their wings there over the course of the war, including two thousand Free French pilots. The influx of construction crews, trainers, and trainees pumped a steady flow of new money into Orangeburg. After the war, the Hawthorne School closed, and the land was bought by the city; it is now the site of a seven-hundred-acre retirement home called the Oaks.

My father was still in the army right after the war ended, stationed not far from Atlanta. My mother, having graduated from South Carolina State, was earning a degree in library science at Atlanta University. They met at a dance. Louisa was brilliant and beautiful; Harold looked sharp in his lieutenant's uniform and had dreamy "apricot eyes." Both were educated and ambitious. They fell in love.

Harold Robinson soon became one of more than a million Black men and thousands of Black women discharged from military service after World War II. A quarter century earlier, African Americans had come home from World War I brimming with new confidence and bristling with new demands—only to be met with the brutal repression of the Red Summer. Now the numbers of former soldiers, sailors, and marines was far greater; the Black communities they returned to had more capacity and less patience; and the president of the United States was not Woodrow Wilson, a staunch segregationist, but Harry Truman, an unexpected ally in the crusade for equality.

This time, African Americans would press far more insistently for the freedom and opportunity whose outlines they had glimpsed during the war. This time, their demands would be confronted—as so many times before—with violent, implacable resistance. The epic story of the civil rights era—effectively, a third founding of the republic—was set to begin.

Chapter Ten

WHITE SUPREMACY DIGS IN

In January 2012, I wrote a *Washington Post* column that caught my mother's eye. The Martin Luther King Jr. Memorial, with its towering likeness of the civil rights leader, had opened the previous summer and was drawing surprisingly large crowds. I went for a visit and was deeply moved. King's memorial, stretching along the bank of the Tidal Basin, is on a direct line between the marble temples honoring Thomas Jefferson and Abraham Lincoln—architects of the nation's birth, rebirth, and second rebirth, arrayed in an axis of eloquence, all of them inscribed with words that never fail to stir and inspire, no matter how many times you read them. The federal holiday in honor of King's birthday seemed like the right moment for a column that reflected on the new memorial and the universality and timelessness of King's vision.

After the piece appeared, my mother called with a critique: "That was good, but I wonder why you left out that you saw Dr. King speak in person." I reminded her that I had never had that honor—and I wondered, though not out loud, if her steel-trap mind, at ninety, might finally be losing its edge. "Oh yes, you did," she replied without hesitation. "He came here to Orangeburg, to speak at Claflin and Trinity. You were little, but Harold and I went to hear him, and we took you with us."

I was in my late fifties when we had that conversation. It was the first I'd ever heard of Dr. King visiting our city. And it was definitely the first time anyone had suggested, much less insisted, that I had been in his presence.

In journalism, there's an old saying about the imperative of pinning down every single fact: "If your mother says she loves you, check it out." So, I did. I found stories in the archives of the *Times and Democrat* confirming that in 1959, when I was turning five, Dr. King came to Orangeburg. The visit was at the invitation of our pastor at Trinity Methodist Church, the Reverend Matthew D. McCollom, who was a leader of the local NAACP and an active figure in King's civil rights organization, the Southern Christian Leadership Conference. The Reverend McCollom strategized and worked with all the major figures of the movement—Dr. King, Roy Wilkins, Medgar Evers, Ralph Abernathy, Ella Baker, Joseph Lowery, Fred Shuttlesworth, Hosea Williams, John Lewis.

My next step was to call Cecil J. Williams, a remarkable man whom I have known all my life. Cecil is a brilliant photographer who has documented the civil rights movement in South Carolina from the 1950s, when he was a student at Claflin, to the present day—and who ultimately turned his vast, meticulously catalogued archive into the state's only civil rights museum, housed in a striking modern building of his design on the outskirts of Orangeburg. In short order, Cecil tracked down a black-and-white image he had captured of King's 1959 visit to the Claflin campus. It was taken either just before or just after King's speech. Seeing the picture failed to surface any buried memories for me, at least not of King; but shown with him were two men I immediately recognized: the Reverend McCollom, who was tall and thin and wore browline horn-rimmed glasses, just like Malcolm X; and Hubert V. Manning, Claflin's longtime president and my mother's longtime boss. The camera's field of view did not take in the crowd, so there is no photographic evidence that my parents and I were there, but I take my mother's word on that. Later that evening, King gave a second speech at Trinity, hosted of course by the Reverend McCollom.

Today, King is remembered as a martyr for justice, an orator whose speeches schoolchildren learn by heart, a national hero whose contribution and sacrifice we celebrate with the ultimate honor, a holiday of gratitude and contemplation. But in 1959, when I was taken to hear him speak in Orangeburg, he was a highly controversial figure, believed by most white Americans, and some Black Americans, to be pushing too hard for too much too soon. Organizations such as the NAACP and the National Urban League were pressing their demands for racial equality in the halls of power—government offices, federal courtrooms, boardroom suites. King was taking direct action, sending the masses into the streets of southern cities in a campaign of radical, confrontational nonviolence. FBI director J. Edgar Hoover thought King dangerous enough to keep him under surveillance and try mightily to discredit him. King exasperated three presidents—Eisenhower, Kennedy, and Johnson—who all, at times, expressed the wish that he would settle for incremental progress and temper his demands. He was seen not as a statesman but as a revolutionary.

Dr. King returned to Orangeburg in 1964, speaking again at Trinity to civil rights leaders and foot soldiers during an intense wave of protests, sit-ins, and arrests. On that second visit, he lodged with the Served Sultons, the Black family who had owned the big sawmill. My friend Jim Sulton, who is four years my senior, told the *Times and Democrat* that he remembered being annoyed that day at being called inside from the backyard football game he had been playing with siblings, cousins, and neighborhood friends—only to be rendered speechless when he was invited to meet the family's honored guest for the night.

Dr. King's visits to my hometown and my church came when the conflagration of the civil rights movement was roaring full blast. That righteous fire had been sparked nearly a decade before I was born, as the country demobilized from the cataclysmic Second World War. The

United States was wealthier and more powerful than ever before, and a changed nation was about to undergo a wrenching transformation.

ISAAC WOODARD JR. WAS one of the million-plus Black veterans returning to civilian life. Born in South Carolina, Woodard joined the army in 1942 and was shipped off to the Pacific Theater in a labor battalion, a segregated, all-Black unit, where he rose to the rank of sergeant. His was not a combat unit, but nevertheless he spent time in harm's way; he was awarded a commendation, a battle star, for unloading supplies in New Guinea while under enemy fire. Woodard served his country with bravery and distinction. On February 12, 1946, he was given an honorable discharge at Camp Gordon, Georgia, and boarded a Greyhound bus for the three-hundred-mile trip home to Goldsboro, North Carolina, where the family had moved when he was young. He was twenty-six years old.

On the road outside Augusta, early in the bus journey, Woodard had an argument with the white driver: He wanted to stop at a rest area to use the toilet, and the driver wanted to keep going. The driver relented, Woodard relieved himself, and the trip continued without incident—until the bus reached its scheduled stop in Batesburg, South Carolina, about twenty miles west of Columbia. There, the driver had Woodard forcibly removed from the bus by local police, led by Chief Lynwood Shull. The white officers demanded to see Woodard's discharge papers, which were in order, and then took him to an alleyway, where they beat him bloody with nightsticks before formally arresting him for disorderly conduct. That night, in the Batesburg town jail, Shull and his officers clubbed Woodard senseless. During the savage and unprovoked assault, they gouged both his eyes, leaving him permanently blind. (His purported offense, Woodard later testified in court, was at one point responding "yes" to Chief Shull rather than "yes, sir.") The following day, a local judge found Woodard guilty and fined him fifty dollars. He was left to suffer in his cell for two more days before the police finally arranged for a doctor to treat his injuries. Three weeks later, distraught family members who had been searching for Woodard finally found him in a hospital in Aiken, a bigger town not far from Batesburg. Only then was he slowly beginning to recover any memory of what had happened.

The NAACP quickly learned of what had been done to Woodard, and the atrocity was reported widely in the Black press. But it wasn't until white celebrities heard about Woodard's ordeal that the case began to enter the national consciousness. Filmmaker Orson Welles, who had been alerted by the NAACP, reported Woodard's near-fatal beating on his nationally broadcast radio show and returned to the subject again and again, crusading for accountability and change. Folk singer Woody Guthrie joined the battle, writing and recording a new song, "The Blinding of Isaac Woodard." The case became a cause célèbre for white liberals, a vivid and horrifying illustration of the brutal injustice African Americans faced in the South.

For more than half a year, public demands that authorities in South Carolina investigate the case and bring Woodard's torturers to justice were met with stony silence. Finally, in September—a full seven months after the horrific assault—NAACP executive secretary Walter White brought up Woodard's maiming during an Oval Office meeting with President Harry Truman, who knew vaguely of the case but seemed unaware of the details of what had happened to Woodard and of the refusal of state officials to take any action. Outraged, Truman ordered a Justice Department investigation; if state authorities refused to act, he would. Within weeks, police chief Shull and several of his officers were indicted on federal charges. The indictment asserted federal jurisdiction on the grounds that Woodard's arrest had taken place at a bus stop on federal property and that the just-discharged soldier was still in uniform when he was beaten and blinded.

The jurist presiding at the police officers' trial was U.S. district judge Julius Waties Waring, who eventually would strike mighty judicial blows in support of civil rights, with huge repercussions not just in South Carolina but also across the nation. Recalling the case of the Woodard assault years later, Waring denounced the perfunctory case presented by the prosecution as a "disgraceful" sham. The local U.S. attorney was not inclined to disturb the Jim Crow status quo, no matter what President Truman might have wanted; the prosecutor did not even bother to interview potential witnesses, apart from the bus driver. The jury was all white, given that it was unthinkable, in 1946, that African Americans would be empowered to sit in judgment of white men in a South Carolina courtroom. Shull's defense was based on a preposterous claim of self-defense, along with an explicit call for the perpetuation of white supremacy. "If you rule against Shull, then let this South Carolina secede again," Shull's defense lawyer thundered. After deliberating for less than half an hour, the jurors returned the inevitable verdict. Shull and his officers were found not guilty on all charges.

The message sent by this undisguised miscarriage of justice could not have been clearer: Welcome home, Black soldiers, sailors, and marines. For your own sake, we hope you haven't forgotten your place.

In Orangeburg, college students who had served in the military were coming back to the Claflin and South Carolina State campuses to finish their studies. Their numbers, plus the concentration of brainpower at the two colleges, made our town the nerve center and brain trust of the civil rights struggle in South Carolina. One of those returning Black servicemen who came to Orangeburg was an Army Air Forces veteran named John Howard Wrighten. No one assaulted him on his way across the state. Quite the contrary: He was the one who went on the attack.

Wrighten's target was Jim Crow segregation, and the battlefield he chose was federal court. Born on Edisto Island, near Charleston, Wrighten was a graduate of the Avery Institute—the school Major Fordham had attended—and came from a family with a history of activism on behalf of civil rights. After his discharge, he chose a curriculum at South Carolina State that would advance him toward his goal of becoming an attorney. His time at SC State overlapped briefly with my mother's. I never got the chance to ask her about him, but I would be surprised if they had not known each other, at least in passing. At historically Black colleges, everybody knows everybody.

In 1946, Wrighten completed his bachelor's degree and applied for admission to the law school of the University of South Carolina, the state's flagship institution of higher learning. He knew in advance what the response would be: As had been the case with every Black applicant to the state's white colleges and universities, he was rejected because of his race.

Wrighten sued the university in U.S. District Court on grounds that his rejection violated his constitutional right to equal protection under the law as guaranteed by the Fourteenth Amendment. The NAACP saw this as an important test case, and one of the organization's bravest and most brilliant lawyers, future Supreme Court justice Thurgood Marshall, was sent down to South Carolina from New York to argue on Wrighten's behalf. It was one of the many times Marshall and other NAACP lawyers risked their lives in the South, where they were in constant danger, in order to speak truth to power.

The federal judge who presided over the case was none other than Waring, from the Isaac Woodard case. On Wrighten's suit, Waring declared in his ruling that the issue of racial segregation was "of immense interest and importance under the American constitutional guarantees and the American idea of liberty and equality"—a statement that sounds tame and tentative today but was controversial, and even dangerous, for a white man to make in the South in 1946.

Waring wrote that he was forced to ignore that fundamental question of constitutional rights, however, because the Supreme Court had blessed separate-but-equal segregation in *Plessy v. Ferguson* and had upheld that precedent in subsequent cases. And there was no doubt that as far as the state of South Carolina was concerned, segregation was the law: The state constitution mandated that "no child of either race shall ever be permitted to attend a school provided for children of the other race." The University of South Carolina's charter specified that it be operated "exclusively for white students." And another state law—as if further clarification were needed—made it "unlawful for pupils of one race to attend the schools provided by boards of trustees for persons of another race." There was nothing simply circumstantial or de facto about the university's whites-only policy; it was de jure, by law, specified in triplicate. Waring felt he could do nothing about it.

However, he wrote, the separate-but-equal doctrine required that the state provide Wrighten and other African Americans with legal education of "complete equality and parity with that furnished to whites." He found it inconsistent with the Supreme Court's prior rulings for the state of South Carolina to offer Black students no legal education at all, while offering white students a fully accredited public law school with state-built facilities and state-subsidized tuition. Waring decided not just to take the words of *Plessy* and other Supreme Court decisions literally but to put them into action. He ordered that the state choose and proceed with one of three options: It could establish a law school for Black students that was the equal of the law school reserved exclusively for whites. It could admit Wrighten and other qualified African American applicants to the University of South Carolina School of Law. Or it could close the whites-only law school and offer legal education to neither race.

As far as the governor and state legislators of South Carolina were concerned, the simple and cost-free option of granting Wrighten admission was every bit as unthinkable as shutting down the state's most prestigious law school. Instead, they went with the separate-but-equal option. In the fall of 1947, just months after Waring's ruling, a hastily built law school exclusively for Black students opened its doors in Orangeburg at South Carolina State. The school consisted of a dean, three faculty members—graduates of such top-ranked universities as Harvard and Howard—and a grand total of four students.

Wrighten was not one of those students; he refused to enroll, arguing that the new school was not "substantially equal" to the University of South Carolina law school, which had 342 students and a full complement of faculty and administrators. In the end, though, Waring ruled that at present it was "almost impossible to intellectually compare" the two schools, since the SC State law school was just getting off the ground. He found, reluctantly, that the state government had done enough to keep the federal judiciary at bay.

Was the outcome of the *Wrighten* case a win or a loss for the movement? On balance, definitely a win. The NAACP and Wrighten managed to get the case heard by Waring, a judge known to be sympathetic to their cause. The ideal result would have been a decision that undermined the legal foundations of racial segregation. In that sense, the plaintiffs failed; Waring did not challenge precedent and make a far-reaching ruling that mandated integration. But he did push the envelope by insisting on a literal interpretation of the "equal" part of separate but equal, and he did it in a way that cast the absurdity of *Plessy v. Ferguson* in stark relief. The state was forced to quickly cobble together a whole new law school to avoid letting one young Black man sit in a classroom with whites. That was good enough to pass legal muster for now, but Waring had laid the groundwork for a potential future lawsuit forcing the state to demonstrate that the SC State law school had "complete equality and parity" with the whites-only law school.

Meanwhile, it had cost the state government $200,000 for the building that housed the new law school in Orangeburg, along with a further $30,000 to fill the shelves of its law library. Judge Waring, who continued to monitor the state's compliance with his ruling, observed that this was a remarkable amount of money to spend for no purpose other than "to prevent the meeting of whites and Negroes in classrooms." Even some white law school students complained that building a duplicative Blacks-only facility was needlessly wasteful. When state legislators held a hearing about the costs, the dean of the University of South Carolina law school, Samuel Prince, replied, "Gentlemen, well, I'll tell you, the price of prejudice is very high."

In the end, most African Americans in South Carolina who wanted to become attorneys continued to go away to well-known, long-established law schools outside the segregated South. In its brief existence—the University of South Carolina law school finally integrated in 1964—the SC State law school graduated fewer than a hundred lawyers. Its graduates did include some prominent, barrier-breaking jurists, however, including Matthew J. Perry, the first African American lawyer from the South to be appointed to the federal bench; and Ernest A. Finney Jr., who eventually became chief justice of the South Carolina Supreme Court.

The *Wrighten* case was important, but it turned out to be a warm-up act before the main event: Thurgood Marshall was back before Waring in 1950, representing the plaintiffs in a federal lawsuit, known as *Briggs v. Elliott,* that changed the nation. It was the first of several cases that were eventually consolidated under the title *Brown v. Board of Education*—the first direct, frontal constitutional challenge to the separate-but-equal doctrine and of racial segregation itself in U.S. public schools.

The plaintiffs were the parents of twenty Black students in Clarendon County, which abuts Orangeburg County to the east; the name of Harry Briggs, a gas station attendant, came first in the list. The defendant was R. W. Elliott, chairman of the Clarendon County school board. Originally, the suit's demand was the same as in the *Wrighten* case: literal enforcement of the requirement that public services for African Americans be equal to those for whites. In Clarendon County, typically for the state, white students rode buses to clean, well-supplied schools that were fully staffed. Black students were offered no transportation to makeshift school buildings, where a single teacher might be responsible for instructing more than sixty students, using a handful of tattered, hand-me-down textbooks. Marshall filed the case knowing that Waring would be the judge who heard it and who would likely issue an order forcing Clarendon County to provide much better facilities for African American students.

But when *Briggs v. Elliott* arrived on his docket, Waring did something highly unusual—and, strictly speaking, highly improper. The judge invited Marshall to a private meeting, ex parte, just the two of them. Waring urged him not to file another separate-but-equal lawsuit, like the *Wrighten* case, but to go much farther. He believed the time had come to make a "frontal attack on segregation" by starting a process that would force the Supreme Court to reconsider *Plessy v. Ferguson.*

It was an invitation Marshall could hardly refuse. He rewrote the lawsuit, making it into a demand to outlaw segregation in the schools, and filed it anew in 1951. The case was argued before a panel of three U.S. District Court judges, one of whom was Waring, and the plaintiffs lost 2–1. Marshall and Waring had anticipated this would happen, as the other two judges considered themselves bound by the long-standing *Plessy* precedent. Believing the time had come for *Plessy* to fall, Waring wrote a thunderous dissent in which he made a historic pronouncement that crystallized the stakes of the great civil rights struggle—"segregation is *per se* inequality." Marshall's appeal of that adverse ruling was lumped together with four other suits that similarly challenged the *Plessy* separate-but-equal precedent, including one from Kansas called *Brown v. Board of Education*; for procedural reasons, that became the umbrella title for one of the most important cases ever decided by the U.S. Supreme Court. In 1954, the year of my birth, the Court ruled in *Brown* that government-mandated segregation in public schools violated the Constitution. It was the original *Briggs* case—arising from the county next door to Orangeburg—that marked the beginning of the end for Jim Crow apartheid in the United States.

By then Judge Waring was receiving frequent death threats at his home in Charleston. His skin color and official position gave him a measure of protection that a target like Marshall, an "uppity" Black man from the alien North, could never enjoy. Still, the judge had put himself and his family at considerable risk by challenging white supremacy so directly. The judge eventually moved to New York and became a vocal proponent of radical change. "The cancer of segregation," he once told an audience in Harlem, "will never be cured by the sedative of gradualism." His ultimate vindication in his hometown took another half century to arrive: In 2015, during the second term of the first Black president of the United States, the federal courthouse in Charleston was renamed the J. Waties Waring Judicial Center.

HAVING MADE THE GREAT Migration trek as a child, from northeastern Georgia to southeastern Michigan, my father did something unusual, something almost incomprehensible as an army veteran in his thirties: He traced the Great Migration route in reverse and moved permanently to South Carolina, returning to the second-class citizenship he had once escaped, just as the unholy system of Jim Crow segregation was making its desperate and violent last stand.

He did it for the woman he loved, with whom he would go on to happily spend the rest of his life, and I don't believe he ever had a moment's regret. A disinterested observer might have seen his decision as a sacrifice. My father had done most of his undergraduate studies at the University of Michigan, then finished his degree at Wayne State University in Detroit. He had gone on to Wayne State University's law school and graduated with the degree of Juris Doctor. His older brother, my uncle Franz, was a University of Michigan Law School graduate and already working as a successful Detroit attorney, and he could have opened doors for my father in the city's legal community. Harold Robinson could have had a career as a big-city lawyer, and I have no doubt he would have done well. He had an elephant's memory and seemed to know everything about everything, from history to geography to literature to chemistry to physics. If he had been fated to stay in Michigan, he still would have faced racism and discrimination. But as far as the law was concerned, at least, he would have been the equal of any other man. And whenever he boarded a bus, he would have been able to sit wherever he damn well pleased.

The 1952 wedding of Louisa Gertrude Smith and Harold Irwin Robinson was reported in the society pages of the African American press. They "were united in marriage at the home of her parents," reported the *Pittsburgh Courier*, a widely circulated Black weekly. "The vows were spoken in a double-ring ceremony before the Rev. Matthew D. McCollom, pastor of Trinity Methodist Church." My mother was described as "lovely in a ballerina-length dress of white nylon net and Chantilly lace over white satin, designed with close fitted bodice and lace bolero with long sleeves ending in points over the hands." Her cousin, army lieutenant Dorothy Fordham, served as the maid of honor; she had come all the way from California, where she was posted at the time, for the ceremony. My father's best man was Eugene Montgomery, my mother's cousin on her father's side. Louisa was given away, of course, by her father, Eugene Smith. A photograph above the story in the *Courier* shows the smiling couple in the traditional pose with their tiered wedding cake.

A family photo shows them leaving the house after the ceremony and reception, coming down the front steps as guests and family see them off. They were hardly kids—she was about to turn thirty-one, he was already thirty-six—but it was the first marriage for each. This would seem to suggest a measure of independence and autonomy in both their natures, but I think the fact that they married late had more to do with the way the war interrupted so many lives. From that day forward, until parted by death, they were all but inseparable for the next fifty-seven years.

After their postwar first meeting in Atlanta, Louisa and Harold had kept in touch, mostly through correspondence. While he completed his education, she finished earning her second bachelor's degree, this one in library science, from historically Black Atlanta University. She got a job as a librarian at Allen University, a small HBCU in Columbia, but decided that to have a meaningful career in her chosen field she needed a master's degree. There was no nearby Black college that offered the kind of program she wanted, which meant she would have to go to some faraway school. Surely with the most ulterior of motives, her suitor Harold strongly urged her to consider the University of Michigan. The great institution of higher learning that just happened to be up the street from his mother's house, where he just happened to be living while commuting to Detroit for law school, also just happened to offer an advanced master's degree in library science. And because the practice in Ann Arbor was that African American students did not reside in the dormitories—discrimination was practiced in the North as well as the South—Harold, with all his family's local connections, would have no problem finding a respectable Black household where Louisa could find room and board at a reasonable price.

My father was a good salesman. In 1950, Louisa left her job and headed to Michigan. It was her first experience being in an integrated situation of any kind. In an oral history recorded half a century later, she recalled—it would be hard to forget—that she was the only African American in many of her classes. When students were assigned to work on projects in groups, she told the interviewer, she was left on her own—at first. "When they found that I could carry my weight, all of that changed," she said. She reported not having felt discriminated against in any way by her professors, and it took her just a year of hard work to earn the degree. Louisa went back to working at Allen University. But by then she and Harold were engaged—and planning a future together far away.

After the wedding in 1952, she resigned from her job in Columbia, and the couple attempted—Louisa, perhaps half-heartedly—to live in Harold Robinson's world. They moved to Detroit, where he started the process of establishing himself as an attorney. Unable to find work in any of Detroit's university libraries, Louisa took a job as librarian at George Washington Carver Elementary School, located in an African American neighborhood of Oak Park, a Detroit suburb. Louisa described her year of working in Michigan as an ordeal she was glad to survive and leave behind. She was accustomed to dealing with civilized college students, not with children whom she found bratty and disrespectful. That was bad enough, but in the oral history, she complained more about the weather. Having spent her whole life in the South, she found the frigid, endless, snowbound, bleak, punishing Detroit winter to be simply intolerable.

Life intervened to short-circuit the couple's plans, and ultimately to change the trajectory of their lives. First, Louisa got pregnant with me.

And then, in January 1954, two months before I was due, the father who had doted on his only child, Eugene Smith, suddenly died. Harold and Louisa went home for the funeral, and she began to feel that Orangeburg was the place she needed to be. Her mother, Sadie, and her Aunt Doc were both past retirement age, and now they were alone in the big Fordham house—without her father to take care of all the maintenance the house required. And in any event, it hardly seemed to make sense to go all the way back to Detroit when she was expecting a baby to arrive within weeks. After I was born, Claflin University offered Louisa a position in its library, and as a sweetener, they offered Harold an adjunct teaching job. He agreed that he and Louisa should give living in Orangeburg a try, and they never left.

I've always wondered whether my father's lifelong commitment to putting family first, above ambition or work or pleasure or anything else, was at least in part a reaction to his own father's absence. He adored my grandmother and great-aunt; and while he had brothers and a sister back in Michigan to help with his own aging mother, Louisa was an only child who now felt responsible for a widowed mother in her sixties and a never-married aunt in her seventies. Harold and Louisa moved into the front upstairs bedroom, overlooking Boulevard, where they could see the Claflin campus through the window. Decades earlier, my father had escaped Jim Crow. Now, by moving south, he was enlisting in the fight to end it.

IN 1944, DURING THE war, the South Carolina legislature had passed a resolution upholding "White Supremacy as now prevailing in the South." In language that deliberately echoed that of the Declaration of Independence, the lawmakers pledged their "lives and our sacred honor" to maintain white supremacy, "whatever the cost, in War and Peace." Since the system of white rule was maintained through the enforcement of laws, it was a vital imperative to keep those laws unchanged. And the way to keep the laws in place, and also to ensure they were enforced in a way that preserved the status quo, was to erect as many barriers as possible between African Americans and the ballot box, where they might elect the "wrong" people to office. Where they might even, unthinkable as it was, elect their own kind.

The separate-but-equal *Plessy v. Ferguson* framework did not permit the denial of voting rights to African Americans, but the states of the former Confederacy had always been creative in getting past that inconvenience. Because the Democratic Party was all-powerful in the South, winning the Democratic nomination for almost any office was tantamount to election. When the Supreme Court ruled in 1944 that whites-only primary elections were unacceptable, the South Carolina state legislature rushed to amend or repeal any laws on the books dealing with primaries—not to comply with the Supreme Court decision but to defy it. The pretense was that the South Carolina Democratic Party was nothing more than a private association, akin to a social club, and thus had the right to choose the "members" who were allowed to vote in its primaries. The Charleston *News and Courier* applauded the effort:

> Were hordes of negroes admitted to white primaries in South Carolina, it would cease to be a commonwealth safe for respectable persons, white or colored, to live in. The News and Courier advocates greatly increased restrictions of suffrage. . . . Until the people shall arrive at the conclusion that voting is a privilege, not a right, and act upon it, complete political separation of the white and colored people, in party activities and primaries, must continue, must be maintained.

But in 1947, a Black man named George Elmore filed suit in federal court after being barred from voting in the previous year's Democratic primary election. The case was heard by Judge Waring, segregation's nemesis, who called the idea that the Democratic Party was a private social club "pure sophistry." In his ruling ordering the party to open its primaries to all, he wrote that "racial distinctions cannot exist in the machinery that selects the officers and lawmakers of the United States, and all citizens of this state and country are entitled to cast a free and untrammeled ballot in our elections."

The state's fallback position was to turn away any would-be voter who refused to swear an oath to preserve "the social, religious, and educational separation of the races." Waring struck that down, too, in 1948.

Across the state, despite Ku Klux Klan cross burnings and a host of other threats, thirty-five thousand African Americans were brave enough to cast ballots in the 1948 presidential election won by Harry Truman. And in 1950, Black voters provided the slim margin by which Strom Thurmond, the segregationist "Dixiecrat" who was then the state's governor, went down to defeat in his first attempt to win a Senate seat.

Thurmond was defeated in the Democratic primary—no longer legally barred to Black voters—by incumbent senator Olin Johnston, whom Thurmond attacked for not adequately defending white supremacy in Washington's halls of power. Thurmond's loudest complaint was that Johnston had been "silent as a tomb" about the executive order signed by President Truman on July 26, 1948, that mandated integration of the U.S. armed forces. Thurmond portrayed this as the most outrageous insult to white sensibilities since Radical Reconstruction, and he blasted Johnston as "soft on segregation."

That was not true. Johnston, like the great majority of southern elected officials, was a staunch supporter of racial segregation and the eternal supremacy of the white race. He responded by accusing Thurmond of the same unpardonable sin: While he was governor, Thurmond had appointed a Black doctor, T. C. McFall, to the South Carolina state medical advisory board, making him the first African American since Reconstruction to be named to a statewide position, albeit an advisory one. Johnston told a crowd in Charleston that he, for his part, "never would have appointed the nigger physician"—and when African Americans in the audience booed Johnston's slur, he shouted that someone should "make those niggers keep quiet." Black South Carolinians knew about this incident, but they gave Johnston their votes as the lesser of two evils. Johnston had been more progressive than Thurmond on economic issues. More important, Thurmond had used his public platform as governor to make himself one of the country's leading enemies of civil rights, and he had run for president in 1948 as a third-party candidate—representing the States' Rights Democratic Party, the "Dixiecrats"—on a platform that called for eternal segregation. African Americans decided to use their votes to punish him.

Thurmond was a loser that time, but he ran again and won his Senate seat in 1954. After resigning in 1956 for a few months (to fulfill a campaign promise), he won the seat again later that year—and remained in the U.S. Senate, representing South Carolina, until January 2003, when he finally retired. He was one hundred years old. His mental acuity had been declining for years, even by the Senate's geriatric standards. It must have been work that kept him alive, because five months after he went home to Edgefield, South Carolina, the town where he had been born, Strom Thurmond died.

More than any other individual in the state, Thurmond personified implacable white resistance to racial integration. When I was growing up, the adults in my house did not curse. But I recall one exception: My grandmother, talking with one or another of her friends, might refer to "that damn old Strom Thurmond"—especially in the afternoons, after her midday can of beer.

Black South Carolinians may have deemed him evil, but nobody thought Thurmond was stupid. After the Civil Rights Act and the Voting Rights Act were finally enacted, and after it became clear that these laws would be enforced, Thurmond saw the handwriting on the wall. He may have loved segregation and white supremacy, but he loved power and privilege more. And he realized that to keep that power, he would have to win elections in a state where African Americans voted in decisive numbers.

All the while, Thurmond had a secret—a big secret that the world didn't learn until many years later. Most of the world, that is. In 2003, a few months after his death, a colleague of mine at *The Washington Post,* Marilyn Thompson, reported in a stunning front-page story that Thurmond was the father of a daughter he had conceived with his family's Black housekeeper when he was twenty-two. By then in her seventies, the daughter, Essie Mae Washington-Williams, confirmed the story—as did Thurmond's family. I raced to the phone to call my family in Orangeburg and tell them the news.

My mother's reaction was silence. "Well," she finally said, "we thought you knew."

Apparently, the existence of Thurmond's biracial love child was an open secret among my mother's friends in Orangeburg—though not open enough for anyone to mention it to the only journalist in the family. Thurmond had never publicly acknowledged his daughter, but neither had he ever privately denied her. The mother, Carrie Butler, was sixteen when Essie Mae was born; Carrie sent the infant away to be raised by relatives in Pennsylvania, and Essie Mae was thirteen when she learned that her father was one of the most vehement proponents of segregation and white supremacy in the country. When she reached college age, Thurmond paid all costs for her to attend SC State. One of my mother's coworkers at the Claflin University library had attended college with Essie Mae and had told everyone about an occasion when Thurmond visited his daughter on campus. A big black chauffeur-driven car pulled up at the dormitory, a door opened, and there, visible in the back seat for all to see, was the nationally prominent politician who railed against the evils of "miscegenation" and decried the "mixing of the races." Essie Mae got into the car, which drove away, and her father spent the afternoon with her like any visiting parent, asking how she was adjusting to college life and whether she was keeping up with her studies. After the talk was done, the big black car brought her back to campus.

That scene took place in 1947, a year after Isaac Woodard had been bludgeoned and blinded—and a year before Thurmond ran for president on a platform of permanent separation of the races.

"I want to tell you," Thurmond declared in his campaign, "that there's not enough troops in the army to force the southern people to break down segregation and admit the Negro race into our theaters, into our swimming pools, into our homes, and into our churches." He made no mention of bedrooms.

Chapter Eleven

THE MOVEMENT GATHERS STRENGTH

I was born March 12, 1954, in the "Colored" maternity wing of Orangeburg Regional Hospital, which had separate facilities for whites and African Americans. My mother told me that I was born with a caul, a fragment of the amniotic membrane, covering my face, which is a harmless and fairly rare condition thought by some cultures to be a sign of good fortune. She mentioned this only once, late in her life, which makes me think she didn't put much stock in that superstition. (But in Cuba I did happen to mention the caul once to a *babalawo*, a priest of the Yoruba-Cuban faith, who said it meant I was blessed.)

Everyone agrees that I was a hyperactive child—which was just a description at the time, not a diagnosis. If I'd been born a few decades later, the adults surely would have dosed me with Ritalin for breakfast, lunch, and dinner. Back then, other ways had to be found to deal with a smart-aleck kid who was constantly in motion and wouldn't give anyone a moment's peace.

There was the television, of course, a "console" model in the family room—a hulking piece of furniture with a black-and-white screen only slightly bigger than that of a modern laptop. *Captain Kangaroo* and *Howdy Doody* would reliably keep me rapt and motionless for a while. If nothing I wanted to watch was on, I could amuse myself with a length of rope, learning to twirl a lariat like my cowboy heroes; I got pretty good at it, but getting me to play at rodeo bought the adults only a half hour's peace, tops. Sometimes my parents would send me outside to crawl around in the grass and try to find a four-leaf clover, which they told me was very good luck. That could keep me busy for a good while, since we had a lot of lawn, counting both the front yard and the side yard that used to be the Fordham "croquet ground." Once in a great while, I found one, but I never reaped the windfall I thought I'd been promised: the sudden appearance of a rainbow with a leprechaun's pot of gold at the end.

My grandmother, who had the gift of blarney, came up with a diversion that was more creative and amusing, at least for her: She convinced me that I could catch a bird if I got close enough to put salt on its tail. I would grab the saltshaker, run out the back door and down the steps, and spend what seemed like hours trying to sneak up on sparrows, robins, and blue jays to sprinkle their tails with Morton. I couldn't understand why the birds somehow always flew away just before I got within range. Occasionally I'd look up at the kitchen window in exasperation. Sadie would smile and motion for me to try again.

Sadie also used her storytelling talents to keep me safe, which was not a trivial problem, given my propensity to be here one minute and gone the next, heaven knew where. One time, when I must have been three or four, my father took me to the barbershop and left me there for a few minutes; he needed to dash around the corner to the post office while my hair was being cut. I got bored—I hated sitting still with nothing to do—and so, logically, I decided to leave. My father was just coming back from his errand when he saw me running down the sidewalk in the general direction of our house, with the barber's cape flying behind me like a sail. The poor barber was running after me in frantic pursuit.

The railroad tracks across Boulevard from our house were an obvious hazard. They lay between me and the Claflin University campus, where my mother and father both worked, and it was not out of the realm of imagination that some weekday morning, when my grandmother was busy cooking, I might up and decide to pay one of them a visit. To discourage that, Sadie told me a grisly story about the "bad little boy who didn't listen" and ran across those very same tracks, got hit by a train, and "that was the end of him." Another little boy, she said, didn't even make it as far as the tracks, because he was hit by a car when he was disobedient and tried to cross Boulevard without an adult.

To keep me from wandering off down Oak Street—which was only one block long and had little traffic, but got a bit sketchy down at the other end—she told me about another bad little boy who had been killed right there on Oak, just a few houses away, by a pack of ferocious dogs. (The truth was that our own dog, an ill-tempered spitz named Rambler, was probably the most likely canine in the neighborhood to try to bite someone.) And because Sadie worried about thunderstorms—sometimes I would play in the most distant part of our property, the mid-block lots we called "way out back," where I couldn't hear her if she called—she told me the story of yet *another* bad boy who didn't run fast enough to get inside when he heard thunder and who got struck by lightning and killed. None of this gory fiction made me think there was anything wrong with disobedience on the conceptual level. But it did keep me from disobeying in the specific ways these unfortunate little boys had done, because I certainly didn't want to get run over, mauled, or electrocuted.

When my sister, Ellen, came along, Sadie came up with another story to keep her from going up into the attics. She told her that some kind of ogre named Eli lived up there, and at the same time she'd stamp her feet to make ogre-like noises. Sadie's tales were hardly in keeping with modern ideas about child-rearing, but neither of us ended up with any phobias about trains, cars, dogs, lightning, or attics.

Reading came to me naturally, almost automatically, and at an early age. My father claimed that he and my mother didn't really teach me. He said I used to sit on his lap at the breakfast table every morning while he read to me from the *Times and Democrat*, and one day, when I was four, he stopped to eat a forkful of grits—and I just kept reading the newspaper aloud where he had left off. That was surely an exaggeration, but I don't remember ever *not* being able to read. Words on a page just always seemed to make sense.

As soon as I was aware of the world outside our house, I was aware of the strictures of Jim Crow. I understood generally, even before I was old enough to go to school, that white people were powerful and that people who looked like my family were uncomfortable around them. I did not think of us as Black; we were Negroes, or Colored people. And I knew there were privileges white people had that we did not.

There was a movie theater downtown, on Russell Street, but my father said we couldn't go there; Black people were admitted but could sit only in the balcony, and my parents would not accept those terms. There was a swimming pool down near the Edisto River, but we couldn't go there, either; African Americans were not allowed. The county fair we went to every year, the Black fair, was in the northeast corner of town. I loved everything about it except the Ferris wheel, which for some reason I found so terrifying that my father had to get the operator to stop the ride after one revolution to let me off. (I hate Ferris wheels to this day.) The white county fair, in the south end beyond the colleges and the business district, looked much bigger and brighter, and I was sure it would have been even more fun, but of course we were not allowed to go. Sometimes on Sunday afternoons, the family would take a ride around the city, and I could see that the white neighborhoods had bigger, newer houses, with bigger, newer cars parked in the driveways. I knew that there were no Black people living in those neighborhoods, just as I knew that there were no white people living in ours.

My mother liked to go shopping at the stores on Russell Street, and I remember that when we went into Phillips shoe store, we would always be waited on in an area toward the back of the store—not in a similar try-on area near the front. Walking down the street in our little business district, sometimes I'd see something in a window and beg to go inside, but my mother would tell me no, we wouldn't go in, because "they're prejudiced." I didn't know exactly what that meant, but I knew it wasn't good.

When I was five, my whole life changed. Before then, I had a settled routine. The family would all get up and have breakfast, and then my parents and Aunt Doc would go off to their jobs on the Claflin campus. I would spend the morning amusing myself by playing with toys, watching television, and trying to put salt on birds' tails, while my grandmother cooked and baked. If she was making something sweet, like pound cake or gingerbread, she'd call me in and let me use my fingers to savor the traces of batter left in her big earthenware mixing bowl. Around twelve thirty, my parents and Aunt Doc would come home for dinner, the big midday meal, which we would eat at the large table in the dining room. Then my parents and Aunt Doc would go back to work, and I'd spend the afternoon having more fun. At five thirty or so, everyone would come home again; we'd have supper, we'd watch television for a while, and eventually I'd be sent to bed.

The first change was that suddenly I had a sister: Ellen was born the summer of 1959, on July 10. I remember my father driving me, my grandmother, and Aunt Doc past Orangeburg Hospital and pointing up at the window of my mother's room. She was smiling and holding up the newest member of our family. After Ellen came home, I remember that the crying baby seemed to require all the adults' attention, all the time. I remember a stream of visitors coming to make nonsensical noises over Ellen, and I remember that my mother's regular schedule of going to and from work at the Claflin library was disrupted. I loved the new baby. And I also loved the fact that she was the center of attention, which meant I could be in my own world, bringing the shows I watched on television to life. I won gunfights by beating imaginary outlaws to the draw with my twin Roy Rogers six-guns. I brought imaginary cattle rustlers to justice with my Chuck Connors *The Rifleman* rifle. I went swashbuckling around the yard, threatening imaginary banditos with my Zorro plastic sword, which I wielded while wearing my flat-brimmed black Zorro hat, my flowing black Zorro cape, and my identity-concealing black Zorro mask.

The other big change came at the end of the summer. One morning, my parents got me dressed and took me out with them in the morning. They stopped the car at Trinity, our church—but it was a weekday, not a Sunday. They led me down to the big community room in the basement, where I saw some boys and girls my age, and presented me to a lady I had never met before. It was my first day at kindergarten.

Which I absolutely hated. Being in kindergarten was unbearably boring. The lady was always telling me to sit down and be quiet, which was torture. She insisted on teaching us how to sound out and spell words I already knew. She didn't have any books that I wanted to read, and she didn't have any toys that I found interesting to play with. Worst of all, she expected us all to lie down and take a nap, right there in Trinity's basement, in the middle of the day. I thought the whole thing was a waste of my time, so one morning I escaped—as I had done at the barbershop—and ran the three blocks home. Later, I couldn't understand why my grandmother and my parents were so angry. All I had done was make what I saw as a perfectly reasonable decision.

The next day, when my parents called upstairs to wake me so I could be taken back to kindergarten, I ignored them and pretended I was still asleep. The ploy didn't work; my father came and got me out of bed. But I was nothing if not persistent, so I tried the same subterfuge again the following day, and the day after that, both times without success. Then one day, finally, my still-sleeping act worked like a charm: They let me stay in bed. I came downstairs when the coast was clear—after my dad had left for work—and went back to my happy routine of playing around the house. The following Monday, I did the act again. This time, the failure was catastrophic.

My parents got me up, made me put on some new clothes they had bought over the weekend, and took me in the car with them. But instead of heading down Boulevard to Trinity, they crossed the railroad tracks and drove to an unfamiliar building on the South Carolina State campus. I asked where we were, and they said, "Felton." More formally: Felton Training School. Because I had refused to go to kindergarten, they were punishing me by sending me to first grade.

That was what it felt like that first day, punishment by incarceration. Everything at Felton was so regimented and so alien. I had to sit at a desk and stay put; I didn't know any of the other kids; there were certain tasks we had to do at certain times, whether we felt like it or not; we had to keep quiet while the teacher was talking. And the teacher, Mrs. Flossie Clinkscales, was much scarier than the lady at kindergarten. Mrs. Clinkscales threatened to enforce her arbitrary and unfair diktats with an eighteen-inch wooden ruler she carried as she stalked around the room like a prison guard with a nightstick. At lunch, which was in a separate building behind the school, there were even more kids than just the ones in my classroom, and some of them were really big. And the food we were served in the lunchroom wasn't nearly as good as my grandmother's.

On the positive side, though, at least there were some books at school that I hadn't already read. And in the afternoon, we did something I actually enjoyed: Mrs. Clinkscales darkened the room by turning off the lights and pulling down shades to cover the windows, and she projected a filmstrip onto a big screen. I had never seen that done before, and it was like magic. The words in the filmstrip that she wanted us to read were easy, but the pictures and the story were fun. It seemed like an eternity before a loud bell rang, everybody stood up, we all went outside, and we stood there waiting for a while until our parents came to pick us all up. I decided, in the end, that it had been a mixed experience, going to first grade. Not great, but not all bad. It wasn't until my parents woke me up the next morning and took me back to Felton that I realized the deal with this whole first-grade thing wasn't one and done. I was highly upset that I had to do it again—and that this would be my permanent routine. It took me a couple of weeks to settle in.

Felton was better from then on, though. Actually, not just better: It was the best. Felton Training School gave me the kind of rigorous yet nurturing education I would wish for every child, and I would put it up against any elementary school in the world.

Felton was not one of the underfunded "Colored" public schools. South Carolina State had a teachers' college, and Felton was operated as a laboratory school where aspiring young educators could get practical experience and test-run new theories and methods. Constructed in 1925, the building was a "Rosenwald" schoolhouse—one of five thousand schools for African Americans across the South that were designed and financed by Julius Rosenwald, a Chicago philanthropist whose fortune came from his ownership stake in Sears, Roebuck and Company. Felton had just four huge, airy classrooms, with big windows to admit lots of natural light. In each classroom, a single full-time teacher—one experienced, professional, utterly brilliant teacher—gave instruction to two grades. Mrs. Clinkscales taught first and second grade; Mrs. Lovely M. White taught third and fourth; Mrs. Gwendolyn Edwards taught fifth and sixth; and Mrs. Alba Lewis, who lived two doors down Boulevard from our house, taught seventh and eighth. They were assisted, at times, by young SC State education students, whom we called "practice teachers." The principal, who had an office at one end of the building, was Mrs. Maxine Crawford—a member of the Sulton family and one of my mother's oldest and best friends.

Having just one teacher and one classroom for every two grades might sound like a deficit or a hardship, but in the Felton teachers' expert hands, the system worked brilliantly. The classes were small, roughly fifteen students per grade. When Mrs. Clinkscales was actively engaged with the first graders in their cluster on one side of the room, she would have the second graders doing a quiet assignment in their workbooks. Any talking or laughing behind her back would be squelched by a withering stare and a flourish of that long, stinging eighteen-inch ruler. The genius of the system was that she had the flexibility to move students around. A student who had mastered first-grade arithmetic could be taken by the hand and led over to the second graders' cluster for math lessons with them.

A second-grade student who needed remedial work in reading could be taken to the first-grade side of the room to review fundamentals. And for some activities, like filmstrips or craft projects, the two classes could be blended into one.

I got taken over to the second-grade side of Mrs. Clinkscales's room a lot. Finally, after a few weeks, she just left me there—for the rest of the school year. And after the summer break, when the new school year began, I was sent on to third grade.

I was six, and my classmates were eight. I assume that there must have been discussion among my parents, the teachers, and the principal to decide whether it was right to lock in that two-year age gap between me and the rest of my cohort. I was not consulted, but moving me along is the choice I would have made. I had already spent so much time with the rising third graders that I knew them better than the rising second graders, and the older kids had accepted me as a member of their group. It helped that I was tall for my age—tall, in fact, for my new, older cohort: I was one of the few in the class assigned slightly bigger desks because we had outgrown the standard ones. Physically, at least, I wouldn't be a minnow among sharks.

The teachers were strict about keeping order, each in her own way. Mrs. Clinkscales had that ruler; and, yes, she used it. Mrs. White would grab a misbehaving student by the shoulders and threaten to "shake your liver loose," which I absolutely believed she was ready and able to do. Mrs. Edwards had a way of freezing you with a stare she must have learned from Medusa; the kids all said she had "the evil eye." And Mrs. Lewis, who had the seventh and eighth graders, the oldest kids, practiced a kind of pedagogical jujitsu, treating pubescent boys and girls as if we were young adults and expecting us to display preternatural maturity and seriousness of purpose. She, especially, didn't have to worry about any trouble from me, since she lived practically next door and also went to our church. Between her and Mrs. Crawford, news of any misbehavior reached my parents before I got home from school.

My best friend in the lower grades was Jimmy Sherman, and thinking of him reminds me of the kind of expectations that weighed on us and that ultimately lifted us up. Jimmy's father, who taught at SC State, felt he needed a PhD to further his academic career. Since South Carolina's comprehensive universities, USC and Clemson, admitted whites only, Mr. Sherman—like most of the scholars at State and Claflin, including my mother—had no choice but to pursue his studies far from the segregated South. He chose the University of Oklahoma, and for several years while I was at Felton, Jimmy's dad would periodically spend weeks or months halfway across the country, leaving his wife to manage the household and their three sons. One afternoon, as all the parents were picking us up after school, I remember hearing several of them chatting about my friend's father in a way that struck me as cruel, even at my young age. They were asking what was "wrong with Sherman" that it was taking him so long to complete that degree. Surely he must be done with all the coursework, so was he having some kind of issue with his thesis? I remember one parent sniffing, "Hmmph. Why doesn't he just go ahead and finish?"

In other words, it wasn't enough to seek the academic world's highest distinction at one of the nation's flagship state universities. You had to earn that fancy PhD in short order, or you would be gossiped about. The Orangeburg of my childhood was basically a college town, with all the intellectual pride and arrogance that entails.

Every year progressed according to the rhythms of the academic calendar, beginning in the fall, when students moved into the dormitories on the SC State and Claflin campuses. Then it would be football season, and we always went to at least a few games—not just to watch the teams, which had their ups and downs, but also to see and hear the marching bands, which are held to the highest standards at historically Black colleges. Halftime was often the highlight of the game, especially on the one Saturday each year when SC State was playing rival Florida A&M University. State's band was excellent, but the FAMU band was in another universe, with its thunderous drum section, its horns that could wake the dead, and its high-stepping choreography worthy of a

Broadway stage, with troupes of dancers and baton twirlers always led by a drum major who had the magnetic presence and dorsal flexibility of a Baryshnikov. Those FAMU drum majors could bend over backward so far that their tall bearskin hats almost touched the ground.

The world of my childhood was as bookish as anyone could imagine. On my way home from Felton, I would take the shortcut through the Claflin campus and sometimes stop by the university library, which was my mother's domain. I was allowed to go back into the shelves and read any book I wanted, provided I put it back exactly where I'd found it. If it was a book I wanted to finish, my mother would check it out for me. At home, there were shelves full of classics that I could read whenever I wanted. And I remember how excited I was when my parents ordered the latest edition of the *World Book Encyclopedia*. On rainy days when I had nothing else to do, I'd pick a volume—a thick one, like "C" or "M," or a skinny one, like "E" or "W-X-Y-Z"—and thumb through it, pausing to read any entry that piqued my interest. I was raised to believe that everyone should want to know everything about everything.

I WAS FORTUNATE THAT my home, my school, and my church gave me a safe space in which to grow up. All around me, meanwhile, the South was on fire.

On May 17, 1954—two months and five days after I was born—the U.S. Supreme Court issued its landmark 9–0 decision in *Brown v. Board of Education*. "Separate educational facilities are inherently unequal," Chief Justice Earl Warren wrote, echoing Judge Julius Waties Waring's pronouncement that "segregation is *per se* inequality."

Black parents in Orangeburg petitioned the school board to comply with the ruling and integrate the public schools. The city's white power brokers had no intention of complying. The business leaders who made up the local White Citizens' Council—part of a network of such groups, across the South, that have often been described as "the Ku Klux Klan in suits"—responded by pressuring the petition's signers to withdraw their names, targeting leaders with punishments that included firings, evictions, and foreclosures. African Americans answered that assault with a boycott of businesses owned by White Citizens' Council members, urging Black people to do their shopping in Columbia, Charleston, or Augusta, carpooling if necessary, and to buy locally only from Black-owned establishments.

The tit-for-tat struggle continued. In 1955, the White Citizens' Council enlisted wholesalers to cut off the flow of goods to Black retailers so that African Americans in Orangeburg would have no choice but to buy at white-owned establishments. Our family friend James Sulton could not buy gasoline for his Esso service station, which my father always patronized, because the regional distributor wouldn't sell to him. He posed for a picture, taken by the photographer Cecil J. Williams and published in *Jet* magazine, of his new soft drink vending machine, which was completely empty because the regional Coca-Cola distributor wouldn't sell to him. Black people in Orangeburg answered this strangling of Black businesses by boycotting specific brands that were being withheld from African American merchants, including Coca-Cola products, Sunbeam Bread, and Paradise Ice Cream. SC State students held protests and staged a walkout. "Everywhere there are signs of pluck, determination, and courage," *Jet* reported on October 20, 1955.

In the end, this battle led to a stalemate. The White Citizens' Council realized that its initial goal—coercing the African Americans who had signed the desegregation petition into withdrawing their names—would never be achieved, so council members ceased the coercion. Our minister at Trinity, the Reverend McCollom, who was president of the local NAACP, claimed victory. "The merchants, all of them, began hurting," he said. "The net result was that the economic pressure on the Blacks eventually dissipated, and the petition of the Blacks remained intact."

But so did separate-but-equal segregation. The school board in Orangeburg, like most throughout the South, simply refused to comply with *Brown v. Board*. Racial segregation in virtually all aspects of life remained the law and continued to be enforced. Jim Crow would not go gently. It would have to be constantly pushed, shoved, confronted, harassed, obstructed, inconvenienced, and defied. It could not be given a moment's peace.

On February 1, 1960, while I was being led back and forth across my Felton classroom by Mrs. Clinkscales, four students at North Carolina Agricultural and Technical State University—the state's leading historically Black college, located in Greensboro—sat down at the whites-only lunch counter at the local Woolworth department store and asked to be served. When they were denied service, as they had anticipated, they refused to leave and sat stoically at the counter until the store closed for the evening. The following day they came back, but this time there were not just four Black students demanding coffee and doughnuts; there were twenty. On February 3, more than sixty students joined the Woolworth sit-in; on February 4, there were more than three hundred. By February 6, the number of Black protesters and white counterprotesters jammed into the little Woolworth exceeded one thousand—and the events in Greensboro were headline news across the country. It wasn't the very first sit-in of the civil rights movement, but it was the first to capture the nation's imagination. The bravery of those North Carolina A&T students led to the creation, later that year, of one of the movement's most forward-leaning and effective organizations, the Student Nonviolent Coordinating Committee. A section of that Woolworth lunch counter is now exhibited in Washington, D.C., at the Smithsonian National Museum of American History.

In Orangeburg, students at SC State and Claflin were electrified by the Greensboro sit-ins and formed their own group to coordinate action between the two campuses, calling it the Orangeburg Student Movement Association. The SC State president, Benner C. Turner, was unwilling to frontally challenge the segregationist power structure; it is, after all, a state university, beholden to the governor and state legislature. Turner was so cautious that he would not even allow students to establish an NAACP chapter. This meant that meetings and training sessions for protesters had to be held on the Claflin campus next door.

The target that Orangeburg students chose was S. H. Kress and Co., a five-and-dime downtown with a segregated lunch counter. I remember my mother taking me to Kress, with its creaking wood floors and its eclectic jumble of merchandise—including shelves full of toys. I have no mental picture of the lunch counter, probably because eating there was simply not an option for my family. The Orangeburg Student Movement Association began by politely asking Kress's management to desegregate the counter. When the store refused, as the students had expected, they staged sit-ins on February 25 and 26—to no effect. The next escalatory step came on March 1, when four hundred students marched downtown, peacefully but insistently, carrying signs that read, "Segregation Must Die." Kress and a competing five-and-dime across Russell Street, Fersner's, responded by shutting down their lunch counters for two weeks.

Under pressure from SC State's board of trustees, President Turner prohibited "demonstrations which involve violation of laws . . . or which disrupt the normal College routine." The city of Orangeburg—heedless of the First Amendment—made picketing illegal. None of this worked: When the lunch counters opened again on March 15, protest leaders sent more than one thousand Black students marching toward downtown in groups of about seventy-five. To reflect their sense of purpose, the young men and women dressed in their Sunday clothes. They looked as if they were heading to church, not to a confrontation.

One group turned back when they were met on Russell Street by police. All the others walked on toward the heart of the business district, steely in their determination, careful to do nothing to provoke the police officers and state troopers who awaited them en masse.

No provocation was needed. Police ordered the students to disperse. When the demonstrators refused, police suddenly attacked them with fire hoses and tear gas. The students kept their discipline; they did nothing to fight back as they were shoved and soaked. The powerful spray from the fire hoses slammed the demonstrators into walls and pummeled them to the ground. They tried to shelter one another and scrambled for cover. A blind student, disoriented, was washed down the street like a piece of trash. Some of the students managed to retreat and make it back to campus. The rest were forcibly herded into smaller groups and ultimately taken into custody.

Three hundred and eighty-eight protesters were arrested. That was far more than the county jail—the medieval-looking Pink Palace—could hold, so police put most of them in an outdoor enclosure near the courthouse. It had been an unusually cold late-winter's day, about forty degrees, and a steady rain was falling. It took until late that night for all the students to be arraigned and for the NAACP, working with faculty members at the colleges, to organize the needed bail money. The students passed the time by singing the national anthem and "God Bless America." A huge photograph of the corralled students was published the next morning, above the fold, on the front page of *The New York Times*. The story, by correspondent Harrison Salisbury, was headlined "350 Negro Student Demonstrators Held in South Carolina Stockade."

One of the SC State students arrested that day and held for hours in the outdoor corral was a protest leader named James E. Clyburn. He was tired, wet, and hungry when well-wishers from the campus arrived with food and blankets. Police tried to keep any relief from reaching the detainees, but a young student, Emily England, passed Clyburn a sandwich—and then playfully pulled the sandwich back, broke it in two, gave him one half, and ate the other herself. After bail was posted, Jim and Emily walked back to campus together. A year and a half later, they married. Clyburn went on to become a longtime member of Congress, representing the Orangeburg area—the most powerful Democrat in the state and the individual most responsible for making Joe Biden the party's 2020 presidential nominee.

Turner, the hapless SC State president, tried to reassert control over his campus by announcing that students who continued to participate in demonstrations would be expelled. The state legislature passed a new law making it a crime to refuse to leave a place of business when asked to do so. Smaller marches and attempted sit-ins continued for a while, but the Orangeburg protests eventually petered out. None of the downtown stores desegregated.

In the upstate city of Greenville, meanwhile, on July 16, eight young African Americans staged a sit-in at the main public library, which admitted whites only. One of them was a college student named Jesse L. Jackson, who was home from North Carolina A&T for the summer. It was the start of a decades-long career of activism in which Jackson would become one of Dr. Martin Luther King Jr.'s chief lieutenants and, later, a titan of the civil rights movement in his own right. His first protest was not a success. Rather than agree to the students' demands, the defiant Greenville City Council closed the main library—and also closed the smaller branch library across town that Black people had been allowed to use. It was deemed preferable for access to books to be denied to everyone, even whites, than for a Black person and a white person to read side by side.

White solidarity was being tested throughout the South. For the most part, it was holding.

Chapter Twelve

THE ORANGEBURG MASSACRE

Twenty classmates and I graduated from Felton on May 18, 1967, in the "Gymtorium" of our brand-new school building. Our little Rosenwald schoolhouse had been deemed no longer adequate, and after spending my cohort's seventh-grade year taking classes in various SC State buildings, as if we were miniature college students, we had settled into a new, sprawling, low-slung, modern Felton. Some of the classrooms had a mirrored wall that was actually one-way glass, which allowed degree candidates from the SC State education school to study us as we were being taught. I think of those classrooms whenever a *Law & Order* rerun gets to the scene where Lieutenant Van Buren phlegmatically observes suspects being questioned in the interrogation room.

As class president, I gave a speech at our commencement ceremony—I recall it containing the customary nostrums about "going forth into the future" and being the "leaders of tomorrow"—and while it is not listed in the program, I remember the singing of the school anthem, "Our Dear Felton," set to the melody of "Danny Boy." We were graduating not from the eighth grade but from the ninth; the extra year at Felton was thought by scholars at SC State to be more in sync with the developmental transition from adolescence to pre-adulthood. This meant that in the fall, we would enter high school not as freshmen but as sophomores.

For a full decade after the 1954 *Brown v. Board of Education* decision, Orangeburg's high schools had remained segregated: White students attended Orangeburg High, which was about a mile north of our house, and Black students were only allowed to attend Wilkinson High, across the railroad tracks and beyond the college campuses, near the SC State football stadium. In 1964, grudgingly, Orangeburg High accepted its first Black students—and some of the more affluent white students promptly decamped to Wade Hampton Academy, a new whites-only private school on the outskirts of town. Similar "segregation academies" had popped up across the South as the federal government, under President Lyndon B. Johnson, pressed harder for adherence to the law of the land.

In the fall of 1967, I enrolled at what had been the whites-only high school, just three years after forced integration. In my class of 203 students at Orangeburg High, there were just 11 African Americans. Among them was Douglas Wells, who had transferred to Felton in the seventh grade and become my closest friend. He and I became co-conspirators. We were determined not to defy the color line but to demolish it, to prove how ridiculous it had always been—and to enjoy the process.

I hadn't known what to make of Doug when he came to Felton. It was the year when we didn't have a schoolhouse, and the first-day-of-school assembly was held in a big lecture hall in one of the SC State classroom buildings. The principal calling the roll got to "Wells," and a voice in the back that sounded like a grown man's answered with a resounding "Present." All heads snapped around. I was eleven, and my voice hadn't changed; Doug was thirteen, his had, and it was precociously deep. On the playground, the guys in our class gave him the new-kid treatment for a while. I remember challenging him to a race and beating him, but only because he didn't know our Felton rules; he bent down to touch the tree root marking the turnaround spot with his hand, rather than tapping it with his foot like a base runner, and that cost him just enough time to give me the win at the finish line. He won the next race, though. And a few days later, Doug beat me on what I considered my home turf, where I had thought I was invincible: He scored higher than I did on an English quiz. Then I beat him on the following one. We became friends out of mutual respect.

Doug lived in the country, miles outside town, which made his daily logistics complicated; his mother or father would take him to school in the morning, but when we got out at three, there was no easy way for him to get home. My parents knew his parents, and Felton families helped each other out. Our whole first year at Orangeburg High, before Doug was old enough to get his driver's license, he and I followed a daily routine: After school we would walk down Boulevard to my house, where we did our homework, ate the sandwiches and pound cake and gingerbread my grandmother made for us, listened to the new Motown records and eight-track tapes we'd bought, compared notes about the girls we liked, played basketball at the hoop my father had put up in the yard near the pecan trees, and generally hung out. Around five thirty, his mother would get off work and come to pick him up. Spending all that time together was good for both of us, and it was good for our shared mission. We strategized our way through our classes and cheered each other on. By going to the white high school and proving ourselves not just academically equal but academically superior, we believed, we were doing what we could to strike a blow for civil rights.

I had thought my white classmates would be hostile to me, and a few were, but most of them ranged from curious to indifferent—though I had no illusions about how they might have talked about me, Doug, and the other Black students when they went home to the white side of town. Almost all were politically conservative. The girls dressed demurely; the boys favored a style that I would call southern prep, involving alpaca sweaters and tasseled loafers. Only one of my classmates—a doctor's son named Mike O'Cain, who lived on Russell Street in a big white house with two-story columns that looked like Tara from *Gone with the Wind*—seemed to have any idea that the year was 1967, that the "Summer of Love" in San Francisco had just ended, and that the times they were a-changin'. Mike had a disability in his legs and walked with an awkward, shuffling gait, which kept him out of the jock clique and the too-cool-for-school clique and even the nerd clique, making him something of an outsider. He chose to be a rebel. Whenever a political topic came up, his was usually the only white voice arguing the liberal point of view. He was the only white classmate who ever came to my house and the only white classmate who ever invited me into his. We went straight up to his room—I never even saw his parents, who I suspect disapproved—and we listened to his Bob Dylan records.

The teachers were another story. Out of nearly seventy teachers, only two were Black—one taught history, the other mechanical drawing. All the rest were white, and some of the older ones obviously had not come to terms with racial integration. Entering as a sophomore, I signed up for tenth-grade French. The teacher, Mrs. Bonnette, gave me a C for the first grading period, which I knew was unjust; I'd already had two years of French at Felton and had done well. In her mind, apparently, there was no way a thirteen-year-old Black boy coming from an all-Black school could be ready for her second-year course. She kept me after class one day and suggested I fall back into the entry-level course for ninth graders. I told her no. My parents, never having seen such a stain on one of my report cards, asked if I wanted them to arrange for a tutor. I don't remember my exact words, but they were the 1967 equivalent of "Nah, I've got this." I went to the library and got a copy of the ninth-grade textbook, spent a weekend going through it, and got A's from Mrs. Bonnette for the rest of the year.

Mrs. Rhame, the geometry teacher, was a member of the Daughters of the American Revolution and the Daughters of the Confederacy who seemed to delight in humiliating any African American student who was struggling in her class. I still vividly remember the day she made Glenn Cain, a friend of mine, stand up in front of the class while she grilled him mercilessly, and endlessly, about some concept he hadn't yet gotten his head around. That made me angry, and I decided then and there that I was going to make Mrs. Rhame give at least one Black student an A-plus. Math was not my strongest suit, but that didn't matter; I would figure it out. Every single night, I spent more time on geometry than any other class. I got to the point where I could have told you in my sleep which angles were congruent when two parallel lines were crossed by a transversal, and I could have told you why. I simply refused to get anything wrong on a quiz or a test. At the end of the year, I got my A-plus.

But there were also white teachers like Mr. Turner, who not only taught me everything I've ever known (and have since forgotten) about chemistry but also was a kind and generous mentor. I did well enough in his class to give him the idea that I should become a scientist. He convinced me to join the Science Club—I was club president my senior year—and as encouragement, he nominated me for a national award given to outstanding high school science students by Rensselaer Polytechnic Institute, which somehow I won. Mr. Turner was mistaken about my aptitude; I was much better with words than numbers. But he was right about the new world that the South was being dragged into, a world in which old barriers and old assumptions were being obliterated.

Mr. Turner was an outlier, though, not just at the school but in the city. Most white citizens of Orangeburg were like the novelist William Faulkner, who resisted desegregation: They believed the past was not even past. The old days when whites maintained political control by simply denying African Americans the right to vote were gone, finally. But there were other ways to keep a monopoly on power. As Orangeburg grew, City Hall quickly annexed new suburban developments whose residents were white—but left new Black suburbs outside the racially gerrymandered city limits. This ensured that what was by then a majority-Black city continued to be run by an all-white government, which oversaw a virtually all-white police department.

And while segregation was no longer the law, it was still the practice.

After the end-of-school bell rang, my white classmates at Orangeburg High went off to one universe, and I went off to another. White students would come in on Mondays talking about the fun they'd had over the weekend "at the country club." I didn't even know where this mysterious country club was, much less what facilities it had—there was a golf course, I gathered, and a swimming pool, and they seemed to have lots of parties out there, wherever it was. The only thing I knew for certain was that the country club had no Black members.

White classmates would also rave about the delicious pulled pork they had eaten at Piggie Park, a joint out on Highway 301 that reportedly served some of the best barbecue in the state. I had no way of knowing whether that was true. Piggie Park was owned by a die-hard white supremacist named Maurice Bessinger, who believed fervently in racial separation. Years after the Civil Rights Act theoretically desegregated public accommodations, including restaurants, Bessinger adamantly refused to seat and serve African Americans at Piggie Park. He argued in court that the Civil Rights Act "contravenes the will of God," and even after he lost the case, he refused to change his policy against Blacks and whites dining together. This was a flagrant violation of the law, but city and state authorities could not be troubled to do anything about it.

There was another thing my white classmates did that I couldn't do because of my skin color: They went bowling. That sounds like a minor thing, but it lay at the heart of a tragic chapter in civil rights history—one that changed the course of my life.

THERE WAS ONE BOWLING alley in Orangeburg, the All Star Bowling Lane, across the railroad tracks and a few blocks down Russell Street from the SC State campus. The establishment admitted only whites. It claimed not to be a public accommodation but instead to be more like a private club that could choose its members. Any white person who came in and wanted to bowl was allowed membership, and any

Black person who did the same was rejected. No ruse was ever more transparent. But the All Star bowling alley had been whites-only before the Civil Rights Act, and it remained whites-only after the Civil Rights Act, and nobody in authority did anything to correct that situation. In February 1968, during the second semester of my battles with Mrs. Bonnette and Mrs. Rhame, student activists at SC State decided to force the issue.

Much had changed on the campus in the years since the 1960 demonstration in which the future congressman James Clyburn was arrested. SC State's longtime president Benner C. Turner kept in the good graces of the state government by maintaining a strict prohibition against student protests throughout most of the decade. By the spring of 1967, however, Turner's stance had become unsustainable; students staged a long walkout that forced Governor Robert McNair's hand and Turner's resignation. His successor, M. Maceo Nance Jr., bowed to reality and allowed students to form political clubs on campus, including an organization called the Black Awareness Coordinating Committee that championed what at the time was a radical concept: Black Power.

Those potent words were a challenge not just to white supremacy but also to establishment civil rights organizations, such as the NAACP and the National Urban League, which initially saw the Black Power movement as rash and counterproductive. Conversely, the firebrands who led the most important Black Power organization, the Student Nonviolent Coordinating Committee—men like John Lewis, Stokely Carmichael, and H. Rap Brown—saw their civil rights elders as overly patient and far too polite.

SNCC's leaders understood that nearly a decade's worth of pent-up energy was ready to be unleashed at SC State. One of SNCC's most experienced itinerant organizers, an Orangeburg-area native named Cleveland Sellers, came home to offer the students strategic and technical guidance. The white authorities in Orangeburg knew who he was and viewed him as a troublemaking "outside agitator," even though he had been born in the town of Denmark, South Carolina, roughly twenty miles distant. A newspaper article called him one of those “long-haired black militants” who were stirring up trouble among “the Negroes.”

On Monday, February 5, 1968, about fifty students from SC State and Claflin went to the All Star Lane to confront the owner, a man named Harry Floyd, and demand that they be allowed to bowl. Floyd refused and called the police, demanding that the students be arrested. Police chief Roger Poston declined to arrest anyone, given that no crime had been committed, but he also declined to enforce the students’ right to be treated the same way white patrons were treated. The students left, unsatisfied.

The next day, February 6, a small group of Black students returned to the bowling alley and staged a sit-in at Harry Floyd’s lunch counter. The business closed for the day, and Floyd called the police again to kick the protesters out. This time, law enforcement got physical. There was pushing and shoving as they tried to evict the demonstrators, and both sides called in reinforcements—more police streaming in to defend the segregated public order, more students rushing over from the campuses. The situation seemed to be nearing the brink, but no one wanted serious violence that day, and the two sides negotiated an end to the standoff: Fifteen students allowed themselves to be arrested, which would lay down a legal marker for the matter to be pursued in court; and the leaders of the protest announced that their goals had been met and urged everyone to return to the campuses.

But then Chief Poston committed a needless act of provocation: He summoned two fire trucks to the scene. Everyone there knew what that meant. Everyone knew how fire hoses had been used against peaceful civil rights marchers in Birmingham and elsewhere across the South. Everyone knew how they had been used right there in Orangeburg, right there on Russell Street, at the last big demonstration, in 1960.

“Hey, man. Where’s the fire?” the students shouted.

Now nobody was inclined to meekly go home to the dorms. More police arrived. The crowd grew to more than a hundred, and protesters broke several shopwindows and rocked police cars. Officers responded by clubbing students with batons, and soon the demonstrators were in retreat, some of them bloodied, all of them enraged at the violence police had inflicted in defense of injustice. On the short walk back to campus, across Boulevard and Magnolia Streets, they threw rocks at anything they saw that was made of glass. In the melee, eight students and one police officer were injured badly enough to be taken to the hospital.

Perhaps because campus activism at SC State had been artificially suppressed for so long, this was the biggest protest Orangeburg had seen in years—and the first ever that was not an orderly, disciplined set piece but a loud, militant, nonviolent-but-unruly Black Power statement. None of it was Sellers's doing; he was encouraging students to think more broadly and systematically about the struggle and had advised them not to waste time and energy on one sad little bowling alley. But the students were passionate about it, and Sellers respected their right to make the All Star Lane their priority. Nobody took orders from him or asked his permission; he had been out of town when the protest began and had no idea anything was going on until he got home on the evening of February 6 and excited students filled him in. Only at that point did he rush to the scene.

Nevertheless, the story that South Carolina officials told the world, and perhaps actually believed, was that the "agitator" Sellers had organized the whole protest and egged the students on, replacing what they saw as an admirable cordiality between whites and Negroes with rage and anarchy. In their minds, they were not up against a few hundred students. They imagined themselves as being at war with the radicals of SNCC, led by the hated and feared Stokely Carmichael. They saw themselves as holding the line against the dangerous ideology known as Black Power. Perhaps because of this mindset—or perhaps because they so sincerely believed in white supremacy and could not bear to see it challenged—they responded with overkill. In a display of massive force, authorities deployed hundreds of state troopers and National Guardsmen to set up roadblocks at all the entrances of the SC State and

Claflin campuses. They decided to surround the students, isolate them, and lock them down.

To keep cars from going in and out of the campuses was not a difficult tactical problem. The two campuses, separated only by a fence, formed essentially a single complex stretching along Magnolia Street, roughly between Goff Avenue to the north, Chestnut Avenue to the east, and Russell Street to the south. Claflin occupied just a corner of the total area, its classrooms and dormitories arranged tightly around an irregular circle. The school's one entrance for vehicles was on Magnolia. SC State, much larger, sprawled beside and behind Claflin in a loose grid; its main entrance, also on Magnolia, was flanked by expansive campus greens. There were a couple of other vehicular entrances to the SC State campus, both of them on the eastern side of the property, away from downtown Orangeburg. Four roadblocks were enough to seal off the campuses to anyone traveling by car.

Foot traffic was a different story, however. There were pedestrian entrances to the campus complex—one, leading into Claflin, was directly across the railroad tracks from our house. Gaps in the fence made it easy to walk from one campus to the other, and everyone knew the footpaths that led out to Russell Street or Goff Avenue. Police had established a cordon, but it leaked.

After the clash at the bowling alley, students gathered for an impromptu meeting in an SC State auditorium to try to decide what to do next. They agreed on their anger and outrage at the way protesters had been assaulted by police, but came to no firm consensus on what would be the most effective course of action. Shortly before midnight, they finally decided to call for a demonstration the next day in the downtown business district. Left undecided was whether they would ask for a permit for the rally or hold it without official permission—but by morning, the new protest had been called off, or at least postponed. City officials had agreed to talk with the students about the persistence of racial segregation.

On the following afternoon, Wednesday, February 7, Orangeburg mayor E. O. Pendarvis and city manager Bob Stevenson went to the SC State campus for what students believed would be negotiations. The encounter, held in a packed auditorium, ended up aggravating tensions rather than easing them.

The city officials came not to negotiate but to justify. They showed no regret for the way protesters had been treated at the All Star Lane, which angered the crowd. The mayor wanted peace but was unwilling even to discuss the students' list of demands, which now went beyond the question of the bowling alley. They wanted movie theaters integrated as well; they wanted an end to racial segregation at Orangeburg Regional Hospital; they wanted an end to police brutality; they wanted the establishment of a biracial city committee to chart the path toward full integration as required by federal law. Mayor Pendarvis didn't want to talk about any of these demands. Nor would he approve a permit for students to hold a protest march the following day. Orangeburg's power brokers were clueless as to how to speak to a hall full of irate young African American students who wanted the civil rights they were guaranteed by the Constitution and by law, all of them, and who wanted those rights immediately—young, educated Black men and women who were demanding change, not asking for it. The meeting ended when Pendarvis and Stevenson were hooted off the stage. Afterward, the students delivered a formal list of their demands to City Hall, where it was ignored.

After sundown, with police blockading the campus, three students decided to sneak out to a sandwich shop by hopping a fence and cutting through a residential backyard. The white homeowner greeted them with a shotgun blast, claiming later that he thought the young Black men were coming to rob him. Fortunately, the students' injuries were minor. Later, around eleven p.m., a car with two white men inside came barreling through the SC State campus. One of the men leaned out the car's window and fired wildly with a pistol in the direction of students. No one was hit. Students threw rocks and bottles at the car and tried to detain the men, but they managed to speed away. This incident frightened the student protesters less than it further angered them. There seemed to be only one way the car could have entered the campus, given all the roadblocks: The police must have intentionally let it through.

Since the first clash at the bowling alley, Orangeburg had been all but paralyzed. Classes were canceled at the public schools, including Orangeburg High, so I was at home all day. My mother and father stayed home, too; they couldn't have made it through the police barriers to their offices if they had wanted to. The phone rang constantly as my mother exchanged news and rumors with her friends around town and her colleagues on the two campuses.

Our house at Boulevard and Oak has a clear line of sight to the Claflin campus and a corner of the SC State campus beyond. I remember waking up on Thursday morning, February 8, and immediately heading to the best vantage point—the front upstairs window, in my parents' bedroom—to see if anything was happening. My father, who happened to be walking past the foot of the stairs, noticed me standing at the window and yelled at me in a tone of voice I'd never heard from him before: "Get down! Get down from that window right now!"

He rushed upstairs, crouching as he came into the room, and let me peek over the sill at the scene that he, my mother, my grandmother, and my great-aunt had been viewing with alarm. Across the street, on the wide railroad right-of-way, was a line of four parked SC Highway Patrol cars, angled toward a house two doors away from ours. The troopers were out of the vehicles, crouched behind the open front doors, aiming rifles or shotguns at the front door of the little house. That was where Cleveland Sellers had been staying, and those officers were prepared to take him into custody, dead or alive.

He wasn't there. Warned on Wednesday afternoon that law enforcement was constantly watching the house, Sellers had decided to spend the night on campus in one of the dorms, so there was no bloodshed that Thursday morning. Death came to Orangeburg hours later, after dark.

Much of the day was spent in preparation for what might happen after nightfall. The dreaded precedents on the minds of state and city officials were Newark and Detroit: Seven months earlier, in July 1967, sixty-nine people had been killed in those cities, and hundreds of buildings destroyed, in the nation's worst urban riots in decades. The lesson South Carolina officials took was that authorities in those cities had let containable disturbances get out of hand. Determined to prevent any such uprising in Orangeburg, Governor McNair mobilized more than a hundred additional National Guard troops and beefed up the roadblocks that penned students inside the campuses with additional personnel and military equipment.

The students, meanwhile, were still furious about the shooting incidents of the previous night. Nance, the SC State president, issued a statement calling on students to refrain from throwing projectiles at police or anyone else. For their own safety, Nance cautioned, all students should remain in the central part of the campus. They had little choice, given that police would not let them leave, so they stayed put—but continued their protest.

As night fell, the temperature plummeted; Orangeburg was in a cold snap, with lows in the thirties. To stay warm—and also to send a message of defiance to the police and National Guard keeping them from leaving the campus—the students lit a big bonfire near the Magnolia Street campus entrance, fueling it with street signs and wood from a construction site. The sight of flames alarmed police officials, who feared a Detroit-style orgy of arson was about to begin, and they sent yet more officers and troops to keep the protesters confined to campus. Students responded with taunts and jeers, and a few grabbed burning pieces of wood from the fire and threw them in the direction of the police line. J. P. "Pete" Strom, chief of the South Carolina Law Enforcement Division, gave the order for a fire truck to come put out the students' blaze. That provoked the students, who yelled and cursed at the state troopers. The troopers became visibly unnerved; they were untrained in crowd control, had bayonets fixed to their weapons, and now anxiously looked around for someone to tell them what to do. Students reignited the bonfire in defiance. The standoff looked set to explode—but then, somehow, tempers seemed to cool a bit. In his memoir, *The River of No Return,* Sellers recalled walking up to the scene and thinking the threat of violence had passed.

That was just moments before the shooting started.

As Sellers recalls the massacre, one student stepped forward and threw something onto the fire. A state trooper, taking that gesture as a challenge to authority, fired warning shots into the air. Other troopers panicked at the sound, not knowing where the shots were coming from, and began firing their shotguns into the crowd.

Sellers was among the victims, shot in his left shoulder. Students were scrambling to get away, helping the wounded escape, heading through the darkness toward the middle of the campus. Sellers wanted to run, too, but he was sure the troopers would recognize him in silhouette by his hair, which he wore in a towering Afro. The governor had made him public enemy number one, and "I knew that if they caught me they would kill me," he wrote. He dragged one wounded young man as far away from the front of the campus as he could, and then crawled away from the gunfire on his own, afraid he would pass out before he reached safety. When he finally made it to a dormitory, he collapsed as soon as he got inside.

Sellers rested for a few minutes, but he was bleeding and knew he had to make his way to the campus infirmary. "Although I had expected things to be bad, it was worse than I had imagined," he wrote of the scene. "Blood was everywhere, on the floor, the walls, the chairs; and everyone was working with the wounded. Most of the forty to fifty students in the infirmary were quiet, though some were weeping softly. One of the students, I think he was the quarterback on State's football team, was paralyzed. He had been shot in his spine."

In all, thirty-one protesters were wounded by state troopers firing shotgun blasts into an unarmed crowd. Many were shot in the back as they tried to run away. Three of them—SC State students Henry Smith and Samuel Hammond and Wilkinson High School student Delano Middleton—were killed.

THIS SPASM OF DEADLY Jim Crow police violence is remembered as the Orangeburg Massacre—to the extent it is remembered at all, that is. When most people think of unarmed college students being killed during the tumultuous years of campus protest, they think of the Kent State massacre of 1970, when four unarmed students demonstrating against the Vietnam War were killed by soldiers from the Ohio National Guard. Does the nation's historical memory give primacy to Kent State because those victims were white? Because that outrage produced the indelible, Pulitzer Prize–winning photograph of an anguished young woman kneeling over her classmate's corpse? Because Crosby, Stills, Nash and Young wrote a song about Kent State, "Ohio," that became a counterculture anthem?

The slain students in Orangeburg were Black, their lives were taken in the dark, and nobody wrote a song about them. But the main reason the Orangeburg Massacre is not better known might simply be that it happened in 1968, when absolutely *everything* happened. U.S. forces were besieged by the North Vietnamese Army's Tet Offensive, the biggest of the Vietnam War. President Lyndon B. Johnson, tormented by war overseas and ceaseless protests at home, abandoned his bid for reelection. The Reverend Martin Luther King Jr., the nation's leading civil rights leader, was assassinated in Memphis. Senator Robert F. Kennedy, campaigning to replace Johnson, was assassinated in Los Angeles. The Democratic National Convention was utter chaos, days of rage, with antiwar protesters clashing with Chicago police and the party bitterly divided over the war. Republican Richard M. Nixon was elected to begin what would be a consequential and uniquely shameful presidency.

That sequence of world-changing events began right after Orangeburg, before the killings on the front lawns of South Carolina State had had time to sink in. And press coverage of the massacre was at best desultory. Reporters from the wire services and the major papers flocked in, but only a few of them bothered to look deeper than the official story being told by Governor McNair, which was that Black Power militants had instigated the deadly clash. McNair's spokesman maintained that Cleveland Sellers was ultimately responsible for the deaths, calling him "the biggest nigger in the crowd."

The aftermath of the massacre took years to play out. Nine state troopers were tried on federal charges of violating the students' civil rights, and all of them were acquitted. Sellers was tried on state charges of failing to disperse when ordered, and he was convicted and spent seven months in jail. When SC State built a new basketball arena, it named the building the Smith–Hammond–Middleton Center in honor of the victims. And an essay I wrote about the massacre during my first semester in college impelled me to become a journalist.

The immediate impact of the massacre felt to me like a raising of the stakes. They were raised even higher two months later, on April 4, when King was assassinated at the Lorraine Motel in Memphis, Tennessee, and devastating riots erupted in Black urban centers around the country. In Orangeburg, about four hundred students from the colleges marched to the city's central plaza, where the Confederate memorial stands, and knelt in a silent vigil before peacefully returning to the campuses. The city was placed under curfew. Two days later, a hulking old wooden warehouse on Boulevard, just a block from our house, caught fire and burned to the ground. I remember that day vividly because the adults were debating whether we should evacuate. The blaze was towering, and it was easy to imagine that if the wind were to shift, the flames could easily jump to a wooden house across narrow Peasley Street, and then to the next wooden house, and then to the next, and then to ours. Firefighters eventually managed to contain the fire, leaving the charred embers to serve for many months as a reminder of that tragic week.

To me, it felt even more important not just to excel at Orangeburg High but to dominate. I joined a group of Felton alums who met a couple of times, with the idea of forming some sort of high school Black Power organization, but nothing came of that. The way I believed I could contribute to the movement was to force as many white people as possible to acknowledge that a Black student could dazzle academically. In my senior year, I got the chance to do just that.

There was a weekly show on NBC, *College Bowl,* in which teams of university students competed to answer high-level trivia questions. The NBC-affiliated local station in Columbia decided to organize a similar statewide tournament called *High School Bowl.* Orangeburg High was one of the competing schools, and our team members were chosen by an objective criterion: the four seniors with the highest PSAT scores. That included me.

I was the only Black member of the Orangeburg High School team. As far as I can recall, I was the only Black student on any of the teams from any of the schools. And, for what it's worth, I became a *High School Bowl* star.

The matches were held in the WIS-TV studio in Columbia, and the emcee was a longtime anchorman, weatherman, and children's show host named Joe Pinner. After letting the first few questions go by—nerves, I guess; I'd never been on television before—I started ringing the buzzer confidently and giving the right answers again and again. All those idle hours I had spent reading the *World Book Encyclopedia* and accumulating random facts had been worthwhile.

I went on a roll, and we won that match. A week later, I went on a roll again in the next match, and we won that one easily. The same thing happened in the third match. Our team went undefeated—and for a brief time, I was a celebrity among African Americans within the reach of the powerful WIS broadcast signal, which blanketed almost the whole state. Strangers recognized me in public. The effect faded quickly enough, but for a while, wherever I went in Orangeburg and across South Carolina, I was "that Black boy who beat all those white children on that show."

That same year, 1970, I was one of three graduating high school seniors from South Carolina chosen as Presidential Scholars—an honor, established by President Lyndon B. Johnson, meant to recognize academic success, leadership skills, and community service. There were 119 of us that year, two or three from each state, and we were invited to come to Washington, meet with our representatives in the House and Senate, and visit the White House to be congratulated by the president. It was a sign of the times that my cohort of scholars, meeting late into the night at the George Washington University dormitory where we were housed, drafted a petition to President Richard Nixon demanding an end to the war in Vietnam—which the White House was not happy to receive. The other two scholars from South Carolina were white, as were almost all the rest of the young honorees. One of the other rare exceptions, I later learned, was a young Black woman from Ohio, Rita Dove, who wanted to be a writer—and who would go on to win a Pulitzer Prize and become poet laureate of the United States.

When our little South Carolina delegation arrived at the Capitol, the House members who represented our districts were polite and cordial but clearly had more important things to do. Over on the Senate side, I have no clear recollection of a meeting with one of our senators, Fritz Hollings, a Democrat whom my parents liked, or at least didn't dislike. But I will never forget our meeting with our other senator, Strom Thurmond, who by then had switched to the Republican Party. He had all the time in the world for three kids who were not even old enough to vote. He showed us around his office, which was palatial, and I recall that he made a special point of highlighting the dumbbells on the floor behind his desk, telling us several times that he used them every day. At the time, he was sixty-seven—and married to a former Miss South Carolina less than half his age. Thurmond was always a peacock who wanted the world to know of his strength and virility. After chatting for a while, inviting us to ask question after question—and making a point to treat me no differently from my fellow white scholars—he grandly invited us to lunch in the Senate Dining Room. I remember that the famous Senate Navy Bean Soup tasted no different from any other navy bean soup. But the surroundings were impressive.

TWO WEEKS LATER, A large envelope arrived at our house in Orangeburg. Inside was a picture taken by Thurmond's photographer during that

Senate lunch. It is inscribed, in Thurmond's hand, "Best wishes to my good friend Eugene Robinson. Strom Thurmond, U.S.S.-S.C." My parents thought it was so hilarious to be offered "best wishes" from such an unlikely source that they framed the picture. For decades now, I've kept it on a bookshelf in my study.

Indeed, the times they were a-changin'. But not for the last time.

Chapter Thirteen

A WINDOW OF OPPORTUNITY

Like John Hammond Fordham's generation a century earlier, my cohort came of age at one of those episodic moments when the window of opportunity for Black Americans was briefly pried open. We squeezed, scrambled, and barreled our way through.

On March 6, 1961, six days before my seventh birthday, President John F. Kennedy signed Executive Order 10925, establishing the President's Committee on Equal Employment Opportunity and mandating that federal contractors "take affirmative action to ensure that applicants are employed, and that employees are treated during employment, without regard to their race, creed, color or national origin." The young president had been inaugurated just six weeks earlier, and African American leaders were pushing hard for the aggressive use of federal power to advance the cause of civil rights. Kennedy's order is often cited as the first use of the term *affirmative action* in the context of race.

Despite that acknowledgment of systemic racial discrimination and the imperative to do something about it, revolutionary progress would not come until after Kennedy was tragically assassinated and his vice president was sworn in. Once a powerful senator from the Jim Crow state of Texas, Lyndon B. Johnson wrestled Congress into approving the landmark civil rights laws that changed the nation—the Civil Rights Act of 1964, the Voting Rights Act of 1965, and the Fair Housing Act of 1968. By the time I was ready to go to college, the techniques long used to relegate African Americans to second-class status had been outlawed, at least on paper.

In the real world, there was resistance—not just fierce defiance in the former Confederacy but also tribalism and inertia in the rest of the country. Massachusetts, for example, was a liberal stronghold that in its history had opposed slavery, sent its sons to fight and die in the Civil War, backed Radical Reconstruction, abhorred Jim Crow, and championed civil rights. But when whites in Boston were faced with plans to achieve racial balance in the public schools by busing white and Black students among neighborhoods, they reacted with violence more characteristic of Birmingham or Biloxi.

My acceptance letter from the University of Michigan arrived at a time when the campus was in an uproar: A student group called the Black Action Movement, with support from many white students and some faculty, was staging a strike to force the university to increase Black enrollment. I didn't know any of this had happened until I got to Ann Arbor in the fall, and I never stopped to wonder whether I might owe my place in the freshman class to affirmative action. With race very much on the university community's mind, and with administrators largely sympathetic to the strikers' demands, might the fact that I am African American have been what tipped the scales in my favor?

I'll never know. If I did benefit from an affirmative action program, it was probably the one that has benefited white students for many generations: I was a "legacy." My father had gone to Michigan, my mother had gotten a master's degree at Michigan, my uncle Franz had earned his undergraduate and law degrees at Michigan, my aunt Primrose had gone to Michigan. And in any event, I had an impeccable GPA, had SAT scores in the 1400s, had been named a National Merit Scholar, and had been honored in Washington as a Presidential Scholar. I got accepted everywhere I applied, including at schools that were more selective than Michigan—but also more expensive, which was a factor in my deciding where to go.

But if the admissions office at Michigan did give my application extra points for my race, then affirmative action worked precisely as intended. I wrote an essay for my freshman English class about the Orangeburg Massacre, and it won a prestigious campus-wide Hopwood writing award. I began working at *The Michigan Daily*, arguably the best student newspaper in the country, and rose to become co–editor in chief. And I went on to have a journalism career that the university chose to honor in 2011 by awarding me an honorary doctorate. Opportunity does not guarantee outcomes, but outcomes necessarily begin with opportunity.

The only time I know that I benefited from affirmative action, I found out after the fact. Coming out of Michigan, I had job interviews lined up with two employers I was pretty sure were ready to hire me: the *Detroit Free Press*, which was a terrific regional paper; and the *San Francisco Chronicle*, whose reputation was a punch line in *All the President's Men*, the great film about *The Washington Post* and Watergate. Jason Robards, playing legendary editor Ben Bradlee, listens to a pitch about a new daily feature: "Yesterday's weather report, for people who were drunk and slept all day." With a twinkle, Robards-as-Bradlee growls, "Send it to the *San Francisco Chronicle*. They need it." The *Free Press* was the correct choice as a career move, but I'd never been to California—the Golden State, the epicenter of the cultural revolution, the paradise where summers were endless and possibilities unbounded. I drove across the country with two friends who also had reason to visit the Bay Area, made a good impression in my interview at the *Chronicle*, and accepted on the spot when they offered me the job.

As soon as I showed up for my first day as a cub reporter, the city editor—the boss who had hired me—took me into his office. "I think I mentioned," he said, "that you were hired under our minority training program."

He had not mentioned. No one had mentioned it. What this meant in practice was that under the terms of the *Chronicle*'s contract with the Newspaper Guild, the journalists' union, the paper could fire me without cause for up to nine months; until then, I would be a probationary hire. Normally, the *Chronicle* had just three months to dismiss a new hire without any sort of documentation or process. Surprise! I had just turned down a better newspaper, burning bridges in the process, and moved to the other side of the continent, only to learn that I was on extended probation and that for the next three-quarters of a year, I could find myself unemployed if my boss came back from lunch one day with indigestion. I was angry. Someone should have told me this beforehand. But I knew it would not be a problem.

When I turned in my first story, one of the editors came over to my desk. "You can write!" he announced with an air of surprise.

"Thanks," I replied.

What I didn't say, but wanted to, was "I went to the University of Michigan, I was editor of the best college daily in the country, I sent you clippings of front-page stories I wrote during internships at *The Washington Star* and the *Detroit Free Press*, which are both much better papers than the *Chronicle*. Why does it surprise you that I can handle a ten-inch news story?"

But I kept my silence. I came in early every day, stayed late, bonded with my colleagues over drinks at the local bar, and wrote stories onto the front page. After one month, not nine, the boss called me back into his office and told me my probation was officially over. In five years at the *Chronicle*, I climbed all the way up the reporting ladder—from the night police beat, writing blurbs on murder and mayhem from six in the evening until two in the morning, to chief city government reporter, covering then-mayor Dianne Feinstein following the shocking murders of her predecessor, George Moscone, and the gay rights pioneer Harvey Milk in their offices at City Hall. All young reporters have to prove themselves. My burden of proof was heavier than it should have been, at first—and, of course, I had much to learn about the arts of reporting and writing. But the burden did get lighter as I showed what I could do.

I paint the outlines of my own experience in the affirmative action era because it was representative. My generation of African Americans was given unprecedented opportunity, which was often accompanied by extraordinary scrutiny. In 1980, after five years at the *Chronicle*, I was hired by *The Washington Post* to cover the District of Columbia's mercurial and scandal-plagued mayor, Marion Barry. In a city whose population was more than two-thirds African American, the *Post*'s newsroom was much farther along the diversity curve than the *Chronicle*'s. Eight years earlier, in 1972, a group of Black reporters known as the "Metro Seven" had filed a complaint with the U.S. Equal Employment Opportunity Commission alleging discrimination in the competition for promotions and plum assignments—at a time when hardly any American newspapers even had seven Black reporters on staff, much less reporters with the confidence and self-possession to confront management so aggressively. My predecessor at City Hall and immediate supervisor, Milton Coleman, was Black; the editor who ran all coverage of the city, Herb Denton, was Black; some of the paper's most celebrated writers—Leon Dash, Courtland Milloy, Jacqueline Trescott—were Black. I was aware of the issues raised by the Metro Seven, and I could see that the ranks of upper management were overwhelmingly white and male, so I knew from the beginning that the *Post* hadn't arrived at the promised land of racial equality. But it seemed to be on the right road.

Because of our race, we all believed we had to be not as good as our white counterparts but better. And we were right. The *Post* was at the top of the newspaper food chain, which meant that everyone who got hired there had exceptional strengths or exceptional promise. But everyone had weaknesses, too. Some staff members were dogged and resourceful reporters but only pedestrian writers; others were stylists who wrote like a dream but whose reporting skills were nothing special. Some were wizards at connecting the dots, able to tease coherent narratives out of budgets and balance sheets; others were empathetic interviewers who could coax the most reluctant sources to bare their souls. I noticed a subtle pattern, though: There was a tendency to expose and critique the weaknesses of Black reporters and editors rather than play to their strengths. There would be a Black reporter who covered his beat—say, the local criminal courts—perfectly well, but who wrote in prose that was just workmanlike. Editors would tend to harp on his wooden writing rather than celebrate his excellence at the most important requirement of his job, which was not getting beaten on stories by his competitor from the rival *Washington Star.* The reporter's career might stall—while a white reporter with a similar skill set might be promoted to the National or Foreign staffs.

I saw this disparity clearly when, two years after coming to the *Post,* I became an editor on the City desk. You learn a lot about journalists when you handle their raw copy—who writes with clarity and style, and who doesn't; who sticks carefully to the facts, and who draws conclusions that the facts don't justify; who puts maximum effort into every story, and who tends to coast. The overall level of talent, accomplishment, and rigor at the *Post* was higher than I'd seen at the *Detroit Free Press*, the *Washington Star*, or the *San Francisco Chronicle.* But within that context, there were white reporters who were allowed to be journeymen whose useful stories ran on inside pages, year after year. Black reporters, by contrast, tended to be seen either as stars or as failures.

As I said, the pattern was subtle, and it did attenuate over time. And there was one glaring and disastrous counterexample, in which an African American reporter's talent and integrity were wildly overestimated. Janet Cooke started working at the *Post* in January 1980, the same month I started. The executives who hired her had been dazzled by her looks, her charm, and her glittering résumé: a degree from Vassar, further study in Paris at the Sorbonne, fluency in French and Spanish. In interviews, she had even mentioned that she was proficient at tennis, the preferred sport of *Post* upper management; Ben Bradlee had a court in his backyard.

Cooke was assigned to a junior position, writing for a weekly local news section focused only on the District of Columbia, and she was in a hurry to advance to the regular Metro staff, where I worked. On September 28, 1980, she got her wish: The *Post* published "Jimmy's World," Cooke's stunning profile of an eight-year-old heroin addict, given the pseudonym "Jimmy," who lived in a crime- and drug-ridden neighborhood of Southeast Washington.

The story was so vivid in its imagery, so compelling in its narrative, that it had a massive impact. Cooke instantly became not just a star but something of a celebrity, as reporters at other publications wrote stories about the shocking "Jimmy" story. Every day for weeks, my editors sent me to the District Building, Washington's City Hall, with instructions to press Mayor Barry on what the city government was doing to find the heroin-addicted little boy and get him the help he so desperately needed. After police conducted a thorough search and came up empty, Barry finally said he doubted the veracity of the story. He said he believed "Jimmy" did not exist.

Cooke's first editor at the *Post*, an African American woman, also had doubts about the story, which she had not overseen. And one of Metro's most experienced Black reporters, who knew the city's streets better than anyone else at the *Post*, believed there was no chance that Cooke, with her patrician ways, could ever have gained access to a household like the one she described "Jimmy" living in. Despite these serious reservations, however, the newspaper's top editors—among them, some of the greatest journalists I've ever known, including Bob Woodward, who was then in charge of the Metro staff, and Bradlee—not only stood by the story but also decided to nominate Cooke for a Pulitzer Prize, which she won.

Within hours of the Pulitzer announcement, Cooke's résumé and career fell apart, and the *Post* suffered the worst embarrassment in its storied history. Reporters at other papers trying to write feature stories about her—she was now very much a celebrity—were unable to confirm the college degrees cited in her biography. Only then did the *Post* investigate and interrogate. Under questioning by Bradlee, Cooke admitted that she had not graduated from Vassar, she had not studied at the Sorbonne, she did not speak the languages she had claimed to speak. She did not even play tennis. And later, finally, she admitted that "Jimmy's World" was not journalism but fiction. She had made it up.

How had such legendarily hard-nosed journalists been so fooled? They wanted to believe. They wanted to believe they had been clever enough to find and hire a unicorn—a young and attractive African American woman with impeccable credentials, familiarity and ease with the world of white privilege, genuine writing talent (which Cooke certainly had), and an eye-batting coquettishness they found irresistible. And they were too enchanted with their unicorn to hear the warnings from the Black staff members who worked most closely with Cooke, had serious doubts about the "Jimmy's World" story, and could have saved the newspaper from its mortification.

The point of all this is that, yes, mistakes were made during the early years of affirmative action in the workplace. African Americans given opportunity in white institutions were often underestimated and held to a higher standard—and they were occasionally overestimated. Not every individual effort to offer previously denied opportunity to Black people was successful.

In the aggregate, though, affirmative action objectively benefited not just African Americans and other minorities but also the universities that admitted them and the employers who hired them. In my industry, newspapers became much better when they diversified their reporting and editing staffs—measurably better, by any standard. At the *Post*, Black reporters allowed the paper to cover aspects of life in the majority-Black city of Washington with depth and insight that white journalists, no matter how talented, could not have achieved.

One classic example is the work of Leon Dash, one of the original Metro Seven reporters. Dash became a pioneering Black foreign correspondent who covered West Africa for the *Post* with great sensitivity and understanding. Back in Washington, on the Special Projects staff, he spent a year living in Clifton Terrace, one of the city's worst housing projects, a place riddled with drugs and crime and every other pathology you could think of, to produce a remarkable eight-part series about one Black family's struggle. The series, headlined "Rosa Lee: A Mother and Her Family in Urban America," won both a Pulitzer Prize and a Robert F. Kennedy Journalism Award, and later was made into a book and an Emmy-winning documentary. Among the many insights Dash gained from his deep reporting was that the impoverished teenage mothers he met were not having babies because of any ignorance about birth control; they had babies as a way of striking out on their own and establishing their own households. Another twist that confounded readers' initial assumptions was that the central character in Dash's series, the matriarch Rosa Lee Cunningham, was at the time in a committed lesbian relationship. No white reporter could have learned as much about the daily and inner lives of the people who lived in that housing project. No white reporter would have been able to spend even a day there.

Black editors similarly improved the *Post*'s coverage, when they were listened to. African American journalists introduced readers to people and places they never would have known otherwise—middle-class Black neighborhood leaders, the city's growing Latino community, gay and lesbian activists. A similar broadening of horizons took place at businesses in other sectors of the economy and at colleges and universities. There was ample evidence that taking steps to make a staff or a student body better reflect the nation's diversity turned out to help the institution better carry out its mission.

Not everyone agreed, however. Affirmative action had barely begun before an angry backlash arose.

The stage for this reaction had been set in 1968 by Richard Nixon, who saw political opportunity for himself and the Republican Party in stoking white resentment. For the better part of a century, the South had been a Democratic Party stronghold—and powerful southern Democrats in Congress had been the guarantors of racial segregation. Veteran senators such as James Eastland and John Stennis, both of Mississippi, staunchly opposed civil rights legislation, even as Democrats from other parts of the country came to embrace the goal of racial equality. Measures by Democratic presidents weakened the party's bond with white voters in the South—Truman's desegregation of the armed forces in 1949, for example, and Kennedy's use of federal power to force the integration of the University of Alabama in 1963. When Lyndon Johnson, himself a southern Democrat, shepherded Congress into passing the transformative civil rights laws of the 1960s, divorce between his party and whites in the former Confederacy became all but inevitable. Republicans, led by Nixon, saw an opening that they exploited via Nixon's "Southern Strategy."

One of Nixon's political gurus, Kevin Phillips, explained the strategy in a 1970 interview with *The New York Times*: "From now on, the Republicans are never going to get more than 10 to 20 percent of the Negro vote and they don't need any more than that . . . but Republicans would be shortsighted if they weakened enforcement of the Voting Rights Act. The more Negroes who register as Democrats in the South, the sooner the Negrophobe whites will quit the Democrats and become Republicans. That's where the votes are. Without that prodding from the blacks, the whites will backslide into their old comfortable arrangement with the local Democrats."

While Nixon was stoking the backlash in the political sphere, the Supreme Court—led by Chief Justice Warren E. Burger, a Nixon appointee—was doing the same on the legal front.

In 1974, a white former marine named Allan Paul Bakke was rejected for the second time for admission to the University of California, Davis, medical school. He sued the university, claiming that its policy of reserving a certain number of slots for minority students violated his constitutional rights. *Regents of the University of California v. Bakke* went all the way to the U.S. Supreme Court, and in 1978 the Court issued a decision that in retrospect was the beginning of the end for affirmative action. The *Bakke* decision held that the university could take race into account in admissions decisions, along with other factors, but that numerical quotas such as the one set by the UC Davis medical school—out of one hundred entry slots, sixteen were reserved for minorities—were unconstitutional.

Affirmative action continued for decades, in weakened fashion, but *Bakke* was a harbinger. Without quotas or mandates—but with old-school, unvarnished racial discrimination legally outlawed and now socially unacceptable—some African Americans did rise to previously unimagined heights of wealth, power, and influence. Many others did not, and on average there remained large and persistent gaps between whites and Blacks in income, net worth, life expectancy, and a range of other socioeconomic indicators. But highly visible examples of Black success were seen, by some, as white deprivation.

THE CULTURAL ARTIFACT THAT perhaps most vividly tells this story—Black advancement, followed by white resentment—is a political ad known as "Hands" from the 1990 midterm election.

Senator Jesse Helms of North Carolina, one of the last Democrat-turned-Republican dinosaurs from the South, found himself in an unexpectedly tough reelection campaign. Like Thurmond, Helms had realized that the time for overt race-baiting had passed; the GOP's Southern Strategy was more subtle than that. He had even made a show of hiring James Meredith, the first African American to attend the University of Mississippi, onto his Senate staff. Still, Helms was seen by Democrats, especially Black Democrats, as a staunch defender of white privilege and primacy. In his most recent reelection bid, six years earlier, he had won by just four percentage points. This time, his opponent was a rising star in the Democratic Party: Harvey Gantt, the first Black mayor of Charlotte, whose life story embodied African American progress in the post–civil rights era.

Gantt was originally from South Carolina, born in 1943 in Henry Fordham's hometown of Charleston. He grew up when the city, like the rest of the state, was segregated and unequal and when the civil rights movement was gathering steam; his father, a shipyard worker, took young Harvey with him when he went to NAACP meetings. Gantt graduated second in his class at Burke High School in 1960 and went away to Iowa State University to study architecture. After a few months in frigid Iowa—and after learning that there was a more highly regarded architecture program at a college much closer to home—he applied to transfer into Clemson University, South Carolina's big land-grant public university, located near Greenville, in the northwestern corner of the state. Like its in-state rival, the University of South Carolina, Clemson was established and operated for white students only.

For more than two years, Clemson denied Gantt's application without explicitly rejecting it. The school did not respond at all for months, then demanded SAT scores and transcripts that Gantt hadn't been told were required, then informed him that there was not enough time to process his application for the 1961 school year. The school's next step was to demand that Gantt appear for an in-person interview. Then it canceled his original application, saying he could begin the whole process again and submit another application if he cared to. While continuing his studies at Iowa State, Gantt did all the paperwork and once more applied to transfer into Clemson, this time seeking to enter the school in the fall of 1962. He heard nothing for five months, and then Clemson told him his new application was incomplete—but did not tell him what was supposedly missing.

Gantt got in touch with a civil rights lawyer he had met when he was involved with the NAACP Youth Council: Matthew Perry, the future federal judge who had received his legal education in Orangeburg at SC State's court-mandated law school. In July 1962, Perry filed a discrimination lawsuit on Gantt's behalf in federal court. Gantt lost at the District Court level, but won on appeal before the U.S. Fourth Circuit Court of Appeals, which ordered the university to end its discriminatory practices and promptly admit Gantt. In February 1963, at the beginning of the spring semester, Gantt became the first African American to attend Clemson University.

He graduated from Clemson with a degree in architecture, earned a master's degree in urban planning at MIT, and then moved to Charlotte, North Carolina's largest city, where he cofounded an architectural practice that played a big role in shaping the rapidly growing metropolis. He went into politics in 1974, winning a seat on the city council—and then setting his sights higher. In 1983, he took office as Charlotte's first Black mayor. In 1990, at a time when the idea of a non-racist "New South" was ascendant, Gantt sought and won the Democratic nomination to run against Helms, who was the epitome of the "Old South." As Gantt campaigned across the state and was warmly received, including in many majority-white communities, change seemed to be in the air. With a week and a half to go before Election Day, he was leading Helms in the polls.

But then the Helms campaign began airing one of the most infamous political ads in U.S. history. In it, a man wearing a red flannel shirt sits at a table. His face is not shown; the viewer sees only his torso and his hands, which show that he is white. The hands open an envelope, take out a letter, hold it in position to be read, and then crush the letter in frustration or anger. An unseen, deep-voiced narrator says, "You needed that job, and you were the best qualified. But they had to give it to a minority because of a racial quota. Is that really fair? Harvey Gantt says it is."

The word *minority* is emphasized into a sneer. The message to white voters is unmistakable: Gantt, a Black man, wants to take away your jobs and give them to Black people who have not earned them. The ad's premise is a lie; racial quotas of the kind being implied had been ruled out more than a decade earlier in the *Bakke* decision. But Gantt did support affirmative action measures that passed constitutional muster, and the Helms campaign had identified this stance as a vulnerability that could be exploited.

The "Hands" ad was immediately controversial, seen by many as an undisguised appeal to racism. Helms ended up defeating Gantt by five percentage points, 52.5 percent to 47.4 percent. It could be that the polls were wrong all along—that a considerable number of white voters, when asked whom they would vote for, gave what they considered the "correct" non-racist answer rather than the true answer. Or it could be that the "Hands" ad really had that much impact—that it spurred whites who rarely voted to turn out this time and vote, not so much for Helms as against Gantt.

Either way, the "Hands" election was a reality check. The civil rights revolution and the affirmative action measures that followed had changed the nation enough that an eminently qualified African American candidate could seriously contend for a Senate seat in one of the states of the old Confederacy. But not enough that such a candidate could actually win.

I WATCHED THAT ELECTION unfold from far, far away. Along with Avis and our two sons, Aaron and Lowell, I was living in a suburb of Buenos Aires, Argentina, which was my home base as South America correspondent for *The Washington Post,* a posting I held from 1988 to 1992. My job was to cover the entire continent, which meant constant travel with pit stops at home to reintroduce myself to my family. The big stories I covered included the tumultuous end of Augusto Pinochet's brutal rule in Chile, the height of the drug wars in Colombia, a coup against the longtime dictator of Paraguay, a "self-coup" by the president of Peru against his legislature, several fizzled attempted coups by right-wing military officers in Argentina, deadly urban riots in Venezuela, and a murder trial held in a small town in the remotest part of the Amazon rain forest. Avis called those four years my "cowboy" phase.

I will highlight just a couple of moments from this adventure that are relevant to this American history.

The first requires a bit of context. When I was in grade school at Felton, among the supplemental materials the teachers used was a publication called *My Weekly Reader.* It was almost like a little *Time* or *Newsweek* for kids, with brief news and feature stories targeted at various levels of reading comprehension. Now, many years later, I have a vivid memory of only one thing I ever read in the *Weekly Reader*: a story about Brasília, the new capital city built in South America's biggest country. I was dazzled by the pictures of the striking modern buildings, all glass and concrete, some with curving forms augmenting their clean, straight lines. I had never seen buildings so beautiful, never imagined they could exist. Then and there, I decided I wanted to be an architect. I was disabused of that notion by my dismal performance in Architecture 101 at Michigan, where I was at the bottom of my class; I would have been a terrible architect. But I never lost my appreciation for great architecture, and I never lost my sense of childhood wonder at what the great architect Oscar Niemeyer and the great city planner Lúcio Costa had achieved in Brasília.

Magically, in 1988, I was there. I went to Brasília on a reporting trip and got to see those iconic modern structures firsthand. The whole time I was there, I spent much more time admiring architectural details than doing journalism. I saw how the major buildings—the congress, the presidential palace, the supreme court—were meant to speak to one another across their wide plaza, in democratic conversation. I got to walk inside Niemeyer's amazing Metropolitan Cathedral, there on the grand esplanade, and appreciate the way its curving supports, like concrete tepee poles, framed the building's stained-glass walls, whose swooping designs were tinted in the most heavenly shades of blue. And sitting there in a pew, I thought of my family. I thought of how far I had come from Orangeburg, how I was getting to see and experience a place I had only dreamed of, and how fortunate I was to have been launched on this journey by the hard work and sacrifice of my ancestors. In my grandparents' and great-grandparents' and great-great-grandparents' time, Black boys from a Cotton Belt county in South Carolina did not become foreign correspondents for major American newspapers and get sent halfway around the world to exotic places. Yet there I was. And I owed that fact to those who had come before me, who had built a foundation and, if it was demolished, built it again, and ultimately made my career possible. I felt tremendously proud and profoundly humbled.

The other moment came when my sister, Ellen, flew down to South America for a visit. Avis and I had urged any and all family members to take advantage of the fact that we lived in a fascinating, faraway place. By then our parents were retired; Louisa had spent three decades as head librarian at Claflin, and Harold had ended up being a civil servant, running the Orangeburg office of the Social Security Administration. They had plenty of free time for travel, but no great desire to see South America. (They did visit us at our next posting, in London.) Ellen had always been adventurous, though, and she jumped at the chance to come to Buenos Aires. By then she had graduated from Spelman College, in Atlanta; done graduate study in marketing at the University of Illinois; and embarked on what would become a distinguished career in academia as a professor and administrator. Avis would have said she still had a lot of "cowgirl" in her.

I decided to take her on an excursion to a natural wonder I had not yet seen: Iguazu Falls, the vast and awe-inspiring cataracts on the Iguazu River near the point where the borders of Argentina, Brazil, and Paraguay meet. On the road from the airport, still miles away, we could hear the thunder of the waters and see the ever-present plume of mist rising to the heavens. We stayed on the Brazil side, in the grand old Hotel das Cataratas, which overlooks the waterfalls in their majesty—taller than Niagara, twice as wide, mesmerizing in their power. After seeing this natural wonder from all angles, we had to do one more thing while we were in the neighborhood: I had mentioned to Ellen that Asunción, the capital of Paraguay, was a fabulous place to buy high-quality leather goods at ridiculously low prices. She wanted to go there.

We were "in the neighborhood" only relatively speaking. Asunción was across an international border and more than two hundred miles from our hotel. Still, we piled into our little rental car, and I drove us all the way across a strange and unfamiliar country. And we had the greatest time. I had estimated that it would take between three and four hours; it took closer to five. We got to Asunción barely a half hour before the stores were going to close, and Ellen gave me a master class in just how many leather shops can be visited, and just how many beautiful bags of all shapes and sizes can be bartered for and purchased, in thirty minutes' time.

As we drove back to the hotel with our haul, I had another of those long-way-from-Orangeburg epiphanies. What would our great-great-grandfather Henry Fordham have thought of us in that moment? What about John Hammond Fordham and Louisa Fordham, our great-grandparents; or Sadie Fordham Smith, our grandmother? Would they have thought us spoiled and frivolous? I hope not. The Fordhams always did like nice things, after all, when they could afford them. I like to think they would have seen this moment of carefree privilege as theirs as much as ours.

Chapter Fourteen

THE OBAMA MOMENT

In 2007, I spent much of the week between Christmas and New Year's driving from small town to small town across the frozen tundra of eastern Iowa, trying to dispel what logic and history told me was an illusion. I failed. I left believing that the illusion might just be real.

I had become a twice-weekly columnist at the *Post*, and the most compelling story at the moment was the presidential election campaign, which was in full roar. There were open primary contests in both parties—the Republican incumbent, George W. Bush, was finishing his second term—but most of the electricity and excitement were on the Democratic side. Senators Joe Biden of Delaware and Christopher Dodd of Connecticut were in the race, as was New Mexico governor Bill Richardson, but polls showed all of them lagging well behind the three leaders: former senator John Edwards of North Carolina, former First Lady and senator Hillary Rodham Clinton, and first-term senator Barack Obama from Illinois. For the party to nominate either Clinton, a woman, or Obama, an African American, would be an epic milestone. The first-in-the-nation Iowa caucuses were scheduled for January 3, and the major Democratic candidates were all crisscrossing the state in their campaign buses, appearing at five or six events a day in search of every persuadable voter between the Mississippi and the Missouri.

I had written *Washington Post* columns about the race and talked about it in MSNBC appearances throughout the year. I knew all the Democratic candidates, and I spoke regularly with sources in their campaign operations. My view of the contest basically conformed to the conventional wisdom, which was the following: Edwards had a distinctive and appealing message, centered on the urgent need to address rising inequality, but he was falling behind; the Clinton campaign was a juggernaut, powered and funded by the huge political machine of the candidate's husband, Bill Clinton, and was probably unstoppable; and Obama was something we had never seen before—an African American presidential candidate who had broad mainstream appeal and who was gaining ground on Clinton, but who in the end would probably fall just short.

At a holiday gathering, friends quizzed me on what was happening in the Democratic race, and I told them the above. When Avis and I got home, she looked at me and said, "How the hell do you know what's happening in Iowa? Your ass is here in Arlington, Virginia."

She was right, of course. I remembered an old saying from my years as a foreign correspondent: "If you don't go, you don't know." Even in the internet age, when all of us have the whole world at our fingertips, there is always more for a journalist to learn by witnessing events firsthand. There is nuance; there are sights, sounds, and smells; there is a tone of voice or a raised eyebrow that doesn't come through in a transcript. Avis reminded me that when we lived in Buenos Aires, if big news broke in the middle of the night—a bombing in Bogotá, say, or an oil spill in Patagonia—I would grab the bag I always kept packed with a few days' clothes, head immediately for the airport, and figure things out as I went along.

For my Iowa trip, the one thing I arranged in advance was the flight, simply because I had to decide where to land. I knew that Des Moines would be saturated with political reporters from around the country and the world, making the whole city a conventional wisdom echo chamber, and I wanted to base myself on ground less trampled. I saw that there was a nonstop flight to Cedar Rapids, a smaller city in the eastern part of the state, and I guessed the candidates would be in that general vicinity. So, I flew there on the day after Christmas, rented a car, and drove off to discover what it was I didn't know.

I caught up with Edwards in a little town called Washington, about sixty miles south of Cedar Rapids, where the former senator was scheduled to hold a roundtable with undecided caucus-goers at the public library. When I got there, I was surprised at the size of the crowd waiting for the candidate; the consensus narrative back in D.C. had been that his campaign was leaking oil and losing steam, but apparently nobody had told these Iowans. I reminded myself that Edwards had done very well in the Iowa caucuses four years earlier, finishing a close second to eventual Democratic nominee John Kerry; he had a history of support in the state. I should note that all this was before a tawdry "love child" scandal ended Edwards's political career.

Politics in Iowa is a tactile pursuit. When Edwards arrived, he had to squeeze his way through the knot of people gathered at the library's narrow entrance. This was just his second event of the day, and I could tell. He seemed fresh, his white shirt and navy blazer were unwrinkled, and clearly he was energized by the big crowd. With his boyish good looks and movie-star smile, Edwards lit up the room. He gave a brief, informal version of his "two Americas" speech, about how this was becoming a nation of haves and have-nots, and I could see that much of the audience was nodding in agreement. By the time he had answered questions and was ready to move on to his next stop, the crowd had grown to the point that it took him and his aides ten minutes to disentangle themselves and make an escape. I hadn't eaten all day, so I walked to a Chinese restaurant across the town plaza to fuel up and plan the rest of my day. I made a note that the Edwards campaign in Iowa didn't look as dead as I'd expected.

I found Clinton at a rally in a high school auditorium in Vinton, a little town on the Cedar River, where I beheld the mass and momentum of the vaunted Clinton machine. I arrived well before the candidate did, and this was a much bigger venue than the one where I'd seen Edwards; it was set up for at least five hundred people. Neat rows of folding chairs were already filled with supporters eager to see their candidate, and quite a few in the expectant audience were wearing sweatshirts with one of the campaign's slogans, "Ready for Change, Ready to Lead." Security arrangements for the former First Lady were more elaborate than those for her rivals, and attendees had been told to be sure to arrive on time. But Clinton was running late. While the crowd waited, I noticed that members of the campaign's advance team were removing an unoccupied row of chairs at the very back, which was a textbook move. No candidate wants television cameras covering a campaign stop to pan across a line of empty chairs.

Clinton finally swept in with an entourage—her security detail, a phalanx of campaign aides, fifteen or more reporters and photographers. Everything about the rally itself was utterly professional. I had heard Clinton deliver her stump speech before, and while she is not what anyone would call a soaring orator, on this occasion I thought she was quite good. Seeing and hearing the enthusiasm of women in the audience especially, I could feel how historic it would be for one of our two major political parties to nominate a woman for president. Clinton had plenty of energy, her smile positively beamed, her applause lines landed, and the crowd roared with enthusiasm when she left the stage. The event had projected the confidence of a winning campaign, and I left with a new understanding of why the conventional wisdom was so sure that the Clinton machine would prevail in the end—that Clinton would likely win Iowa and then roll on to become the Democratic nominee.

But I also went to an Obama rally. In Ottumwa, a small city about eighty-five miles southeast of Des Moines, the senator was scheduled to hold a nighttime rally. I got there early, as usual, and the high school gymnasium where he would speak was already packed with hundreds of people. Advance staff were not removing empty seats; they were setting up more. Obama's crowd looked much the same as Clinton's crowd, but did not sound the same: There was a constant hum, a buzz, of anticipation. A section of the bleachers was roped off for media, and I ran into a couple of reporters I knew from Washington. To pass the time before the candidate's arrival, we played a game: Try to find a non-white person in the audience. We couldn't do it. Every person of color one of us spotted turned out to be a journalist or campaign worker from out of town. Iowa is one of the least diverse states in the country. Every four years, questions are raised about why an objectively unrepresentative set of voters is given such an outsize role in choosing the presidential nominees of both parties. And every four years, inertia prevails and Iowa again goes first.

Like Clinton at her rally, Obama arrived with a substantial coterie of aides and traveling journalists in tow. That is where any similarity between the two events ended.

By this point, Obama had polished the standard stump speech he gave four or five times a day into lapidary perfection. It was a thing of beauty. The point, obviously, was not to list policy positions or attack his opponents; Edwards and Clinton had both been more specific and more aggressive. Obama's aim was more ambitious: What he did masterfully was invite those Iowans to imagine a better America—and, most important, to envision their own better selves. It was a stirring message, and he delivered it expertly, varying his cadence and volume in a way that took his listeners on a journey; the crowd was pin-drop silent when he lowered his voice, and thunderous when he raised it. When he exhorted the crowd to be "fired up," the gymnasium seemed ready to ignite. When he flashed what is often described as his million-dollar smile, its radiance seemed more in the billion-dollar range. Toward the end, the speech built and built until Obama came to his exit line: "This is our time to unite in common purpose to make this century the next American century. Let's go change the world!"

I had the sense that those mild-mannered Iowans would have

marched off to storm Ottumwa's City Hall, if Obama had asked them to. The crowd almost seemed to float out of that gym. Obama had delivered the kind of speech Sarah Palin would later deride as "that hopey-changey stuff." But what had floored me was not what Obama said to those Iowa voters. It was how he made them feel.

I flew home in time to go with Avis to a small New Year's Eve gathering at the home of some good friends. The guests were almost all African American, and everyone there was active in politics to some degree. Two former Cabinet secretaries were in attendance. When Avis mentioned that I'd just returned from Iowa, the group wanted to know what the race looked like. Could Obama finish a close-enough second to make it a two-person race between him and Clinton? Would his showing be respectable enough to give him a boost in New Hampshire and beyond?

I told them I thought Obama could win in Iowa. I said I wasn't sure and wouldn't put money on it. But I had watched as Barack Hussein Obama—a Black man, in America, with a name that might have come from the Guantánamo prisoners' list—enchanted and inspired a gymnasium full of white voters in one of the whitest states in the nation. After seeing that, I couldn't be sure my old assumptions were still valid.

Those assumptions were about Clinton's inevitability and about race in America. I had assumed that Democratic voters, like the party establishment, would see the 2008 cycle as Clinton's turn to run. I had assumed that the historic "first" the nation was more likely prepared to countenance was the election of a woman as president. I had assumed that Obama, having used this campaign to introduce himself to the nation, would be in a good position to run again in 2012 if Clinton lost the general election, or in 2016 if she won. I had assumed that only then might I have to seriously ponder whether this nation, with its centuries-long history of slavery and Jim Crow, could ever send an African American to the White House, not as head butler but as commander in chief. I didn't know whether I believed that was possible. Up to that point in my life, I'd never had reason to think about it.

Three days later, Obama won the Iowa caucuses. The process for calculating results there is numbingly complex, but in the closest thing to a one-person, one-vote tally, Obama finished with 39 percent, Edwards with 30 percent, and Clinton with 29 percent. As the primary season unfolded, it turned out that Obama was a generationally talented orator and that his brilliant young campaign gurus had shrewdly charted a path to the nomination. Obama overwhelmed Clinton in the states that chose their Democratic convention delegates in caucuses, at least held his own in the states with primaries, and eventually amassed such a lead that Clinton had no chance of catching up.

For the rest of the year, all the way through November, everything I wrote or said about the election was informed by what I had experienced at that Obama rally in Iowa. I knew that he had an incredible balancing act to perform, a long walk along a knife's edge. He had to project strength, but he could never come across as an Angry Black Man. He had to acknowledge the nation's long history of racism, but he could never seem resentful. He had to always look forward, never backward. I wrote in one column that he had to be seen as "the least-aggrieved Black man in America." When a moment of crisis came—controversy over very angry, very aggrieved remarks by his pastor, the Reverend Jeremiah Wright—Obama defused it not by forsaking his Black identity but by expanding it to embrace the white side of his family. I knew that he might actually win. I knew because, in Iowa, I had seen it with my own eyes, that the universe of the possible had been expanded.

Still, even after Obama had taken a decisive lead in the polls, on Election Night there was a little voice inside my head that kept saying, "But history, history, history . . ."

I spent that evening in New York, in a third-floor television studio at Rockefeller Center, doing commentary for MSNBC. As the numbers came in and the NBC Decision Desk called the eventual outcome in state after state, it became increasingly clear that Obama would indeed defeat his Republican opponent, Senator John McCain of Arizona, and win the presidency. But the little voice saying "history" wouldn't be quiet. Finally, at roughly 10:50 p.m., those of us on the anchor set were told through our earpieces that, at 11, the network was going to announce that Obama had won the election.

I had two immediate thoughts. First, I looked around the set at my colleagues—David Gregory was directing traffic in the anchor role, and I was providing analysis along with Rachel Maddow, Chris Matthews, and Keith Olbermann—and I realized that when Gregory announced the election of the first African American president, he was going to quickly turn to the only African American at the table for comment. I made a mental note of what I might say.

My second thought was to reach for my phone. There was a commercial break before the top of the hour, and I used those few off-air minutes to call my parents in Orangeburg. I had the privilege of telling Harold Robinson, who was ninety-two years old, and Louisa Robinson, who was eighty-seven, that they had lived to see a Black man elected president of the United States. They had been watching MSNBC's coverage all night, and I pictured them there in the sitting room, with the portraits of Major Fordham and Louisa Fordham looking down on them. When I ended the quick call, my concern was no longer what I might say on the air. It was whether I could keep from tearing up.

I was right: Gregory did come to me after announcing Obama's victory. My voice caught several times as I struggled to channel a flood of thoughts into some semblance of a coherent stream. This is what I said, or tried to say:

"I can't get to what the rest of the world is thinking, I'm just trying to deal with what I'm thinking at the moment. It is a moment that I will always remember. It is an amazing moment in American history, going back three hundred eighty-nine years. To think that a Black man, a man of African descent, represents this nation not only as head of government but as head of state. To think that when we tell our children, as I told my sons, that you can grow up to be anything, you can grow up to be president, I am now telling the truth. I spoke to my mother and father a few minutes ago during a break. They were still up; they were excited; I am so happy that they lived to see this moment. And I miss others who did not live to see this moment, my dear mother-in-law and father-in-law, I wish they were here to share it. Maybe they're looking down from somewhere and sharing in a moment that not only will I never forget, but that—I think the world will never forget this moment, because it is a moment of demarcation. There was a before and an after. We don't know what happens in the after, but we know it's different from the before. And it feels different, to me, to be an American tonight."

I kept my composure, barely, the rest of the time we were on the air. MSNBC had asked me to stay in New York the following day to do more commentary. Wednesday wasn't one of my regular days to write my *Post* column, but no force on earth was going to keep me away from the keyboard, so the network gave me an office where I could work between my television hits. I wrote about the huge expectant crowd that had gathered in Chicago's Grant Park. I wrote about seeing the Reverend Jesse Jackson in that crowd with tears streaming down his face as Barack and Michelle Obama took the stage. I wrote about my on-air conversation with Georgia congressman John Lewis, one of our bravest civil rights heroes. I wrote about my phone call to my parents. And I tried to capture what Obama's election meant to me:

"I can't help but experience Obama's election as a gesture of recognition and acceptance—which is patently absurd, if you think about it. The labor of black people made this great nation possible. Black people planted and tended the tobacco, indigo and cotton on which America's first great fortunes were built. Black people fought and died in every one of the nation's wars. Black people fought and died to secure our fundamental rights under the Constitution. We don't have to ask for anything from anybody. Yet something changed on Tuesday when Americans—white, black, Latino, Asian—entrusted a black man with the power and responsibility of the presidency. I always meant it when I said the Pledge of Allegiance in school. I always meant it when I sang the national anthem at ball games and shot off fireworks on the Fourth of July. But now there's more meaning in my expressions of patriotism, because there's more meaning in the stirring ideals that the pledge and the anthem and the fireworks represent."

Producers interrupted my column writing three times to take me out to the set to do on-air segments. Each time, they had to take me to the makeup room for emergency repairs. Without realizing it, I had been crying.

The column ended, "Now I know how some people must have felt when they heard Ronald Reagan say 'it's morning again in America.' The new sunshine feels warm on my face."

LATER THAT MONTH, AVIS and I and our son Lowell, then eighteen, went to Orangeburg for Thanksgiving. During this period, we were visiting as often as we could because my father's health was poor; he had chronic obstructive pulmonary disease—during my youth, he had been a heavy pipe smoker, never far from his ashtray and his tin of Carter Hall tobacco—and he had heart problems as well. For more than a year, he had required supplemental oxygen. Through it all, he had been his regular self, razor-sharp and always good-natured. This time, though, he was different. He hardly moved from the recliner that was his customary throne in the sitting room, right beneath Major Fordham's portrait, and he didn't join the general conversation the way he always had.

At Thanksgiving dinner, he sat in his usual seat at the head of the table. As always, we all waited for him to say grace. Instead of his usual brief prayer, he spoke slowly and softly about our family and our many blessings. He hardly touched his turkey, hardly ate anything at all except one of the yeasted cloverleaf rolls Avis had made especially for him because he loved them so. After dinner, we went back into the sitting room to watch football, and he fell asleep in his chair, which was what always happened after Thanksgiving dinner. But late in the afternoon, when it was time for a bite of supper, we couldn't wake him up.

We called an ambulance and took him to the emergency room. The physician on duty told my mother that they could try putting him on a respirator, sedating him for the night, and try to wake him in the morning, but made clear that he probably would not revive. "Do it," my mother said. Avis and I spent the night at the hospital, and we feared the worst when a nurse on the morning shift came to take us to his room. He was on a respirator, with tubes and monitors everywhere, but he was wide awake, his eyes smiling. When my mother, his sweet Louisa, rushed to the hospital and came into the room, those eyes positively beamed.

He never left that hospital bed, though. On January 2, 2009, Harold Irwin Robinson died. In his lifetime, the limit of how high a Black man could climb had reached the apex of American power. And like Major Fordham and Eugene Smith, the previous patriarchs of the house at Boulevard and Oak, he had provided big shoulders for the next generation to stand on.

Chapter Fifteen

THE BACKLASH—AND THE CYCLE CONTINUES

The day of Obama's inauguration was cold and blustery—the temperature in Washington at noon on January 20, 2009, was twenty-eight degrees, with wind gusts of more than twenty miles an hour. Still, for me, the day was dreamlike, full of sights and sounds that previously had been beyond the range of possibility. The best estimate of the number of people gathered on the National Mall was 1.8 million, according to *The Washington Post*, which made it the largest crowd on record in the city's history. On or near the West Front of the U.S. Capitol was gathered a shivering who's who of African American celebrities and heroes—among them Oprah Winfrey, Tiger Woods, Beyoncé Knowles, Muhammad Ali, and scores of surviving Tuskegee Airmen, the pioneering Black aviators from World War II. Obama gave an inaugural speech that dwelled on history and tradition rather than chart some program of bold initiatives, as if to reassure the nation that the radical step of electing the first Black president would not lead to radical change. I spent that day in the relative warmth and comfort of a temporary studio erected on the Mall for MSNBC's coverage of the inauguration. It was hard for me to believe what I was seeing, and I said so on the air. Repeatedly.

That evening, after a suite of inaugural balls in which guests danced to more soul and funk music than at any previous such galas, a Black family took up residence in the White House—Barack and Michelle Obama, first daughters Malia and Sasha, and first mother-in-law Marian Robinson. Op-ed writers and television commentators wondered whether the nation, at last, had entered a "post-racial" era. It was a reasonable question. An African American was now the most powerful man in the United States, which made him the most powerful man on earth. He had been given that awesome power by American voters, two-thirds of whom were white. Clearly, attitudes about race in this country had changed. But exactly how? And for how long?

One of the biggest and most star-studded Inauguration Week parties celebrating Obama was hosted by Harvard University professor Henry Louis Gates Jr., who was a friend of the new president. For many years, Gates had been the best-known and most influential Black scholar in the nation. His leadership of the African American Studies department at Harvard, his documentaries on PBS, his articles in *The New Yorker*, and his other high-profile work had focused new attention, resources, and rigor on the study of the Black American experience. I had first met Gates in December 1993, in Stockholm, Sweden, where I was covering novelist Toni Morrison's acceptance of the Nobel Prize in Literature—the first such honor for an African American. Gates and I rode on the same shuttle bus from our hotel to the grand hall of the Swedish Academy, where Morrison gave her laureate's address. Gates is a slight man of less than average height. Because of a childhood injury, he walks with a limp and uses a cane.

Six months after the inauguration, on July 16, Gates was arrested at his home in Cambridge, Massachusetts. Then fifty-eight, he was returning from a trip to China when he tried to open his front door and found that the lock was jammed. He asked the driver who had brought him from the airport to wait while he went around to the back door and let himself in. Then he went back outside and, with the driver's help, forced the front door open.

A neighbor watched this sequence of events from a distance and called Cambridge Police, believing a burglary was taking place. Police sergeant James Crowley, who is white, soon arrived to investigate the suspicious activity by "two Black males." When Gates answered the door, Crowley instructed him to step outside and told him to present proof that this was his residence. An indignant Gates did so, and Crowley became satisfied that Gates indeed lived there. Nevertheless, Crowley put Gates in handcuffs and arrested him for disorderly conduct. The two men agreed that all this happened. What they, and the nation, disagreed about was why it happened.

Gates, the respected and famous public intellectual, was tired, jet-lagged, and outraged at being accosted in his own home. Gates is four years older than I am; he grew up in segregated West Virginia and remembers the humiliations of Jim Crow segregation. He believed—as I would have believed, in the same circumstances—that he was being racially profiled, and he let Crowley know it, demanding of the officer, "Do you know who I am?" Crowley had no idea who Gates was, did not know if the second of the reported "two Black males" might still be in the house, bristled at the way his authority was being challenged, and believed that Gates's sustained verbal abuse crossed the line. Crowley could have just said "good day" and left, having ascertained that Gates was in his own home. Gates, for his part, could have just shut up. Instead, the eminent professor was taken into custody, handcuffed, bundled into a squad car, and hauled off to the police station for booking. The incident was first reported by Harvard's student newspaper, *The Harvard Crimson*, and then picked up by the national media. The disorderly conduct charge against Gates was quickly dismissed, but not before Obama, at a July 22 news conference about health care reform, was asked to comment on the arrest of his friend. The president's answer became a national Rorschach test about race.

"I don't know, not having been there and not seeing all the facts, what role race played in that," Obama said. "But I think it's fair to say, number one, any of us would be pretty angry; number two, that the Cambridge police acted stupidly in arresting somebody when there was already proof that they were in their own home; and, number three, what I think we know separate and apart from this incident is that there's a long history in this country of African Americans and Latinos being stopped by law enforcement disproportionately."

Years later, Obama wrote in his White House memoir, *A Promised Land,* that those remarks caused a bigger drop in his support among whites than any other single event. The Pew Research Center measured the tumble in white voters' approval of Obama at seven full points, from 53 percent to 46 percent. For the president and his political aides, the sharp decline was alarming. On July 24, Obama came unannounced to a White House press briefing to explain what he had meant, saying he "could have calibrated those words differently." But by then, he had a genuine controversy on his hands.

Many African Americans saw Obama's initial assessment—that Crowley had acted "stupidly" in arresting Gates in his own home—as the self-evident truth. Many whites did not see it that way at all, and some police groups were irate that, in their view, Obama had reflexively taken sides against the officer without knowing all the facts. Congressman Steve King of Iowa, a conservative Republican firebrand notorious for giving voice to white nationalist views, laid out the white complaint against Obama in unapologetic language: "The president has demonstrated that he has a default mechanism in him that breaks down the side of race that favors the black person, in the case of Professor Gates and Officer Crowley."

To stop the political bleeding, Obama invited Gates and Crowley to the White House for a made-for-television "Beer Summit" of reconciliation. Each man issued a statement afterward about understanding the other's point of view, and they ended up on friendly terms. "When he's not arresting you, Sgt. Crowley is a really likeable guy," Gates said.

But the suspicion that the first Black president would use his power to the advantage of African Americans, and the disadvantage of whites, had been aired and, in some minds, validated. The post-racial era, if it ever began, had ended.

AT THE RISK OF understatement, Obama's life story was different from that of most African Americans. He was born in 1961 in Honolulu, Hawaii, thousands of miles away from the southern towns and northern cities where most Black Americans were born. He was the son of a white mother from Kansas, an anthropologist named Stanley Ann Dunham, and a Black father from Kenya, an economist named Barack Hussein Obama Sr. The elder Obama had added the Arabic name Hussein to his own as a young man, during the African struggle for independence from colonial rule, when he converted from Roman Catholicism to Islam; later, he converted back to Christianity, and later still, he became an atheist. The couple divorced in 1964, and in 1965, Ann Dunham married an Indonesian man named Lolo Soetoro. When Soetoro had finished his studies at the University of Hawaii, he took the family to his homeland. From age six to age ten, young "Barry" Obama lived with his mother, stepfather, and infant half sister, Maya, in Jakarta, the Indonesian capital. Barry went to local schools and became fluent in the Indonesian language. In 1971, he was uprooted again and spent the next eight years back in Honolulu. Ann Dunham was away for much of that time, doing anthropological fieldwork, which meant that Barry and Maya were left in the care of their white maternal grandparents. With the aid of a scholarship, Barry attended and graduated from Punahou, Hawaii's most elite private prep school.

In his first book, *Dreams from My Father*, Obama describes his long and difficult struggle to make sense of his exotic heritage. From all those bits and pieces, he somehow had to construct an identity. Between graduating from Columbia University and enrolling at Harvard Law School, he worked as a community organizer in Chicago, and that is where he finally could see himself clearly: He was a Black man, and the African American community was his home.

Obama had no lingering doubt about who he was. But during his 2008 presidential campaign, fringe conspiracy theories began to percolate: He was secretly a Muslim, just like his father, and his middle name was the clue that gave it away. Or he hadn't actually been born in the United States, and instead was born in Kenya, which made him ineligible to serve as president. Or perhaps both. No one could ever point to a single fact that supported either of these fantasies, because neither contained a shred of truth. Still, the idea that Obama was some sort of impostor was stubbornly persistent. To put to bed what was clearly a non-issue, in June 2008 the Obama campaign released his birth certificate. It proved that he had been born, as he said, in Honolulu.

Some skeptics refused to be convinced. At a town hall during the general election campaign, Republican candidate John McCain had to correct a woman in the audience who had claimed Obama was "an Arab." In the end, Obama was elected, he took office, and a lawsuit seeking to challenge his legitimacy based on his birthplace was quickly thrown out of court. The "birther" conspiracy theory looked like a minor historical footnote.

It never completely went away, however. By March 2011, Obama's pristine political standing had been battered and bruised by two years of incumbency. He had orchestrated controversial spending measures to keep Americans afloat during the worst financial crisis since the Great Depression. He had pushed through Congress the Affordable Care Act—the biggest expansion in health care access since Medicare and Medicaid—over the vehement objections of a strident new conservative movement that called itself the Tea Party. And he had seen his party suffer a huge defeat—he called it a "shellacking"—in the 2010 midterm elections.

As Obama struggled to regain momentum, a new antagonist revived the "question" of whether he had been born in the United States: Donald Trump, the flashy New York developer and self-promoter who had swung for the fences with heavily mortgaged casinos in Atlantic City, failed and declared those projects bankrupt, and then reinvented himself as a television star with his *Apprentice* and *Celebrity Apprentice* reality shows. Using his generational talent for drawing attention to himself, Trump summoned reporters and claimed—without producing an iota of factual support—that there were "real doubts" about the birth certificate Obama had presented three years earlier. Trump announced that he was sending a team of private investigators to Hawaii to discover "the truth."

Trump never revealed the fruits of any investigation, and there is no reason to believe he ever commissioned one. The announcement was part of a constant drumbeat of noise that did not so much raise Trump's already high profile as radically change it. Before, he had been a wealthy and somewhat louche celebrity; now, with these relentless attacks, he was becoming a political actor on the biggest stage. In the past, he had made campaign donations to Democrats; now he was trying to delegitimize a Democratic president—an African American president—to the delighted cheers of the most conservative anti-establishment Republicans. White House aides I spoke to at the time were convinced that Trump was appealing to racist attitudes some whites still held but were uncomfortable airing publicly—saying, effectively, that while a Black man might be working at the big desk in the Oval Office, he didn't really belong there. Obama abstained from responding to Trump directly, fearing that to do so would only give Trump's false claims more oxygen.

The definitive response came on April 27, 2011, when Hawaii officials released yet another Obama birth certificate: the "long-form" original version, which Trump had darkly suggested did not exist. It was identical in its particulars to the shorter version Obama had released earlier, proving that the president had indeed been born where and when he said he was. Three days later, Obama and Trump crossed paths—perhaps fatefully.

Their very public encounter took place in the cavernous ballroom of the Washington Hilton Hotel, where the White House Correspondents' Association was having its annual awards dinner. Often called the "nerd prom," the dinner is the Washington media establishment's biggest social event of the year, with up to two thousand attendees, decked out in black tie and formal gowns. Major news organizations compete to host the fanciest pre-dinner receptions, secure the most prominent tables, and land the most buzzworthy guests. *The Washington Post*'s big shiny object was Trump. The late Katharine Graham's daughter, Lally Weymouth, a doyenne of the New York social scene, had extended the invitation, and Trump had accepted, bringing his wife, Melania. Some journalists in the *Post* newsroom objected—not to supping with Trump the television celebrity, but to publicly embracing Trump the "birther" conspiracy theorist. The *Post*'s guest list, however, was above the newsroom's pay grade.

What gave the yearly dinner its prominence, and its newsworthiness, was that every sitting president since Calvin Coolidge had attended. The custom was for the president to give a humorous speech, one that skewered political opponents, gently ribbed political allies, and roasted the journalists who would spend the rest of the year roasting him. Obama, in his two previous appearances, had shown considerable talent for delivering barbed jokes with impressive comedic timing. That night, Obama warmed up with other topics before turning his focus on the guest at the *Washington Post* table.

"Donald Trump is here tonight!" Obama said. "Now, I know that he's taken some flak lately, but no one is happier, no one is prouder to put this birth certificate matter to rest than the Donald. And that's because he can finally get back to focusing on the issues that matter—like, did we fake the moon landing? What really happened in Roswell? And where are Biggie and Tupac?"

Looking at Trump, Obama addressed him in a tone of mock seriousness: "But all kidding aside, obviously, we all know about your credentials and breadth of experience. For example—no, seriously—just recently, in an episode of *Celebrity Apprentice*, at the steakhouse, the men's cooking team did not impress the judges from Omaha Steaks. And there was a lot of blame to go around. But you, Mr. Trump, recognized that the real problem was a lack of leadership. And so ultimately, you didn't blame Lil Jon or Meatloaf. You fired Gary Busey. And these are the kind of decisions that would keep me up at night. Well handled, sir. Well handled." (This swipe at Trump—I do important things, you do trivial things—was supported by a circumstance that no one appreciated at the time: Obama had just secretly given the go-ahead for the raid that killed Osama bin Laden.)

Trump managed to keep a fairly neutral expression through Obama's routine, looking neither amused nor enraged. But another tradition at the dinner was to invite a well-known comedian to do a more professional job of skewering Washington's egos and pretensions. And Trump visibly seethed when *Saturday Night Live* "Weekend Update" anchor Seth Myers went after him.

"Donald Trump has been saying he will run for president as a Republican—which is surprising, since I just assumed he was running as a joke," Meyers said. "Trump owns the Miss USA Pageant, which is great for Republicans, because it will streamline their search for a vice president. . . . Donald Trump said recently he's got a great relationship with 'the Blacks.' Unless the Blacks are a family of white people, I bet he's mistaken." By the end of Meyers's routine, Trump was glowering. Guests often linger after the dinner to mix and mingle; Trump left immediately. He complained the following day about how untalented Meyers was.

Some journalists and biographers have speculated that sitting through that evening—and reading stories about how he had been "humiliated" to his face by Obama—angered Trump so much that he decided, then and there, to make a serious run for the White House. He has denied that the dinner had anything to do with his launching his political career. Historians will someday reach their own conclusions.

A COINCIDENCE OF UNRELATED events can sometimes, in retrospect, take on larger historical meaning: On Tuesday, June 16, 2015, in New York, Trump rode down the golden escalator at his eponymous Manhattan tower and announced his candidacy for the Republican nomination for president. On Wednesday, June 17, in Charleston, a racist white man named Dylann Roof took a handgun into historic Mother Emanuel AME Church and murdered nine innocent Black worshipers.

The twenty-one-year-old Roof fled by car and was captured the next morning in North Carolina. What had spurred him to kill without mercy or remorse was his belief that white people are the superior race. His rage was fueled by a perception that Black-on-white crime was ubiquitous and worsening—although crime rates were at fifty-year lows—and he was proudly unrepentant. "I would like to make it crystal clear I do not regret what I did," he wrote in his prison journal after his arrest. "I am not sorry. I have not shed a tear for the innocent people I killed. I do feel sorry for the innocent white children forced to live in this sick country and I do feel sorry for the innocent white people that are killed daily at the hands of the lower race. I have shed a tear of self-pity for myself. I feel pity that I had to do what I did in the first place. I feel pity that I had to give up my life because of a situation that should never have existed."

For many, including me, this massacre was more devastating than most other tragic mass shootings because of the unmitigated racial hatred that had inspired it. I could not help but think of the lynchings that had plagued the South a century earlier, and the underlying assumption that whites had the right to take African American lives whenever they wanted, for any reason or even for no reason at all. One of the victims was the church's well-known pastor, the Reverend Clementa Pinckney, who was a longtime Democratic state senator and an influential figure in South Carolina politics. Obama, who had met Pinckney, decided to go to Charleston to speak at his funeral. The nation's first African American president was about to eulogize the Black victims of a white racist killer in the city where my great-grandfather Henry Fordham had won freedom from slavery. No force on earth could have kept me from witnessing that moment.

I booked the Mills House hotel on Meeting Street because it seemed to offer the best combination of comfort and convenience. I was unaware at the time that it was the hotel founded in 1853 by Otis Mills, the merchant who purchased Henry Fordham, my great-great-grandfather, in 1848 and who was his last enslaver. Grand enough to have hosted Robert E. Lee during the Civil War, the Mills House had thrived, faded, crumbled, and finally been faithfully rebuilt to Mills's original plan. Late July was the apex, or the nadir, of Charleston's hot and muggy summer, and on the way to the College of Charleston sports arena where Pinckney's funeral was to be held, I tried my best to follow my grandmother Sadie's instruction: Walk slowly and stay in the shade. Still, in my funeral-appropriate suit and tie, I was sweating profusely and must have looked a mess by the time I arrived.

I was an emotional mess as well. Thinking about the massacre ripped me apart—all the senseless deaths, all the lives unfairly cut short. The victims, attending Wednesday-evening Bible study, had seen the unfamiliar young white man come in and had invited him to pray with them. They were obeying Jesus's instruction to welcome the stranger, and in return, Roof had killed them. The fact that the atrocity had happened in Charleston, where my family had lived so much of its history, made it even worse for me.

The arena was already quite full, and I ended up finding a seat in the upper tier, amid a group of older men and women who could have been the trustees and usher board at Trinity Methodist Church in Orangeburg—proud dark ladies wearing fine hats, brown-skinned gentlemen in their most elegant suits. Once the service got under way, it felt familiar; I knew the hymns, I knew the responses. This was an African Methodist Episcopal funeral, meant to be not a mournful farewell but a joyous homegoing. I felt as if I had come to a place where I belonged. When the choir launched into the gospel standard "Goin' Up Yonder," and the whole crowd in its thousands joined in, I put down my reporter's notebook and added my voice. We swayed together and clapped together, and we sang another chorus, and another, and yet another. My eyes welled with tears.

Finally, it was the president's turn to stand at the pulpit. The theme of Obama's eulogy was divine grace. He preached in the call-and-response cadences of the Black church, and his pauses were answered with shouts of "amen" and arpeggios from the organist. It was a powerful tribute that built and built until finally he electrified the arena, and the millions watching on television, by breaking into song:

Amazing grace, how sweet the sound
That saved a wretch like me.
I once was lost, but now I'm found,
Was blind, but now I see.

First the musicians joined in, then the choir, and then the whole audience in the packed arena was singing "Amazing Grace." And then Obama named the victims: "Clementa Pinckney found that grace. Cynthia Hurd found that grace. Susie Jackson found that grace. Ethel Lance found that grace. DePayne Middleton-Doctor found that grace. Tywanza Sanders found that grace. Daniel L. Simmons Sr. found that grace. Sharonda Coleman-Singleton found that grace. Myra Thompson found that grace. Through the example of their lives, they've now passed it on to us. May we find ourselves worthy of that precious and extraordinary gift, as long as our lives endure. May grace now lead them home. May God continue to shed His grace on the United States of America."

After the funeral, I went back to the Mills House to work. I did an MSNBC appearance, wrote a column, grabbed something to eat. As evening fell, I was feeling restless and decided to take a walk. I went past the Custom House, where Major Fordham had worked. I went past the Old Exchange Building where slave auctions were held on the steps. I had come to this place of my origins, this place where my great-great-grandfather had been enslaved, to witness a speech by a Black man who had risen to the very pinnacle of American power. But the event that had occasioned the president's visit—unspeakable racial violence—was old and familiar.

TRUMP, POSITIONING HIMSELF AS Obama's antithesis, won the 2016 election in an upset over Hillary Clinton. Four years later, in 2020, he lost his reelection bid to Joe Biden. Trump's false claims of election fraud—unanimously disproved in scores of court cases—culminated in the shocking and violent U.S. Capitol insurrection on January 6, 2021. A massive mob of Trump's Make America Great Again supporters stormed the citadel of U.S. democracy in a last-gasp attempt to prevent Congress from certifying his defeat. Members of the Senate and the House had to barricade themselves inside their chambers before fleeing to safety; at least 140 police officers were injured by protesters, and African American officers said they lost track of how many times they were called "nigger" and spat upon by rioters. After the building was finally cleared, Congress was able to return late that evening and make Biden's victory official.

Four years later, in 2024, Trump won the presidency again—defeating Kamala Harris, the first Black vice president. It was the way Trump began his second term that made those two successive days a decade earlier—Trump's entry into politics and the Mother Emanuel killings—look like historical inflection points. For nearly half a century, the nation had been on a trajectory that led to the election of the first African American president. Now a serious attempt was being made to reverse that long arc.

The second Trump administration began with a "shock and awe" blitzkrieg of executive actions, some of which seemed to pull and tug in conflicting directions. Among the most consistent, and potentially most consequential, were efforts to delegitimize and outlaw the affirmative action concepts known as "diversity, equity, and inclusion." This erasure had implications for all racial and ethnic minorities and also for women, gays, lesbians, and transgender Americans; but in the context of this family history, the impact on Black people was salient. The crusade to eliminate DEI took aim at efforts that boosted Black university admissions and corporate hiring, policies that supported Black businesses, lesson plans that taught "uncomfortable" American history in schools at every level, and even museum exhibits that presented the African American experience in ways the Trump administration considered "divisive."

The country had twice elected a president whose slogan, Make America Great Again, explicitly promised a return to the past. Taken literally and seriously, that meant an America that would once again be less diverse, less equal, and less inclusive. And from the speed and sweep of its actions, the second Trump administration appeared to be both serious and determined. To many African Americans, it seemed that the wheel of American history—which had been turned back and forth, in their favor and against their favor, so many times—was turning again.

FOUR DAYS AFTER TRUMP'S election in 2016, *Saturday Night Live* featured a skit that became an instant classic, at least in my family, because it offered perspective that still serves me well. In it, six young urban, liberal friends—four white cast members along with Black comedians Dave Chappelle and Chris Rock—are gathered to watch television coverage of the Election Night vote count. At the beginning of the evening, the whites are certain that their candidate, Clinton, will win and become our first woman president. Chappelle and Rock are not so sure. As the night rolls on and Trump wins key states, the white yuppies become increasingly distraught. At two a.m., when Trump's victory is finally sealed, cast member Beck Bennett exclaims, "God, this is the most shameful thing America has ever done!" Chappelle and Rock look at each other and break into hysterical laughter. The unspoken history lesson is clear: *As if.*

In 2020, toward the end of Trump's first term, a Minneapolis police officer killed a Black man named George Floyd by kneeling on his neck for nine minutes, ignoring his repeated pleas of physical distress. The murder, which was captured on cell phone video, followed a series of high-profile killings of unarmed African Americans by law enforcement and sparked massive demonstrations across the country. The crowds in the streets were strikingly diverse—Black, white, Latino, Asian, old, young, progressive, conservative. But Trump's reaction to this unjust killing was radically different from Obama's reaction to Mother Emanuel: Trump saw the protests not as a cry for justice, not as a call for change, but as a threat to law and order. Many elected officials from both parties disagreed. Even Senator Mitt Romney of Utah, Obama's Republican opponent in the 2012 election, marched in a protest. And on June 5, at the height of the uproar, Washington, D.C., mayor Muriel Bowser had the demonstrators' message painted in fifty-foot yellow letters on the pavement of the southernmost two blocks of Sixteenth Street NW, right across Lafayette Square from the White House: BLACK LIVES MATTER. The bold statement was positioned so that Trump would see it if he looked out his front window.

A few days later, I went downtown to view the blocks that Bowser had renamed Black Lives Matter Plaza. I was moved by what I considered a powerful work of public art in response to tragic events, following the tradition of masterpieces such as Picasso's *Guernica*. And I dared to hope that finally, 401 years after the first Africans were brought to the British colonies of North America to labor in forced servitude, the nation might be prepared to begin an honest reckoning with our shared history on race.

My hope was in vain. And in March 2025, two months into the second Trump presidency, the Republican-controlled House of Representatives used its power over the federal city's finances to force Bowser to erase the lettering, revert the street to its previous name, and remove all references to Black Lives Matter from city documents. An uncomfortable national conversation about race? As if.

I believe historians will indeed see the Trump years as a turn of history's wheel. The cycle that led to the Obama presidency had ended, and a reactionary counter-cycle had begun. Freedom and opportunity won during the civil rights and affirmative action eras came under sustained, unrelenting attack. Trump and his movement were determined to wrench the nation back toward what they fantasized as a more orderly and prosperous past. For African Americans, that meant a past in which we were supposed to shuffle quietly and complacently to the back of the bus. Once again, as so many times over the past four hundred years, Black Americans are forced to fight for our place in a land we have loved, but that has not always loved us back.

Still, the point that Chappelle and Rock made in that memorable skit in 2016 remains true. Objectively, by any standard, nothing that has happened in this century remotely qualifies as "the most shameful thing America has ever done." My family's long and proud American history proves that fact.

My great-great-grandfather Henry Fordham was sold like a piece of livestock in 1829 and then sold again in 1848. Still, through skill and perseverance, he managed to wrest his own freedom before the Civil War. My great-grandfather Major John Hammond Fordham took advantage of fleeting Reconstruction-era opportunity to become a lawyer, rise to prominence in the Republican Party, raise and educate six children, and build the house in Orangeburg where I grew up. He could have done much more, but his freedom to rise in the world was choked off by the advent of Jim Crow repression. My great-uncle Marion Fordham was one of the thousands of Black soldiers who patriotically fought for their country in Europe in World War I. When they came home, full of new confidence and ambition, they were met by the brutal Red Summer of deadly violence intended to put African Americans back in their place. My father, my three uncles, my godfather, and a million other African Americans served their country in the racially segregated armed forces during World War II. They, too, returned to their communities with new confidence and ambition and were reminded of their second-class status; the blinding of Isaac Woodard, still in his uniform when small-town South Carolina police brutalized him, was just one vicious episode. Yet this generation went on to file the lawsuits, organize the boycotts, and lead the marches that ignited the civil rights movement and changed the nation. My parents' generation dramatically expanded the meaning of Thomas Jefferson's declaration that "all men are created equal" and made it possible for me and my sister, Ellen; my late wife, Avis; my cousins Theresa and Charles and Mary; my sons, Aaron and Lowell; and my grandchildren, Alice and Malcolm, to have opportunities that previous generations of Black Americans only dreamed of.

Another direct descendant of Henry Fordham, my cousin Kara Walker, is one of the most acclaimed American artists of this century. Her powerful and provocative work often refers explicitly to slavery, boldly seizing control of the historical narrative. Our ancestors would have been proud.

I keep in mind what my father told me in early 2008, less than a year before he died. Avis and I were in Orangeburg for a visit. He was ninety-two, and his health was in decline; the rhythms of life at Boulevard and Oak now included the need to periodically make sure that the cannula he wore was giving him the supplemental oxygen he now needed. We were all gathered in the sitting room—Louisa and Harold; Ellen and her husband, Mario Ricoma; Avis and I—and we were talking about the incredible fact that Barack Obama was beating Hillary Clinton in primaries in overwhelmingly white states such as Iowa. Our consensus view was that, in the end, Obama's campaign would fall short.

None of us could get our heads around the idea that a Black man could be nominated for president by one of our two major parties—much less embrace the fantasy that he could be elected. In what was a solidly Democratic household, the only real question seemed to be whether it was already time for the party to begin unifying behind Clinton so that she would be in the strongest possible position to defeat her Republican opponent in November.

It was getting to be time for supper, and everyone started drifting back to the kitchen. My father and I were the last to stir. He had been quiet through most of the political discussion, but now he looked at me and said, "Don't you ever let anybody tell you that nothing has changed."

And so I will not.

ACKNOWLEDGMENTS

This book could not have been written without the constant and loving support, both moral and concrete, of my family. Long before I began working on *Freedom Lost, Freedom Won*, my late wife, Avis Collins Robinson, had the foresight and patience to sit for hours with my mother and fill in details of my family lore that I knew only in broad strokes. Avis also annotated and digitized scores of old photographs that my mother brought out by the box-load. My sister, Ellen R. Ricoma, not only took loving care of our family's house and its antique contents but also let me take advantage of her razor-sharp memory at times when my recollection was vague or errant. And my cousin Theresa Robinson shared copious information about the history of my father's side of the family that otherwise I would never have known.

Knowledgeable staff members at the South Carolina Historical Society Reading Room, a sanctum within the College of Charleston's Addlestone Library, helped guide my search for data points to assemble into a portrait of the life of Henry Fordham. And I offer immense gratitude to the brilliant genealogists at the Columbus (Ohio) Metropolitan Library, who expertly traced my Robinson family lineage much further back than I had dreamed possible.

My agent (and friend) Rafe Sagalyn was with me every step of the way, from germ of an idea to finished manuscript. And my editor (and friend) Mindy Marques is, quite simply, the very best.

NOTES

This book relies on official records of births, deaths, marriages, military service, and business transactions, including those documenting sales of enslaved African Americans. It makes extensive use of letters, speeches, bank statements, and other documents found in the author's ancestral home. Family lore that is stated as fact has been verified against public records. Additional information comes from the following sources:

CHAPTER ONE: A BOY CALLED HARRY

2 *Richard Fordham was*: "Daniel Island African American History," Daniel Island Historical Society, accessed October 20, 2025, https://dihistoricalsociety.com/island-history/daniel-island-african-american-history/.

2 *Not far from the forge*: Mateo Mérida, "Part 1: Old Slave Mart and Charleston's Historic Memory," Avery Research Center for African American History and Culture, College of Charleston, January 18, 2023, https://avery.charleston.edu/part-1-old-slave-mart-and-charlestons-historic-memory-by-mateo-merida/.

3 *$725 for a field hand*: Robert Evans Jr. et al., *Aspects of Labor Economics* (Princeton University Press, 1962), 199.

19 *Researching the Gullah*: Jason Kelly, "Lorenzo Dow Turner, PhD '26: A Linguist Who Identified the African Influences in the Gullah Dialect," *University of Chicago Magazine*, November–December 2010, https://magazine.uchicago.edu/1012/features/legacy.shtml.

21 *Just a few years later*: Thomas Jefferson, *Notes on the State of Virginia* (Mathew Carey, 1794; first published 1785).

CHAPTER TWO: PROUD BUT TENUOUS FREEDOM

26 *Jehu Jones Sr.*: Bernard Powers, *Black Charlestonians: A Social History, 1822–1885* (University of Arkansas Press, 1999).

28 *"kind to his slaves"*: Peter H. Wood, *Black Majority: Negroes in Colonial South Carolina from 1670 through the Stono Rebellion* (Alfred A. Knopf, 1974), 436.

29 *Jones's wife, Abigail*: *South Carolina Encyclopedia*, "Jones, Jehu," by Roberta V. H. Copp, last updated August 5, 2022, https://www.scencyclopedia.org/sce/entries/jones-jehu/.

33 *my ancestor Francis Smith*: Friendly Moralist Society Records, 1841–1856, Avery Research Center for African American History and Culture, College of Charleston, p. 188.

CHAPTER THREE: WAR AND SURVIVAL

42 *Half of Charleston*: William Howard Russell, *My Diary North and South* (Burnham, 1863).

43 *One building in the path*: Marie Ferrara, "Moses Henry Nathan and the Great Charleston Fire of 1861," *The South Carolina Historical Magazine* 104, no. 4 (October 2003): 258.

44 *At the beginning of the Civil War*: "Population of the United States in 1860: South Carolina," https://www2.census.gov/library/publications/decennial/1860/population/1860a-32.pdf, pp. 449–51.

44 *"Not by one word"*: Mary Boykin Chesnut, *Mary Chesnut's Diary* (Penguin Classics, 2011), 33.

46 *"In our veins flows"*: Leon F. Litwack, *Been in the Storm So Long: The Aftermath of Slavery* (Knopf Doubleday, 1980), 17.

51 *Despite any laxity*: Grace Cordial, "Robert Smalls: War Hero, Public Servant, and a Man of Mark, 1839–1915," Beaufort District Collection, June 6, 2023, https://bdcbcl.wordpress.com/2018/12/20/robert-smalls-war-hero-public-servant-and-a-man-of-mark-1839-1915/.

54 *The official record*: *Record of the Service of the Fifty-fifth Regiment of Massachusetts Volunteer Infantry* (Press of John Wilson and Son, 1868).

CHAPTER FOUR: THE MAKING OF MAJOR FORDHAM

63 *The man leading*: Edmund L. Drago and Eugene C. Hunt, *A History of Avery Normal Institute, 1865 to 1974*, Avery Research Center for African American History and Culture, University of Charleston, 2010, 1991.

65 *There were between three hundred*: Edmund L. Drago, *Charleston's Avery Center: From Education and Civil Rights to Preserving the African American Experience*, ed. W. Marvin Dulaney (The History Press, 2006).

67 *The Reverend Joseph Baynard Seabrook*: Mabel L. Webber, "Early Generations of the Seabrook Family (Continued)," *South Carolina Historical and Genealogical Magazine* 17, no. 2 (1916): 58–72, http://www.jstor.org/stable/27569389.

68 *Seabrook was determined*: Richard Reid, "Black History Month/Orangeburg Notebook: Major John H. Fordham," *Times and Democrat* (Orangeburg, SC), February 26, 2014, https://thetandd.com/features/article_08c1953c-92b5-11e3-a5df-001a4bcf887a.html.

72 *The "new" house*: Property Record 85002341, Maj. John Hammond Fordham House, South Carolina, Records of the National Park Service, National Archives at College Park, https://catalog.archives.gov/id/118996490.

75 *Sadie may have misremembered*: Albert Bushnell Hart, Henry A. Wallace, G. S. Dickerman, Frederic S. Monroe, "Communications," *Journal of Negro History* 7, no. 4 (October 1922): 419–26.

79 *"If a majority of people"*: Ronald King "Counting the Votes: South Carolina's Stolen Election of 1876," *Journal of Interdisciplinary History* 32, no. 2 (Autumn 2001): 169–91.

CHAPTER FIVE: "GIVE US A FAIR CHANCE IN LIFE'S BATTLE"

91 *"If we would have"*: *Journal of the Proceedings of the Constitutional Convention of the State of Alabama* (Brown Publishing Company, 1901), 12.

96 *On November 10, a White mob*: LeRae Sikes Umfleet, *A Day of Blood: The 1898 Wilmington Race Riot* (North Carolina Office of Archives and History, 2020).

99 *On Saturday, September 22*: Rebecca Burns, *Rage in the Gate City: The Story of the 1906 Atlanta Race Riot* (University of Georgia Press, 2009).

CHAPTER SIX: DEATH AND THE RED SUMMER

115 *A federal government report*: "For Action on Race Riot Peril," *New York Times*, October 5, 1919, https://www.nytimes.com/1919/10/05/archives/for-action-on-race-riot-peril-radical-propaganda-among-negroes.html.

117 *The ever-observant*: W. E. B. Du Bois, "Returning Soldiers," *The Crisis* 18 (May 1919): 13.

117 *According to most accounts*: Damon L. Fordham, "The Charleston Race Riot of 1919," Explore Black Charleston, accessed October 20, 2025, https://www.exploreblackcharleston.com/article/the-charleston-race-riot-of-1919/.

119 *"When the news"*: Fordham, "Charleston Race Riot."

119 *Next came the first*: Gillian Brockell, "The Deadly Race Riot 'Aided and Abetted' by the Washington Post a Century Ago," *Washington Post*, July 15, 2019, https://www.washingtonpost.com/history/2019/07/15/deadly-race-riot-aided-abetted-by-washington-post-century-ago/.

122 *It was the kind of sweltering*: Julius L. Jones, "The Red Summer of 1919," Chicago History Museum, July 26, 2019, https://www.chicagohistory.org/chi1919/.

123 *Governor Frank Lowden*: Chicago Commission on Race Relations, *The Negro in Chicago—A Study of Race Relations and a Race Riot* (University of Chicago Press, 1922).

124 *And finally, on September 30*: Francine Uenuma, "The Massacre of Black Sharecroppers That Led the Supreme Court to Curb the Racial Disparities of the Justice System," *Smithsonian Magazine*, August 2, 2018, https://www.smithsonianmag.com/history/death-hundreds-elaine-massacre-led-supreme-court-take-major-step-toward-equal-justice-african-americans-180969863/.

CHAPTER SEVEN: THE NEXT FORDHAM GENERATION

134 *Some of the ambulances*: "Oral History: William Knox, 366th Ambulance Company, 92nd Division, American Expeditionary Forces," National WWI Museum and Memorial, collections database, interview by Mark Beveridge, May 23, 1980, https://collections.theworldwar.org/argus/final/Portal/Default.aspx?component=AAAS&record=d8bed590-25fa-42b4-896c-d2e90de852c0.

135 *The most unceasing torment*: "Oral History: William Knox."

136 *"A colored soldier"*: "Oral History: William Knox."

142 *An ancestor of his*: Hattie Mobley, "The J. J. Sulton and Sons Lumber Company, Orangeburg, South Carolina," WPA Federal Writers' Project, 1936–37. https://digital.tcl.sc.edu/digital/collection/wpafwp/id/2167/

CHAPTER EIGHT: THE ROBINSONS MAKE THE GREAT MIGRATION

153 *They and their kin*: *Mississippi Encyclopedia*, "Slave Trade," by Ted Ownby, last updated April 15, 2018, https://mississippiencyclopedia.org/entries/slave-trade/.

154 *Some enslaved workers*: *Mississippi Encyclopedia*, "Slave Communities," by Anthony Kaye, last updated April 15, 2018, https://mississippiencyclopedia.org/entries/slave-communities/.

158 *In 1918, Georgia led*: *Thirty Years of Lynching in the United States, 1889–1919*, National Association for the Advancement of Colored People, 1819.

159 *From the 1920s*: Frank B. Woodford and Arthur M. Woodford, *All Our Yesterdays: A Brief History of Detroit* (Wayne State University Press, 2017), 285–87.

159 *The biggest of all*: "Henry Ford's Rouge," The Henry Ford, accessed October 20, 2025, https://www.thehenryford.org/visit/ford-rouge-factory-tour/history-and-timeline/fords-rouge/.

160 *But when he built*: Beth Tompkins Bates, *The Making of Black Detroit in the Age of Henry Ford* (University of North Carolina Press, 2014).

161 *The great boxer*: Joe Louis, *My Life* (Harcourt, 1978).

CHAPTER NINE: JIM CROW AND HARD TIMES

171 *In World War II, he served*: "352nd Engineers in Iran and CBI: Service On Two Fronts," CBI Order of Battle: Lineages and History, last updated December 23, 2024, https://www.cbihistory.org/data/part_vi_352nd_eng_reg.html.

175 *Once the Depression reached*: Dale Linder Altman, "Hard Times: Remembering the Great Depression," *Times and Democrat* (Orangeburg, SC), October 5, 2008, https://thetandd.com/news/article_d7286b23-b6f3-5123-b43c-3de21dc8e3cb.html.

175 *But in 1935*: "75th Anniversary of the Wagner-Steagall Housing Act of 1937," Franklin Delano Roosevelt Presidential Library and Museum, accessed October 20, 2025, https://www.fdrlibrary.org/housing.

176 *In the 1936 Orangeburg map*: Robert K. Nelson et al., "Mapping Inequality: Redlining in New Deal America," in *American Panorama: An Atlas of United States History*, University of Richmond, 2023, https://dsl.richmond.edu/panorama/redlining/map/SC/Orangeburg/areas#loc=14/33.4923/-80.8574.

179 *The group arose*: Erdmann Doane Benyon, "The Voodoo Cult Among Negro Migrants in Detroit," *American Journal of Sociology* 43, no. 6 (May 1938): 894–907, https://doi.org/10.1086/217872.

CHAPTER TEN: WHITE SUPREMACY DIGS IN

190 *Isaac Woodard Jr. was one*: Richard Gergel, *Unexampled Courage: The Blinding of Sgt. Isaac Woodard and the Awakening of President Harry S. Truman and Judge J. Waties Waring* (Sarah Crichton Books, 2014).

193 *Wrighten sued the university*: Henry H. Lesesne, *A History of the University of South Carolina, 1940–2000* (University of South Carolina Press, 2001), 69–72.

196 *The judge invited*: Chris Lamb, "Thurgood Marshall's Unusual Meeting with a Judge Helped End Segregation," *Washington Post*, May 17, 2022, https://www.washingtonpost.com/history/2022/05/17/thurgood-marshall-waties-waring-brown/.

202 *The pretense was*: Nic Butler, "The Decline of Voter Suppression in South Carolina, 1900–1965," Charleston County Public Library, October 30, 2020, https://www.ccpl.org/charleston-time-machine/decline-voting-suppression-south-carolina-1900-1965.

202 *In his ruling ordering*: *Elmore v. Rice*, 72 F. Supp. 516 (EDSC 1947) https://law.justia.com/cases/federal/district-courts/FSupp/72/516/2238812/#:~:text=Elmore%20v.,Rice.

203 *Johnston told a crowd*: "Race and Political Leadership in the South," John F. Kennedy Presidential Library and Museum, March 10, 1998, https://www.jfklibrary.org/events-and-awards/kennedy-library-forums/past-forums/transcripts/race-and-political-leadership-in-the-south.

205 *The mother, Carrie Butler*: Jack Bass and Marilyn W. Thompson, *Strom: The Complicated Personal and Political Life of Strom Thurmond* (PublicAffairs, 2005).

CHAPTER ELEVEN: THE MOVEMENT GATHERS STRENGTH

214 *the building was a "Rosenwald"*: "Training School State College (Felton)," in Rosenwald Schools Database: Orangeburg, South Carolina Department of Archives and History,

accessed October 20, 2025, https://scdah.sc.gov/sites/scdah/files/Documents/Historic%20Preservation%20(SHPO)/Resources/African%20American%20Heritage/Rosenwald%20School%20Database/Rosenwald_Orangeburg.pdf, p. 11.

221 *The story, by correspondent*: Harrison E. Salisbury, "350 Negro Students Held in South Carolina Stockade," *New York Times*, March 16, 1960, https://timesmachine.nytimes.com/timesmachine/1960/03/16/99852685.html.

CHAPTER TWELVE: THE ORANGEBURG MASSACRE

228 *He argued in court*: Jim Shahin, "A Barbecue Case that Helped the Cause of Civil Rights," *Washington Post*, August 2, 2016, https://www.washingtonpost.com/lifestyle/food/a-barbecue-case-that-helped-the-cause-of-civil-rights/2016/08/01/cc5edcd8-5203-11e6-b7de-dfe509430c39_story.html.

230 *On Monday, February 5*: "The Orangeburg Massacre: Bowling Alley Protests," Lowcountry Digital History Initiative, College of Charleston, May 2013, https://ldhi.library.cofc.edu/exhibits/show/orangeburg-massacre/allstarprotest.

230 *"Hey, man. Where's"*: Ibram Henry Rogers, "The Black Campus Movement: An Afrocentric Narrative History of the Struggle to Diversity Higher Education, 1965–1972" (PhD diss., Temple University, 2009), 90, http://dx.doi.org/10.34944/dspace/2239.

231 *Nobody took orders*: Cleveland Sellers with Robert Terrell, *The River of No Return: The Autobiography of a Black Militant and the Life and Death of SNCC* (William Morrow Paperbacks, 2018).

232 *After the clash*: Sellers, *River of No Return*.

235 *To stay warm*: Sellers, *River of No Return*.

236 *As Sellers recalls*: Sellers, *River of No Return*.

238 *McNair's spokesman*: Jack Bass and Jack Nelson, *The Orangeburg Massacre*, 2nd ed. (Mercer University Press, 1984), 83.

CHAPTER THIRTEEN: A WINDOW OF OPPORTUNITY

243 *On March 6, 1961*: "EO 10925: Establishing the President's Committee on Equal Opportunity Employment," Federal Register 26 FR 1977, National Archives, 1961.

249 *On September 28, 1980*: Janet Cooke, "Jimmy's World: 8-Year-Old Heroin Addict Lives for a Fix," *Washington Post*, September 28, 1980, https://www.washingtonpost.com/archive/politics/1980/09/28/jimmys-world/605f237a-7330-4a69-8433-b6da4c519120/.

252 *One of Nixon's*: James Boyd, "Nixon's Southern Strategy: 'It's All in the Charts,'" *New York Times*, May 17, 1970, https://www.nytimes.com/1970/05/17/archives/nixons-southern-strategy-its-all-in-the-charts.html.

255 *But then the Helms campaign*: "Jesse Helms 'Hands' ad," YouTube video, posted by SnakesOnABlog, October 16, 2006, https://www.youtube.com/watch?v=KIyewCdXMzk.

CHAPTER FOURTEEN: THE OBAMA MOMENT

267 *I wrote in one column*: Eugene Robinson, "Who's Raising Race?" *Washington Post*, August 4, 2008, https://www.washingtonpost.com/wp-dyn/content/article/2008/08/04/AR2008080401824.html.

CHAPTER FIFTEEN: THE BACKLASH—AND THE CYCLE CONTINUES

274 *Six months after*: "On the Gates Arrest and Its Aftermath," *Harvard Magazine*, September 1, 2009, https://www.harvardmagazine.com/2009/09/arrest-of-henry-louis-gates.

275 *He believed—as I would*: Nathan Robinson, "One Year Later, Does the Henry Louis Gates Arrest Mean Anything?," *Huffington Post*, July 22, 2010, https://www.huffpost.com/entry/one-year-later-does-the-h_b_655574.

280 *"Donald Trump is here"*: "'The President's Speech' at the White House Correspondents' Dinner," White House Archives, May 1, 2011, https://obamawhitehouse.archives.gov/blog/2011/05/01/president-s-speech-white-house-correspondents-dinner.

281 *Trump managed to keep*: Roxane Roberts, "I Sat Next to Donald Trump at the Infamous 2011 White House Correspondents' Dinner," *Washington Post,* April 28, 2016, https://www.washingtonpost.com/lifestyle/style/i-sat-next-to-donald-trump-at-the-infamous-2011-white-house-correspondents-dinner/2016/04/27/5cf46b74-0bea-11e6-8ab8-9ad050f76d7d_story.html.

281 *"Donald Trump has been"*: Cleve R. Wootson Jr., "Seth Meyers Invited Trump to Be a Guest on His Show. Trump Wanted an Apology First," *Washington Post,* May 8, 2018, https://www.washingtonpost.com/news/arts-and-entertainment/wp/2018/05/08/seth-meyers-invited-trump-to-be-a-guest-on-his-show-trump-wanted-an-apology-first/.

INDEX

Note: *ER* refers to Eugene Robinson.

ABOUT THE AUTHOR

EUGENE ROBINSON is an award-winning journalist and author. Born and raised in Orangeburg, South Carolina, and educated at the University of Michigan, he is a frequent commentator on MSNBC and was a reporter, editor, and columnist at *The Washington Post* for forty-five years. He was awarded the Pulitzer Prize in 2009 for his columns chronicling the historic campaign of the nation's first Black president, Barack Obama. Robinson is the author of *Coal to Cream*, *Last Dance in Havana*, and *Disintegration*.